# THE OTIS FAMILY

*In Provincial and Revolutionary Massachusetts*

*John and Joy Kasson*
*1975*

PUBLISHED FOR THE
*Institute of Early American History and Culture*
AT WILLIAMSBURG, VIRGINIA

# THE
# OTIS
# FAMILY

## IN PROVINCIAL AND
## REVOLUTIONARY MASSACHUSETTS

*JOHN J. WATERS, JR.*

The Norton Library
W·W·NORTON & COMPANY·INC·
NEW YORK

Books That Live
The Norton imprint on a book means that in the publisher's
estimation it is a book not for a single season but for the years.
W. W. Norton & Company, Inc.

Waters, John J.      1935–
    The Otis family in Provincial and Revolutionary
Massachusetts.
    (The Norton library)
    Reprint of the 1968 ed. published by the University
of North Carolina Press, Chapel Hill; with new pref.
    1. Otis family.   I. Title.
[CS71.088   1975]      929'.2'0973      74–30403
ISBN 0-393-00757-X

Printed in the United States of America
    1 2 3 4 5 6 7 8 9 0

*for*

C N R

# PREFACE TO THE NORTON LIBRARY EDITION

The paperback edition of *The Otis Family* happily provides its author with the opportunity to write a second preface and thus to reflect about what the book means and to refer to recent research on pre-industrial social structures.

Above all, this is a book about patterns, rhythms, and sounds which we no longer easily see or readily hear. Throughout the seventeenth and eighteenth centuries the Otis males named their first sons after themselves; in Barnstable the youngest son lived with the aged father and inherited the homestead. Relatives tendered to cluster in the same neighborhoods, and invariably in each generation the sons would replace their fathers as town selectmen.

Such patterns of name, association, persistence, and service in a community are rare in our contemporary world. Yet it is my belief that these customs obviously reflect past attitudes toward intimacy, personality, and individuality. In that lost world kinship was instrumental before it was expressive. It alone provided the whole range of social functions: care when young, a hearth when old, the shared experiences of plowing together, the expectation of inheritance; and it alone legitimized sexual activity. In part, where one sat in the meeting house followed the community's evaluation of family service. There the communion cup, with its inscriptions and remembrances, symbolically linked the past with the present and the future in ways which are outside the experiences of most modern readers of this book.

The pages of this book are densely populated by presiding Otis patriarchs and their strong-willed women, their children, grandchildren, and a host of uncles, aunts, and cousins. We now know that their experiences as told here were unusual back then: this clan's fertility, its survival rates, its persistence, and its wealth, all were much higher than the norms for that age. We have come to expect a life cycle which will include parents living to see their grandchildren. But two hundred years ago such expectations were atypical and in fact marked the Otis family as exceptional. Recent demographic studies indicate that less than ten per cent of married couples back then would jointly survive to see their first grandchild's second birthday. In today's North America the figure is at least eight times as high. Moreover, the presence of kin in such towns as Hingham, Barnstable, and Guilford indicated wealth and status. In eighteenth-century New England, kin group size correlates with wealth just as surely and accurately as do cattle and plowland. While the sources which tell us this are uneven in range—every adult male would make a tax list while only a third would write wills—they are in general agreement on this major point. That of course is why the colinearity of these variables and the correlates are so high. This book, then, is about the emergence of a pace-setting bourgeois family and its movement in space and time.

The thesis of the book is that such families as the Otises were central in organizing their society's governing institutions. We know that John Winthrop referred to the family as a little commonwealth; this book argues that the corollary is also true, that is, that the commonwealth was a large family. While colonial politicians might write about party and faction, they traded with relatives and they cemented new alliances with marriages. The concept of family dominated the metaphorical world-view of that time. Kinship networks formed the real connecting links uniting that society as well as disturbing it when families feuded over honor, profit, and power. In New England that world ended in the nineteenth century when the industrial revolution changed the very fabric of the social and economic life of that region.

In my quest for meaning I have been helped by the shared perceptions of my colleagues John Demos, Philip Greven, Ken Lockridge, and Dan Scott Smith. Brenda Meehan-Waters has enriched my understanding of change and social process by her own research into eighteenth-century Russian society. In growing up I was privileged to be exposed to four generations of relatives and I now realize how central that experience was to my ability to understand another family in a different time. Lastly, Bob Kehoe of Norton has continued my good luck in having kind editors. I am deeply indebted to all of these friends.

JWJr.

Leningrad
1974

This is the story of five generations of the Otis family in early America. In it I have sought to find out what motivated them to come to the new world in the first place: how did they view reality, what roles did they expect to play, what social and political arrangements did they hope to fashion for themselves and their posterity? It is because we know so little about the old world roots of the first Americans that this book starts with the Otises and their fellow immigrants in their West Country and East Anglian towns. The West Country records show that the Otises were a people already on the move. We can trace them from Glastonbury to Barnstaple in England, and in seventeenth-century Massachusetts from Hingham to Scituate to Barnstable, and to Boston, New York, and Washington in the next century. To use modern phraseology, the Otises were both on the go and on the make, their eyes open for the main chance. When they moved it was for material improvement. The early Otises would indeed be amused if they could hear us talk about the stable past and the good old days.

The first three generations of this family produced marginal historical figures. The importance of John Otis I (1581–1657), John Otis II (1621–1684), and John Otis III (1657–1727) is to be found, not in their individual personalities, but rather in the embryonic family structure they formed and its response to the community needs which helped to shape it. The Otises themselves stressed continuity from generation to generation. A nuclear, responsible, achieving, and successful couple constituted their concept of family. As a rule the males married in their middle or late twenties, for marriage was not to be undertaken until one was established. One expected the aid of relatives, a marriage settlement, and in turn the responsibility of providing for one's own children. The number of children per marriage, which averaged about six, was probably slightly higher than their community's norm—but then, that was one of the prerogatives of the wealthy. (In Scituate and Barnstable the poor had the smallest families.) By the third generation the Otises' concept of family training came to include formal education. A Harvard diploma served to realize the individual's potential, to make him a more valuable member of a mutually reinforcing family clan, and of course to relate him to the larger world beyond the local community. John Otis III's family embodied such modern qualitative goals as personal fulfillment along with the more traditional ideals of family aggrandizement.

While later generations of the Otises would pay lip service to the virtues of order, hierarchy, and stability, the sharp upward mobility of their line occurred during periods of war and crisis. The turmoil of the Glorious Revolution enabled John Otis III to join in displacing the old ruling elite and to move his family into the mainstream of provincial life. He shrewdly channelized the energy inherent in a well-educated and strategically placed family. His sons John Otis IV (1687–1758) and the elder James Otis (1702–1778) continued to represent Barnstable and their family interests as merchants, office-holders, and politicians. In particular, James Otis, Sr., benefited from the fluid structure of provincial politics, the need of Governor William Shirley for a hard-headed lieutenant in the Massachusetts House of Representatives, and the enormous profits to be reaped from office during the French and Indian War.

The careers of James Otis, Jr. (1725–1783), Joseph Otis (1726–

1810), and Samuel Allyne Otis (1740–1814) of the fifth generation testify to the continual soundness of their family entity in politics, law, and commerce. The unique member of the family was
James Otis, Jr. He first saw the challenge that the British fiscal and
imperial demands of the 1760's presented to Massachusetts home
rule. Very early in the crisis James realized that Independence was
a real possibility, that social change was a continuing phenomenon, and that man made his laws and institutions. He believed that
the precedents of the past could guide but not bind future generations. Yet for psychological reasons the younger Otis fled from his
own reasoning. He had come as close to genius as any American of
his period. His brothers, on the other hand, because they saw the
threat which revolution posed to their own privileged status, had
greater concern about the family than any earlier generation. Then
again, they had more to lose. They knew that families fall as well as
rise. Joseph and Samuel Otis considered trade, politics, landholding,
the forging of a new commonwealth, and union itself from the
viewpoint of family profit, stability, continuity, and, in the last
analysis, survival.

For the last three of the five colonial generations the Otis family
formed one of the dominant elements within Barnstable County's
political structure. It is because of my understanding of the Otises'
life pattern within that county that this book has been written as
an exploration in familial formation, influence, and power in provincial Massachusetts. This has helped me to understand Barnstable
on its own terms. If the Otises were secular in their aspirations, the
society they lived in was consciously conservative in matter of religion. Its church, the oldest Congregational establishment in Massachusetts, firmly adhered to the past. It is significant that the Great
Awakening, with its accompanying social fermentation, did not
touch that body covenant. If the shire town of Barnstable was untouched by the religious and social issues of the Great Awakening,
it also remained a stranger to the Land Bank and paper money
issues of the 1740's. Its values were as fundamental as the absolute
law of nature that James Otis, Jr., hurled against the British tax

measures of the 1760's. Among other reasons it was Barnstable's belief in order which caused it to hesitate and become the last known township in Massachusetts to move for Independence. It was at this critical juncture that the Otis family, with its elaborate infrastructure of stores and supplies, relatives, and intraprovincial connections, was able to commit Barnstable to the Revolutionary cause. This move, however, undermined the homogeneous nature of their society. It seriously divided their community along class and ideological lines for the first time in its history. The so-called tories were closer to being revolutionary levelers than the patriot party which represented the propertied and ruling elite. After the 1783 peace there would be an attempt to restore the old mores in Barnstable, but a new order had come into being.

In attempting to reconstruct the history of the Otis family and the communities of Hingham, Scituate, and Barnstable in which they lived, I have used the analytical tools of our own age. Wherever possible I have tried to quantify data on land and office-holding, property accumulation, political service, and family structure. Sociology, economics, and to a lesser extent psychology have shaped my approaches to the sources and have allowed me to broaden the documentary base beyond the traditional letters, memoirs, and sermons which usually constitute the bulk of historical evidence.

This work would have been impossible without the cooperation and assistance of the staffs of Houghton Library at Harvard, the Massachusetts Historical Society in Boston, and Special Collections of the Butler Library at Columbia University. I am especially indebted to Columbia University for permitting me to classify and use its newly acquired Gay-Otis Papers and the Otis Family Manuscripts. Mr. Leo Flaherty of the Massachusetts Archives made me the beneficiary of his documentary lore. The custodians of the Bodleian Library, Oxford, the British Museum, and the Public Record Office, London, were most generous with their resources. A word of thanks is due to the several vicars who opened their parish records to me, as well as to the guardians of the episcopal visitations of Norwich, and Bath and Wells, who allowed me to utilize their documents.

In the realm of ideas Robert D. Cross, Clifford K. Shipton, and Frank Tannenbaum have placed me deeply in their debt. John A. Schutz and Chilton Williamson served as invaluable critics. My mentor and master, Richard B. Morris, served as teacher, director, exemplar, and friend. Richard S. Dunn, Merrill D. Peterson, and Bruce T. McCully graciously served in an advisory capacity. Stephen G. Kurtz and Marise L. Rogge were the best of editors. To all of them, and especially to my wife, Brenda, I owe much more than I can properly express.

JWJr.

Rochester
1967

# ❧ CONTENTS

## ❧ *ILLUSTRATIONS*

*between pages 16–17*

# THE OTIS FAMILY

*In Provincial and Revolutionary Massachusetts*

*And yet they think that their houses shall continue for ever: and that their dwelling-places shall endure from one generation to another; and call the lands after their own names.*

PSALMS 49:11

# ❦ I.

## FIRST PLANTATIONS

      The second and third decades of the seventeenth century were times of difficulty in England. The church wanted reforming, the government wanted mending, the weaver wanted work, and Charles Stuart was king. This unrest, proof visible in this century of the imperfections of the Elizabethan settlement, would eventually overthrow the royal absolutism and replace it with the more efficient despotism of Oliver Cromwell. When the pious John Winthrop wrote that England in the 1620's was a "sinfull lande," he expressed an opinion that was common among the East Anglian puritans.[1] All could see that the Anglican bishops, the true heirs of those other "Ministers of Antichrist" who governed the Roman church, used their energies to persecute godly puritan divines.[2] And did not the dealings of Charles I with Parliament signify a subversion of the political order? The true believer, convinced that the Day of Judgment was at hand, anticipated a "generall distruction"

    1. John Winthrop to Thomas Fones, 29 Jan. 1621/2, *Winthrop Papers* (Boston, 1929——), I, 268.
    2. John Winthrop, "Common Grevances Groanings for Reformation," *ca.* 1624, *ibid.*, 295, 303; Richard Mather, *A Modest and Brotherly Answer to Mr. Charles Herle* . . . (London, 1644), 48; John Cotton, *An Exposition upon the Thirteenth Chapter of the Revelation* . . . (London, 1655), 237.

of the reformed churches of Europe.[3] It was this sense of doom coupled with the expectation of Christ's "Second Coming" that impelled the puritan to his "errand into the wilderness" where, like John the Baptist, he would make straight the way of the Lord.[4] More than forty puritan families from the town of Hingham and its surrounding hamlets in East Anglia left their homeland in the 1630's intending to reform their puritan community in Massachusetts. They were led by the Hobart and Peck families. The spot they picked was "Bear Cove," a little inlet eighteen miles south of Boston, which also hosted twenty families from England's West Country. One of these was headed by John Otis I (1581–1657), who in his individualism, mobility, and land hunger, as well as in his lack of a dominating religious impulse, typified this West Country contingent. These two groups—East Anglian and West Country men—accounted for 55 per cent of the 130–odd planters who came to Bear Cove.[5] They represented different values which led to conflict in the political, religious, and economic life of the new settlement. This plantation, destined as a crucible for these emi-

3. John Winthrop, "Reasons to Be Considered for Justifieinge the Undertakers of the Intended Plantation in New England . . . ," 1629, *Winthrop Papers*, II, 115.

4. John Cotton, *The Churches Resurrection* . . . (London, 1642), 5, 15, 30; Thomas Shepard, *The Parable of the Ten Virgins* . . . (London, 1660), Pt. I, 10, 90–92, delivered as sermons from 1636 to 1640.

5. For Bear Cove identifications I have used Andrew H. Ward's "First Settlers of Hingham," *New England Historical and Genealogical Register*, II (1848), 250–251, rather than the uncritical tabulation in Solomon Lincoln's *History of the Town of Hingham* (Hingham, 1827), 42–49. However, Ward's list must be supplemented with the names of church members recorded by Peter Hobart in his diary, Massachusetts Historical Society, Boston, and landowners in George Lincoln, ed., *Genealogical History of Hingham* (Hingham, 1893), II, III. For English county and parish identifications see Charles E. Banks, *Topographical Dictionary of 2885 English Emigrants to New England, 1620–1650* (Baltimore, 1937), as well as H. A. Whitney, comp., *Extracts from the Minutes of Daniel Cushing of Hingham with a Photograph of His Manuscript* (1865), Boston Public Library, hereafter cited as *Cushing Manuscript*. Of the 131 families that settled in Bear Cove up to 1640, 92 (70 per cent) may be identified by parish or county. Norfolk is clearly in the lead with 45 families out of the East Anglia total of 52 (40 per cent). The West Country's 20 families made up 15 per cent of the Hingham total. However, the Norfolk figures are more complete as they are based upon the seventeenth-century *Cushing Manuscript*. That document, which was written in new Hingham, in its unique listing of "such persons as came out of the town of Hingham, and the towns adjacent, in the county of Norfolk, in the Kingdom of England into New England," epitomizes East Anglian self-consciousness in the new world.

grants, would become a cross for orthodoxy and the Congregational way.

John Otis's West Country, with its rolling hills of Cornwall and its fertile lands of Devon and Dorset, differed in soil and husbandry from East Anglia. Rather than the enclosed-farm Norfolk villages with their broad expanse of flats, Devon and Dorset, marked by open fields, formed in late summer a quilted cloth of green and amber lines. The grain glistened in the sun. Each farmer signed by hedges his parcels of the soft red earth. Those towns that faced the sea, such as Plymouth, Weymouth, and Barnstaple, combined the working of both the sea and land. And in Somerset lay the ancient town of Glastonbury where the people took the new puritan ethos lightly. They raised the May pole, evoking with it merriment and the primitive rites of spring. Pretty girls cast their spells, drunkards crowded the streets, and the barber plied his trade on the Sabbath. It is not at all surprising that the 1620 episcopal visitation to the parish of St. John the Baptist found it without the "booke of sermons and a bible of the last translation."[6] This was the parish of the Otis family. It reflected an open attitude toward life.

John Otis was born about 1581 in Glastonbury. His father Richard lived there as an independent weaver, although he probably tilled at least a garden plot. Richard's will, which is itself evidence of some standing in the community, gave to John and his brother Stephen "all my wearing apparell," while another brother, Thomas, inherited the "frame board" and a chest. The "bedstead in the lower almeshouse," where Richard spent his last days either as a pensioner or minor official, went to his two daughters.[7] John learned to write in the local school, as had his father. About 1602,

6. This analysis of the Glastonbury social scene follows Bath and Wells "Visitation Act Books" 1617 and 1620, D/D/Ca 206, 220, Somerset Record Office, Taunton, England. For the field system see Maurice W. Beresford and John K. S. St. Joseph, *Medieval England, An Aerial Survey* (Cambridge, 1958), 44–45.

7. "Richard Ottis" of Glastonbury, will, 29 Nov. 1611, proved at the Consistorial Court at Wells, transcript from the Somerset Record Office, Taunton. The License Book No. 21, Diocesan Registry, Wells, states that Richard Oates of St. Benignus, Glastonbury, died on the 30th of Nov. 1611. John Otis's birth date follows his Apr. 1657 deposition, Massachusetts Archives, XXXIX, 9, State House, Boston.

when John was in his early twenties, he married a girl known only by the name of Margaret and settled down to rear a family. Their children, Alice, Hannah, Margaret, and Mary, would finally include a son born in 1621, whom they named after his father.[8] Shortly after John's birth the Otises moved to Barnstaple in Devon. By Glastonbury standards it was a quiet town. In 1628 it housed a puritan lecturer by the name of William Crompton, who remained untroubled by the tolerant Bishop Joseph Hall.[9] There is no evidence that John Otis followed Crompton's teachings. And if he had, there would still be no pressing religious reason to explain the elder Otis's decision in 1630 to depart for America. What we do know is that this was a literate family of some prosperity. Its transportation to Massachusetts Bay cost the Otises upwards of £30.[10] They probably sailed from Bristol port on the good ship *Lyon*. Captain William Peirce is known to have made at least four voyages from 1630 to 1632, which brought the majority of these West Country planters to Bear Cove.[11]

Yet the Otis family was neither the richest nor the most important of the score of West Country families that came to Bear Cove. The former would certainly be the Andrews family, who along with the Cades paid the subsidy to King James back in 1624.[12]

8. See entries 1603 to 1620, Parish Register, St. John the Baptist, Glastonbury.

9. See Barnstaple entries for 1622, 1628, and 1631 in Exeter Episcopal Visitations, CCXVII, CCXVIII, Exeter Diocesan Record Office, Exeter. For the policy of Bishop Hall, see Robert J. E. Boggis, *History of the Diocese of Exeter* (Exeter, 1922), 395–404.

10. Nathaniel B. Shurtleff, ed., *Records of the Governor and Company of the Massachusetts Bay in New England* (Boston, 1853–1854), I, 66, hereafter Shurtleff, ed., *Mass. Bay Recs.*

11. The passenger lists for the *Lyon* are either fragmentary or lost. What information we have is summarized in Charles E. Banks, *Planters of the Commonwealth: A Study of the Emigrants and Emigration in Colonial Times* (Boston, 1930), 85–86. Most historians have followed William Tudor's supposition that John Otis "came from Hingham, in Norfolk, England, [8] June, 1635, in company with the Rev. Peter Hobart," *Life of James Otis of Massachusetts . . .* (Boston, 1823), 496. However, Hobart's party did not arrive at Bear Cove until Sept., whereas John Otis's early presence is noted in Hingham's Liber I, "Proprietors Grants of Land," 1 June 1635, "John Ottis . . . for a planting lott four acres of land lying upon weariall hill," in Hingham Town Records, Hingham, Mass.

12. "*Taxacio Tertii Subsidii Trium . . . Jacobo Regi*," (1624), 102/463, Public Record Office, London.

Thomas Andrews, a patriarch in his fifties, must have thought it but natural that his son Joseph should be the town's first clerk, a member of various committees, selectman, and for a brief while representative to the General Court.[13] Then there was William Walton from Seaton Parish. He was a product of Emmanuel College, the cradle of puritanism at Cambridge University. It is more than likely that Walton knew Peter Hobart, also a Cambridge man, who would come to Bear Cove as its first pastor.[14] The shipwright James Cade, a Devon man, held lands in Northam Parish, which provided an annuity of £5 a year. His wife Margaret owned property in her own right at Bideford. By rural standards this was a wealthy family with strong parochial ties as signified by its benefactions to the parish church. In New England James utilized the full regnal citation "Lord Charles by the grace of God King of England," a formula distasteful to the majority of the settlers of the Bay Colony who used the simpler "*annoq[ue] RR. Caroli Angliae etc.*"[15] Cade was no rebel. His position as the second son must have weighed large in his determination to migrate.[16] The gentleman and rich merchant George Strange was his attorney. At Bear Cove they were John Otis's neighbors, as was another West Country man, Thomas Loring, who became the first deacon and held the license "to sell wine and strong water."[17] These families were hardly the underprivileged. Along with the Strongs, Phippenys, and Betscombes, they were people of record, literate, used to owning property, wanting more (probably the key element in their migration), and careful husbanders of the soil. While the West Country men arrived early at Bear Cove—and proof of their coming first is to be found in the

13. George Lincoln, ed., *Hist. of Hingham*, II, 10–11; Solomon Lincoln, "Appendix," in his *History of the Town of Hingham*, 162–163.

14. George Lincoln, ed., *Hist. of Hingham*, II, 335; III, 274.

15. See James Cade's conveyance, 4 Dec. 1638, in Thomas Lechford, *Note-book . . . 1638 . . . 1641 . . .* (Cambridge, Mass., 1885), 42–44, and various regnal citations, 33, 35. For the Cade background see Henry F. Waters, "Genealogical Gleanings in England," *New England Hist. and Gen. Register*, L (1896), 505; Elizabeth French, "Genealogical Research in England," *ibid.*, LXVIII (1914), 61.

16. Charles H. Pope, *Pioneers of Massachusetts . . .* (Boston, 1900), 87.

17. Shurtleff, ed., *Mass. Bay Recs.*, I, 221; George Lincoln, ed., *Hist. of Hingham*, III, 27.

town's place names, such as Walton's Cove and "Weary All" Hill
which John Otis named after a local landmark in his native Glastonbury—they were not to remain alone to fulfill their dreams.[18]

In June of 1633, the *Elizabeth Bonaventure* arrived at Boston
from Yarmouth in Norfolk, carrying sixty-three-year-old Edmund
Hobart and his family with their servant Henry Gibbs, as well as
the Jacobs and Chubocks. Late that summer this advance guard
from old Hingham settled at the Cove. They were heralds of a new
wave of emigrants that would profoundly change the political and
social make-up of this settlement.[19]

In contrast to the general agrarian background of the West
Country men, these East Anglians from Norfolk, Essex, and Suffolk represented an area famous for its weaving industries, although
the trade itself had been in the grips of depression since the 1620's.
The land they left was as flat as fine fustian, while the Norfolk
Broads periodically suffered from "innundations of water." It was
just such a flood that provided the needed pretext for the citizens of
Norwich when they failed to furnish Charles I with £3,000 of
ship money in 1635.

This region, so very much like Holland, had received heavy in-
fluxes of Dutch weavers, whose separatist activities were a thorn
in the side of at least three High Church bishops.[20] The most famous
of those shepherds was the Anglo-Catholic Matthew Wren. It was
his practice to elevate the consecrated host and as master of St.
Peter's College, Cambridge, he had restored the use of Latin in the
Divine Service. "Uniformity in doctrine and Uniformity in discipline," his very own words, indicated what he wanted, and old
Hingham would feel the wrath of his visitation.[21] And Wren

18. George Lincoln, ed., *Hist. of Hingham*, III, 274; *Suffolk Deeds* (Boston,
1880–1906), II, 161; Hingham Town Records, I, 16. For the geography see Jedediah
Lincoln's 1830 map as printed in [Mason A. Foley's] *Hingham Old and New*
(Hingham, 1935), 17.

19. Banks, *Planters of the Commonwealth*, 102–103; *Cushing Manuscript*.

20. William Page, ed., *The Victoria History of the County of Norfolk* (London,
1906), II, 505–506; Wallace Notestein, *The English People on the Eve of Coloni-
zation, 1603–1630* (New York, 1954), 153–154, and petition in *Calendar of State
Papers, Domestic, 1625–1649*, 521.

21. [Anon.], *Wrens Anatomy* (London, [1641]), 3, 12; Louis C. Cornish, "The
Settlement of Hingham" in *Hingham* (1911), 38–39.

authored an early economic interpretation for this puritan migration: "The chiefest Cause of their Departure, was the small Wages
which was given to the poor Workmen, whereby the Work-masters
grew rich, but the Workmen were kept very poor."[22] In justice to
the bishop it should be noted that this explanation, with its critique
of the puritan "Work-masters," was his reply to those parliamen-
tarians who charged that it was his seeking after "Uniformity"
that drove the godly out of Norfolk.[23] Actually, neither an economic interpretation nor a theory of migration based upon religious
persecution *per se* is an adequate explanation for this particular
flight to the Bay Colony.

The key element that brought the Norfolk planters to Bear Cove
is to be found in their historical awareness of themselves as a distinct puritan community. These emigrants, mostly from the neighboring parishes of Hingham, Wymondham, and Norwich, had
shared since 1615 a set of religious experiences that had alienated
them from the traditional poles of English life as symbolized by
king and church. They would separate from the English nation
when they saw their identity as a godly people threatened by the
integrating policies of Charles I and Archbishop William Laud.
Is this not the essence of Peter Hobart's thanksgiving prayer upon
his arrival in New England with its concluding affirmation, "for
ever praysed be the god of Heaven my god and king"?[24] The men
of Hingham did not come to Bear Cove as individual settlers pri-
marily concerned with material gain, but rather as members of a
conscious community of God's people. Their migration formed an
observable plan of three parts. First was Edmund Hobart's landing
party in 1633, seeking a place of settlement; next, a continuing
wave of friends, relatives, and enthusiasts, which lasted until 1637;
and finally in 1638, the flight of the "visible" church.

The coming of the Hobarts as an advance guard in 1633 laid

22. "*The Most Humble Answer of Matthew Wren . . . to the Articles of Impeachment . . . ,*" in Sir Christopher Wren, *Parentalia; Or, Memoirs of the Family
of Wrens* (London, 1750), 101.
23. *Articles of Impeachment, of the Commons . . . against Matthew Wren, Doctor in Divinitie, Late Bishop of Norwich . . .* (London, 1641), Art. 13, p. 9.
24. Peter Hobart, 8 June 1635, diary, Mass. Hist. Soc.

the framework for at least seven subsequent shiploads of human freight. In 1634 the *Elizabeth Dorcas* contributed the recently widowed Mrs. Bosworth and her five children. Her husband, as he sensed death's approach before the voyage's end, requested to be "carried on deck that he might see Canaan, the promised land."[25] His is the religious intensity of ancient Israel. Such a people would not be without a gathered church, as the West Country settlers had been since they settled the Cove. Fortunately, the Hobarts had a candidate for a pastor in their son Peter. He had been guided along the path of puritan righteousness by his pastor, the Rev. Mr. Robert Peck of Hingham, who was himself a graduate of St. Catherine's and Magdalene at Cambridge. The religious vocation of Peter Hobart, which took him to Queen's College in 1621 and finally to Magdalene, where he matriculated in 1626, represented a real social advancement for his family. Peter Hobart received orders in 1627 and then settled down to the life of a nonconforming curate at Haverhill in Norfolk.[26] That he differed from the views of the established church is clear. However, no records exist to substantiate Cotton Mather's belief that it was the "cloud of prelatical impositions and persecutions" that determined his flight to America.[27] A less nebulous reason was the promptings of his relatives to join them in New England. And as new Hingham's pastor, Peter Hobart would now be his own master. This was a real consideration for a man of his strong-willed nature.

The arrival of Peter Hobart in 1635 was not a singular event. It must properly be viewed in the light of the concomitant migration of his friends and neighbors from Haverhill and old Hingham who accompanied him. These East Anglians included Anthony Cooper who came with his wife, four children, and four servants; as well as the Farrows and Larges of lesser station. They had come over on the *Hopewell*, the *Defence*, and the *Elizabeth* (all of London), and were followed in 1637 by the *Increase* and the *Mary Anne*. But the

25. George Lincoln, ed., *Hist. of Hingham*, II, 86–87.

26. John Venn, *et al.*, comps., *Alumni Cantabrigienses* . . . (Cambridge, 1922), Pt. I, II, 423.

27. Cotton Mather, *Magnalia Christi Americana* . . . (London, 1704), III, xxvii, 4.

most important ship to sail since the *Lyon* transported John Otis and the other West Country men in the early 1630's was the East Anglian *Diligent*, which arrived in August of 1638.[28]

The coming of the *Diligent* marked the final chapter in an affair which stretched back to 1615. In that year Robert Peck, the pastor of St. Andrew's in Hingham, was convicted of nonconformity, as he would be again in 1617. The established church did not look favorably upon his teaching parishioners "not to kneel when they came to Church" and that "it was Superstition to bow down at the Name of Jesus." Pastor Peck carefully organized like-minded souls. Under the pretense of catechising and psalm singing this inner parish group held conventicles. In 1622 Peck was caught in the act with twenty-two of his neighbors, some of whom defiantly told Bishop Samuel Harsnett that there was "no Difference between an Alehouse and the Church, till the Preacher be in the Pulpit." While the bishop extracted a public "*I confess my Errors*" from Peck, the degree of penitence must have been small indeed. Peck gave his account of this persecution to influential friends in neighboring Norwich, who then proceeded to enlist Sir Edward Coke to present their petition against Harsnett in the House of Commons. Following the canon, "*Quicunque contristaverit doctorem veritatis, peccat in Christum*," the bishop was accused of simony, idolatry, popery, and persecution.[29]

Robert Peck thus presents an interesting example of the combination of religiosity and precocious political awareness found in the puritan cause. He was the third in a direct line of independent priests who had never favored the royal authority. He intended to resist any concept of the church that did not agree with his own insights, and he did this successfully for almost twenty years.[30] Such

28. Banks, *Planters of the Commonwealth*, 139–140, 144–145, 167–170, 174–176; *Cushing Manuscript*.

29. For the introduction of the petition, see *Journals of the House of Commons*, I, 699, while the petition itself, together with Bishop Harsnett's answer, is in the *Journals of the House of Lords*, III, 388–390.

30. Wren in the *Parentalia*, 95, lists Peck's earlier difficulties. Additional information is in the Norwich Consignation Book, 1629, and Norwich Visitation, Deanery of Hingham, 1633, in Norfolk and Norwich Public Record Office, Central Library, Norwich, Norfolk.

a policy of defiance rested upon consensus within St. Andrew's, the sympathy of well-placed puritan supporters, the inefficiency of the established church, and finally a set of compromises on the part of Peck with the required church rituals. It was this last element which was the most vulnerable point in the system; this was the opening gambit that Matthew Wren, appointed bishop of Norwich in 1635, utilized. It had become traditional for puritan parishes to arrange for two kinds of bell-ringings, one for readings from the *Book of Common Prayer*, and another, "when there were both Prayers to be read, and a Sermon preached."[31] Presumably, the puritan faithful attended only the latter. Wren did away with this device and with the assistance of his able chancellor, Clement Corbett, charged Peck with "contumacious disobedience to the orders and ceremonies of the Church."[32] Nor did the bishop think kindly of Peck's digging a ditch in the east end of the chancel and placing in it the communion table that he had been ordered to set up. Pastor Peck was deprived of his living, but his former parishioners showed their feelings by paying him "their tithes."[33] And when the new vicar had Chancellor Corbett excommunicate two of Peck's supporters for their "factious" activities, they successfully appealed their disbarment in the puritan-controlled Court of Arches, an act so dangerously subversive that Archbishop Laud himself intervened to squelch it.[34]

Chancellor Corbett continued the hunt after that "old Fox" Peck. Although deprived of his parish, Robert Peck ministered in

31. *Articles of Impeachment*, Art. 9, p. 7.

32. Corbett to Wren, 3 May 1637, Tanner Manuscripts, LXVIII, 7, Bodleian Library, Oxford University, Oxford.

33. Corbett to Wren, 29 Apr. 1637, *ibid.*, LXVIII, 7.

34. "The humble petition of Edward Agas" to Archbishop Laud, Hingham, 14 Feb. 1637/8, State Papers Domestic, Charles I, Class 16, Piece 382, 14, P. R. O. Laud replied, "I shall not suffer my Court to be made an Instrument to trouble any man for doing his duty or informing his Ordinary." The suit against Agas is another example of the puritans' genius for nullifying governmental action against their cause by their control of the local process, in this case the Court of Arches. This time they would be opposed by a forceful metropolitan and king, who would utilize the prerogative to stop proceedings in the Court of Arches, if those proceedings aimed to frustrate their policy of national integration. Charles I had done this as early as 1633; see Christopher Hill, *Society and Puritanism in Pre-Revolutionary England* (London, 1964), 336.

secret to his flock, much in the same manner as had his grandfather, who in the days of the Catholic Queen Mary preached the gospel "in woods and forrest places."[35] Corbett now used the threat of action from the Court of High Commission to rid Hingham of that very difficult puritan priest. It was with a sense of accomplishment that the chancellor reported to Bishop Wren in March of 1638 that Robert Peck *"parat se ad fugam in novam Angliam,"* taking with him his rebellious friends.[36] Nearly 120 persons, of whom a sixth were servants, sailed with Peck for what had been Bear Cove and was now known as Hingham in Massachusetts. Those left behind in old Hingham sadly noted in their petition to the House of Commons that "most of the able Inhabitants have forsaken their dwellings and have gone severall ways for their peace and quiett and the town is now left and like to be in misery by reason of the meanness of the [remaining] Inhabitants."[37]

This description of the distressed state of old Hingham was no empty complaint. In the space of six years it had witnessed the decamping of more than forty families, which included the better part of the local wealth. It did not include the titled gentry, nor is there a single name from the 1633 poor relief roll of Hingham Parish.[38] Heading the list of these settlers were Robert Peck with his wife, two children, and two servants, and his brother Joseph Peck, with a family of four and five servants.[39] Joseph Peck brought with him the family plate, silver drinking cups, and his banqueting linens.[40] There was also Henry Smith from Derbyshire (but related to the Smiths of Hingham) with a family of six and five servants, as well as the elder Hobart's son-in-law John Beale, with a family of eight and two servants. While William Ripley's wealth was more modest, his ideological commitment to the puritan cause showed itself

35. Peck Family Pedigree, Tanner MSS, CLXXX, 24–25, Bodleian Lib., Oxford.
36. Corbett to Wren, 9 Mar. 1637/8, *ibid.*, LXVIII, 11.
37. Petition to the House of Commons, Hingham, *ca.* 1640, *ibid.*, CCXX, 54–56.
38. "Norwich Rate Book, 1633/4," in Walter Rye, *History of the Parish of Heigham* (Norwich, 1917), 193–194.
39. *Cushing Manuscript.*
40. Joseph Peck, will, 3 March 1663/4, Wills, II (pt. ii), 11, Old Colony Records, Plymouth Registry of Deeds, Plymouth, Mass.

in his willingness to follow his pastor, and it was no accident that he carried with him John Fox's *Book of Martyrs*.[41] These were the substantial citizenry of East Anglia. Although their estates are rarely counted in the thousands of pounds, some of them, such as the Pecks, were landlords as far back as domesday chronicle. And along with these families of distinction came Samuel Lincorne, weaver and great-great-grandfather of the sixteenth president; Thomas Lincorne, cooper; Henry Chamberlain, blacksmith; Henry Rust, glover; as well as felt makers, carpenters, wheelwrights, agitators, and a host of others essential to the well-being of a community.[42] In short, by 1639 something had happened close to the removal *in toto* of an old English town, physically, mentally, socially, and spiritually, and its transplantation to New England soil. This *en masse* migration of the parishioners of St. Andrew's, although partially paralleled by John Cotton's St. Botolph's flock, is unique in that its reconstruction in Massachusetts perpetuated the norms of old Hingham. It came as a formed body. This immigration was not caused by economic distress, nor may the policies of Bishop Wren be held responsible. After all, the faithful from Hingham and its neighboring parishes started their peculiar flight in 1633, long before Matthew Wren came to occupy the Norwich See in November of 1635. At most the bishop may be charged with the final push that propelled the remaining segment of Hingham's puritan community to depart. Its motivation was that of a godly community seeking a land in which they could forever praise Christ the Lord, their only "god and king," in their particular way.

The continual movement of East Anglians to Bear Cove during the thirties is documented by changes both within and without this plantation. Indicative of the coming direction of things was the renaming of the town as Hingham in 1635, shortly after the Massachusetts General Court had accorded municipal recognition.[43] This

41. Julia C. R. Dorr, *A Book of Remembrance* (Rutland, Vt., 1910), 10.

42. George Lincoln, ed., *Hist. of Hingham*, II, 21, 38, 150, 396, 428, 461, III, 3, 20, 113, 141, 142, 164, 330.

43. Solomon Lincoln, *Hist. of Hingham*, 50.

meant the formation of a *body politic* that would support the
church, enforce law, maintain a militia, and on the provincial level
pay taxes and send representatives to the General Court. Considering that the town had been founded by West Country settlers, and
that they constituted the better part of the electorate until 1639,
it was but natural that they should supply the first slate of town
officers. Joseph Andrews of Devon was the town clerk as well as
constable; and with his gold ring and fancy-dress sword he went up
to Boston as representative in 1636, 1637, and 1638. Andrews used
his influence to obtain the local liquor franchise for his neighbor
Thomas Loring, who came from the same county in England. Anthony Eames, a Somerset man and the West Country's nominee for
the role of natural leader, had led Hingham's seven-man militia contingent during the Pequot Indian difficulties in 1637. He was also
the town's representative to the General Court in 1637 and 1638.
Joseph Hull, likewise from Somerset, completed this list by serving
as the other representative in 1638.[44]

The year 1639 saw the displacement of the West Country men
by the East Anglians. From that year until the Otises left Hingham
in 1661, the representatives were all men from East Anglia, save for
a single exception in 1643.[45] This should not be interpreted as a
planned policy of excluding the West Country planters, but rather
it reflects a changing population ratio based upon the continuing
influx of settlers from Norfolk and the surrounding areas. The arrival of the *Diligent* in 1638, with more than a hundred East Anglians, meant that numerical superiority rested in the hands of the
elders from old Hingham. Due to the community effort in resisting
the ecclesiastical policies of the Norwich bishops for better than

44. *Ibid.*, "Appendix," 163; Hingham Town Records, I, 28; Joseph Andrews,
will, 27 Sept. 1679, No. 1128, Suffolk Registry of Probate, Boston; Shurtleff, ed.,
*Mass. Bay Recs.*, I, 221.

45. Solomon Lincoln, *Hist. of Hingham*, "Appendix," 163, which is a compilation
of the names of office-holders. This does not include the two non-Hingham men,
Mr. John Blackledge, formerly of London, and Jeremiah Houchin, formerly of
Harleston in Norfolk; it is clear that these men acted as surrogates. The single
Hingham exception was Anthony Eames, who served his last term at the 1643
March Court.

twenty years, these emigrants came with a sense of purpose and cohesiveness. Nothing could be more natural than for neighbors and relatives to elect their own to the provincial posts—especially when they were Pecks, Hobarts, Allens, Jacobs, and Beales, the very families that had held positions of leadership in the old country. In fact, the choice of Edmund Hobart, Sr., in March 1635 as constable for Charlestown (the Hinghamites' *entrepôt*) testifies to this solidarity at the beginning of their American experience.[46] If it was a natural impulse to favor one's own, it was also the building stone of a "sad unbrotherly contention" in Hingham that within a decade's time would come close to endangering the very rock of the commonwealth.[47]

If this influx had its repercussions in the more distant halls of the Bay Colony's General Court, its effects were most obvious in this twelfth "Church of Christ" established in Massachusetts. Its pastor Peter Hobart, the Cambridge-educated son of the elder Edmund Hobart, belonged to the Presbyterian wing of the puritan reform movement, as did his spiritual father, Robert Peck, formerly of St. Andrew's. They held that the church officers—the pastor, who ministered and instructed (unless there was an ordained teacher who then instructed while the minister dispensed the sacraments), and the two deacons and elders, who supervised the congregation—constituted a presbytery. Once these officials had received the "gifts" of office, they formed a ruling council over the church. In Governor Winthrop's unflattering portrait, this was a system in which Pastor Hobart "did manage all affairs without the church's advice."[48] With the coming of Robert Peck from old Hingham in 1638, the church divided the ministry by ordaining him as "teacher." Hingham's church was now "double-barreled" and would remain so until Peck returned to England in 1641, where he would try

46. Shurtleff, ed., *Mass. Bay Recs.*, I, 134; "The First Record-Book of the First Church in Charlestown, Massachusetts," *New England Hist. and Gen. Register*, XXIII (1869), 187–191, 279–284, 435–444, testifies to the old Hingham influx.

47. J. Franklin Jameson, ed., *Johnson's Wonder-Working Providence, 1628–1651* (New York, 1910), 116.

48. James K. Hosmer, ed., *Winthrop's Journal "History of New England," 1630–1640* (New York, 1908), II, 244.

WEST PARISH CHURCH OF BARNSTABLE
*Built in 1717*

photograph courtesy Melvin Howard, Hyannis, Mass.

JAMES OTIS, SR.
*by John Singleton Copley*

courtesy Wichita Art Museum, Wichita, Kansas

MRS. JAMES OTIS, SR.
*by John Singleton Copley*

courtesy Wichita Art Museum, Wichita, Kansas

JAMES OTIS, JR.
*by Joseph Blackburn*

Coll. Mrs. Carlos A. Hepp
*Reproduction courtesy Frick Art Reference
Library, New York City*

MRS. JAMES OTIS, JR.
*by Joseph Blackburn*

Coll. Carlos A. Hepp
*Reproduction courtesy Frick Art Reference
Library, New York City*

SAMUEL ALLYNE OTIS
*by Gilbert Stuart*

Coll. Robert H. Thayer, Washington, D. C.

MERCY OTIS WARREN
*by John Singleton Copley*

*courtesy Museum of Fine Arts, Boston
bequest of Winslow Warren*

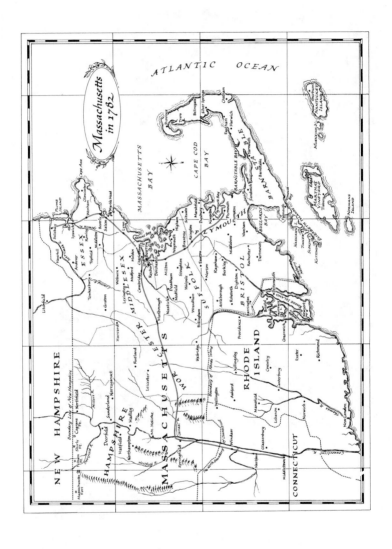

his hand at enforcing Presbyterian uniformity. These two strong-willed men, who had opposed episcopal interference in England, would be just as willing to challenge the Congregational way of the Massachusetts puritans. While that way had started in flux, without a clear-cut policy of separatism from the Church of England, or even an outline of polity, by 1634 it stood for churches "governed by Pastors, Teachers ruling Elders and Deacons" in which the "power lies in the wholl Congregation, and not in the Presbitrye further then for order and precedencye."[49] This was a position directly opposite to the beliefs of Hobart and Peck and their adherents from Norfolk.[50]

Unlike the Boston churches, which by 1640 included less than half the capital's population, the Hingham church encompassed virtually the entire town's 140 families.[51] There was thus an identity between townsmen and church members that gave to the pastor a role of unquestioned authority. The Rev. Peter Hobart was the highest-paid official in his community, receiving £70 to £100 *per annum* from the town, in addition to special land grants.[52] The many bequests from the faithful testify to the general approval his society gave to this status.[53] As pastor, Peter was in a key position to aid both his family and his adherents. The former, headed by his illiterate father Edmund and his brother Joshua, sought to dominate the political life of Hingham, while the latter sought to reconstruct their traditional way of life. The church presbytery mir-

49. John Winthrop to Nathaniel Rich, Boston, 22 May 1634, *Winthrop Papers*, III, 167.

50. For a perceptive account of early church polity in the Bay Colony, see Darrett B. Rutman, *Winthrop's Boston* (Chapel Hill, 1965), 18–19, 98–134.

51. *Ibid.*, 144; while the Hingham estimate is based upon a comparison of baptisms as recorded in Peter Hobart's diary, Mass. Hist. Soc.; and land owners in George Lincoln, ed., *Hist. of Hingham*, II, III.

52. Hingham Town Records, I, 4, 107, 118, 121; and also "Copy of a Record from the Great Book," 17 Jan. 1669/70, Suffolk Court Files, 10: 16 (No. 948), Suffolk County Court House, Boston. At this time the average clerical salary in Massachusetts was £55 *per annum*. At £100 Hobart was one of the highest-salaried men in the Bay Colony: see Joseph B. Felt, *Ecclesiastical History of New England . . .* (Boston, 1855–1862), II, 3, 160.

53. Bozoun Allen's bequest of £10 is the largest on record (No. 123), although the widow's mite of Margaret Johnson, which came to £5, is by no means unusual, Suffolk Registry of Probate, III, 181, Boston.

rored these aspirations. Peter Hobart was its pastor, Robert Peck its teacher, and by 1641 the deaconships, originally held by West Country men, had passed into the hands of Henry Smith from Derbyshire and Ralph Woodward, a merchant from Dublin and representative of the puritan trading community. The most important institution in Hingham now rested in the hands of the East Anglians.[54] In a way the Hinghamites might claim it as their special legacy.

The control of both the two-man Hingham delegation to the General Court and the presbytery by the East Anglians resulted in new judicial and political appointments favorable to their "party." Following their election as deputies in 1639, Edmund Hobart, the pastor's father, and Joseph Peck, the teacher's brother, were nominated along with Anthony Eames as the three commissioners for small causes. This office gave any two of them power to decide at their discretion, and thus without a jury, all legal suits in Hingham in which the damage was under twenty shillings.[55] The deputies then used their positions to award the liquor franchise to Thomas Cooper, and after him their other neighbor from old Hingham, Nicholas Jacob. Of equal import, the three men appointed by the General Court to evaluate property for the province tax came from their adherents, as did the constables elected in 1640.[56] The only important colony office still held by any of the first settlers from the West Country was the militia lieutenancy. With that exception, the East Anglians controlled all major positions of status and profit.

On the town level, the change was equally obvious, as may be seen from the personnel which formed the various governing committees. In 1637 and 1638 the land-grant and rate committees had achieved a form of parity for representation of West Country men and East Anglians. The "great lots division" committee was con-

---

54. Peter Hobart, 29 Jan. 1640/1, diary, Mass. Hist. Soc.; for Ralph Woodward see *Suffolk Deeds*, III, 176–177.

55. Shurtleff, ed., *Mass. Bay Recs.*, I, 255, 259; George L. Haskins, *Law and Authority in Early Massachusetts: A Study in Tradition and Design* (New York, 1960), 34.

56. Shurtleff, ed., *Mass. Bay Recs.*, I, 258, 295, 299, 302.

trolled by the West Country men, who held five out of the seven places. (This probably reflected their initial land holdings and greater familiarity with the land itself.) However, Anthony Eames was the only representative of the West Country settlers on the rate committee. The remaining eight members, headed by the elder Edmund Hobart, as well as Nicholas Jacob, Samuel Ward, and Thomas Underwood, were symptomatic of things to come. These were either East Anglian migrants or their mercantile friends. By 1644 they held absolute majorities on the three major committees which dealt with local taxes, land distribution, and town membership—although the West Country sector could always muster at least one representative on each committee.[57] By and large, West Country representation meant Anthony Eames and John Otis. The main support for Eames came from his leadership in the militia. He also had a team of oxen that he would rent out, certainly an asset in a farming community.[58] In addition to this, he joined the select circle of Hingham men who pooled their capital to erect a town mill.[59]

The case of John Otis is somewhat different, for he was essentially a farmer. Presumably his knowledge of the local land was excellent. He was almost always a standing member of the divisions committee, and his testimony on boundaries was cited in more than one court case. Otis might be considered the spokesman for the old-timers from Devonshire. While this could explain his two elections to the rates committee, he must have had also the respect of the majority of his neighbors, for he was sent to Boston as a grand juror in 1640, receiving six shillings for this service from the "country." And in 1647, long after most West Country men had ceased to play an active role in Hingham politics, he was elected as one of the nine men in charge of the town, as well as serving on the church seating committee along with Anthony Eames, Nicholas Jacob,

57. Based upon analyses of thirteen committees, 1637 to 1647, in Hingham Town Records, I, 28, 38, 46, 49, 58, 70, 81, 82, 83, 97, 98–104.
58. Petition of Anthony Eames, *ca.* 1640, in Lechford, *Note-book*, 405–406.
59. Undertakers, June 1643, Mass. Archives, LIX, 8.

and Ralph Woodward.[60] The inventory of Otis's estate listed £20 at loan in small sums to various townsmen.[61] As one's vote in the town was not secret these unpaid debts were in one respect political obligations. They undoubtedly increased Otis's influence in Hingham. The meaning of his life was as parochial as his debts.

Oddly enough, it would be a marriage in the Otis family that raised the first constitutional challenge to Congregational rule in the Massachusetts Bay Company. In 1641 John Otis's daughter Margaret presented her husband Thomas Burton, former "clarke of the prothonataries office," with a daughter, Hannah. This was the first step in a *cause célèbre* that would bring Burton's signature to Robert Child's *Petition*.[62] It is the third item in that 1646 document, which charged that baptism was denied the children of members of the Church of England until their parents had taken the covenant, that is particularly relevant.[63] To take the covenant meant to become an independent, and we know that Burton had not joined the Hingham Church.[64] Thomas Lechford, the attorney and critic of the Congregational way, who had also refused to take the covenant and separate himself from the Church of England, is our authority on what happened in Hingham. His *Plain Dealing: Or Newes from New-England* recorded the refusal of "master *Hubbard* Pastor, [and] *master* Peck Teacher" to "baptize old Ottis grandchildren, an ancient member of their own Church."[65] John Otis had attempted to gain church standing for his grandchild through his own membership and failed. At this juncture the Hingham Church still followed the Congregational usage which limited the

60. Hingham Town Records, I, 38, 58, 81, 86, 100, 104; Mass. Archives, XXXIX, 11.

61. Otis Inventory, 28 July 1657, Suffolk Registry of Probate, III, 100.

62. "A Declaration of the General Court . . . 1646," in *Hutchinson Papers* (Prince Society, *Publications*, I [1865]), 239.

63. Major John Childe, *New England's Jonas Cast Up at London* (London, 1647), 12–13, as in Peter Force, ed., *Tracts . . . Relating . . . to the Settlement of North America* (Washington, D. C., 1847), IV, iii.

64. George L. Kittredge, "Dr. Robert Child the Remonstrant," Colonial Society of Massachusetts, *Publications*, XXI (1919), 24.

65. Thomas Lechford, "Plain Dealing: Or, Newes from New-England," Massachusetts Historical Society, *Collections*, 3d Ser., III (1833), 93.

sacraments to the "Visible Saints" and their children. This must have been a very difficult decision on the part of the pastor for he was an early champion of the halfway covenant.[66] Then on May 30, 1641, Hobart baptized Hannah Otis Burton, thereby jettisoning Massachusetts's current doctrinal norm which forbade the extension of church membership directly to a grandchild.[67] This action, which upheld and extended the autonomy of the Hingham presbytery, exacerbated relations with the Boston authorities.

If Governor Winthrop's suspicion of Hobart's orthodoxy was still moot, the Hingham militia disturbance of 1645 removed any grounds for further doubt. This dispute involved Anthony Eames, the experienced militia leader and the outstanding West Country man in Hingham, who alone of the first planters had retained his official position in Hingham. In 1640 he had threatened "to looke out for himselfe elsewhere" if he did not receive a larger grant of land, which indicates some disapproval of the East Anglians' land policy. However, unlike several of his friends such as the ex-liquor dealer and former deacon Thomas Loring, Eames did not move, perhaps because he expected promotion to captain, which would bring with it an honorarium in the form of a special land grant. That would have supplied employment for his oxen, the lack of which had led him earlier to think of going elsewhere.[68] Following the

66. As Ezra Stiles put it, the "Boston Church was offended and dealt with Hingham because their Minister practised promiscuous Baptisms, not restraining it to Children of Communicants." See Franklin B. Dexter, ed., *Extracts from the Itineraries . . . of Ezra Stiles . . .* (New Haven, 1916), 259. John Allin in his *Animadversions upon the Antisynodalia Americana* (London, 1664), 5, states, however, that the rank and file at the Cambridge Synod favored the halfway covenant. Hobart undoubtedly had Allin and other ministers on his side (see below, n. 84).

67. Peter Hobart, diary, Mass. Hist. Soc.

68. In the period under study slightly fewer than half of the original West Country men moved elsewhere while slightly more than one quarter of the East Anglian contingent followed suit. If these figures are compared with Kenneth A. Lockridge's "The Population of Dedham, Massachusetts, 1636–1736," *Economic History Review*, 2d Ser., XIX (1966), 321–323, which shows a 25 to 40 per cent change in Dedham's early decades, then Hingham's extraordinary stability becomes evident, even for the West Country men. The real point is that three quarters of Hingham's East Anglian contingent stayed put. The East Anglian rejection of mobility was the major factor supporting the continuation of old Hingham modes and new Hingham's ruling oligarchy.

*cursus honorum* Eames was elected to the captaincy in the spring of 1645. Unfortunately, shortly after this election Eames committed some indiscretion, probably a disagreement with the Hobarts, which offended "the greater part of the town." The militia band then held another election and gave the office to the wealthy Norfolk man and "very good friend" of Peter Hobart, Bozoun Allen. The Boston magistrates, who were the governor's assistants in the Bay Colony and had the right of confirmation, refused to sanction this change until the General Court should meet. All in Hingham were charged to keep their former places. The supporters of Allen now called a training day for the militia. When Eames showed up and told them of the magistrates' position, they accused him of lying and refused to drill under him. The end result was a defection of two-thirds of the band to Allen, while the *de jure* leader Eames, now minus the militia, found himself denounced in church with Pastor Hobart moving to have him excommunicated.[69]

In the minds of the Bay Colony magistrates Peter Hobart's conduct was doubly offensive: it revealed his willingness to use the sacred church censure against Eames for obviously partisan reasons; moreover, when they corrected his actions he slighted their "authority." They feared that unless Hingham was reprimanded the commonwealth would degenerate into a "mere democracy." (And they still had an old score to settle with Hingham because of its religious unorthodoxy.) John Winthrop called the Hobarts to Boston to answer for their insubordination, whereupon far from expressing sorrow, they rejected his argument and charged him with exceeding his authority.[70] As the deputy-governor himself admitted, "many of the deputies were of opinion that the magistrates exercised too much power, and that the people's liberty was thereby in danger."[71] It was precisely this fear that the Hobarts exploited. They introduced a petition, signed by more than eighty of their

69. Hosmer, ed., *Winthrop's Journal*, II, 229–231. The quote on Allen is in Peter Hobart's diary, 14 Sept. 1652, Mass. Hist. Soc.

70. Hosmer, ed., *Winthrop's Journal*, II, 231, 235; Winthrop, [Memoranda of Occurrences, 1643–1647], in Belknap Papers, Mass. Hist. Soc.

71. Hosmer, ed., *Winthrop's Journal*, II, 235.

Hingham supporters, which "complained of their liberties infringed" and asked the deputies for redress.[72] This brilliant maneuver gained the support of fifteen out of thirty-one representatives at its high tide, while the issue paralyzed the central government for three months. Finally, thanks to ministerial pressure, doubting deputies were won over to Winthrop's position and fined the Hobarts and their petitioning adherents from the trainband.[73] The Hinghamites had no intention of paying their fines. They were led in resistance by their pastor, who intimidated the marshal by "questioning the authority of his warrant because it was not in the king's name." Considering the East Anglians' past observances of the royal writs one might be tempted to doubt Peter Hobart's sincerity, but it struck home at Winthrop and his associates, who had altered the Bay Company's oath so as to remove all reference to the king. Hobart's constitutional point was that "Government here was not more than a Corporation in England" and its action against him and the men of Hingham was not "agreeable to the laws of England."[74] Following the trend of events in 1646 this was the opportune time for a congregation organized along Presbyterian lines to appeal to England.

It was at this juncture that the Hobarts allied themselves with Dr. Robert Child and his petitioners, among whom was Thomas Burton, John Otis's son-in-law, who had seen his child initially denied baptism by Peter Hobart in 1641. This petition also declared that the Bay Corporation was but a chartered company and did not have a legal right to govern or to pass laws that infringed the "Naturall rights" of "freeborne subjects of the English nation" (which as a modern critic notes anticipated Locke's position by almost fifty

72. 14 May 1645, Shurtleff, ed., *Mass. Bay Recs.*, II, 97.

73. Hosmer, ed., *Winthrop's Journal*, II, 239; Shurtleff, ed., *Mass. Bay Recs.*, III, 19–26.

74. Hosmer, ed., *Winthrop's Journal*, II, 99, 264–265. Peter Hobart's remarks on the Bay Colony are in Childe, *New England's Jonas*, 6. Hobart's objection to the writs was a brilliant stroke. Judge William Pynchon saw its force and advised Winthrop to follow English usage, for the writs were not legal and it was not possible for Massachusetts to exist without England. See Pynchon to Winthrop, 9 Mar. 1646/7, *Winthrop Papers*, V, 134–137.

years).[75] The General Court recognized behind this defense of "civil liberty" a plot to weaken the autonomy of the colony and subject it to English authority. It ordered a day of fast and humiliation so as to implore God's assistance against those *"that seeke to undermyne the libertyes of Gods people here."* Pastor Peter Hobart, who caught the point, refused to comply, holding that his parishioners "would not fast against Dr. Child and against themselves."[76] Doubtless Perry Miller is correct in interpreting the *Child Petition* as a planned maneuver "to arouse the then Presbyterian Parliament against the Congregational power," but this does not account for the internal difficulties within Hingham.[77]

While Peter Hobart, his brother Joshua, and their friend Bozoun Allen posed now as the defenders of home rule, as well as champions of the Presbyterian viewpoint, the militia dispute in fact reflected the long-smoldering ethnic and political conflicts within their town. It has not been possible to locate the eighty-one signatures on the Hingham petition against Captain Eames, but we do have a list of the nine ringleaders, who were fined from £1 to £20, as well as a petition from five of the rank and file, who claimed their "poverty" prevented them from paying their smaller fines. The leaders are the four Hobarts—Edmund, Joshua, Thomas, and Peter, Bozoun Allen, Daniel Cushing, William Hersey, and John Towers—all from old Hingham, and Edmound Gold, from Kent, as was his servant John Winchester, while the four remaining petitioners were all East Anglians.[78] It is significant that there is not a single West Country man on either list. The split in the trainband reflects the regional origins of the Bear Cove planters. Eames of Dorset *v.* Allen of Norfolk is the West Country against East Anglia. No documents exist to

75. Childe, *New England's Jonas,* 9–10; Loren Baritz, *City on a Hill: A History of Ideas and Myths in America* (New York, 1964), 41.

76. Kittredge, "Dr. Robert Child," Col. Soc. of Mass., *Pubs.,* XXI (1919), 36.

77. Perry Miller, *The New England Mind: The Seventeenth Century* (New York, 1939), 454.

78. Shurtleff, ed., *Mass. Bay Recs.,* II, 113, 164. The court, after examining the petition, correctly held that some of the men "are of good ability." However, for the servant class, if they "will make an open acknowledgment of their offence, upon some lecture day, at Boston," their fines would be remitted. What the magistrates wanted above all from the accused was the acknowledgment of error.

show where John Otis, Sr., stood in this fray, or for that matter his son, who was twenty-five and doubtless an active member of the trainband. It is probably safe to assume that the elder Otis took either a neutral position in this conflict or a pro-Hobart position in spite of his West Country origins. While on the one hand he probably sympathized with Eames, on the other he was personally indebted to Pastor Hobart for having baptized his grandchildren. Moreover, Otis's age—he was now sixty-six—and the fact that his house in 1646 "burnt to the ground" afforded him perfect grounds for ambiguity.[79] It is true that Winthrop recorded that fire in his *Journal* as part of his compilation of events showing the "special providence of God, pointing out his displeasure against some profane persons, who took part with Dr. Child, etc., against the government and churches here."[80] However, Winthrop's remark is in reference to the *Child Petition*, which had been signed by Otis's son-in-law, and only inferentially about the militia dispute. And if Otis, Sr., took either a neutral or pro-Hobart position, his son John, if we might judge from both the absence of his name on the fine lists as well as his future hostility to the Hobarts, probably sided with Eames.

The Massachusetts General Court's solution for this militia leadership squabble was to impose officers from neighboring towns to take charge of the band. This brought about a closing of ranks within Hingham. By November the two former disputants, Bozoun Allen and Anthony Eames, were back again at their milling undertaking.[81] Obviously the desideratum was to regain control of the band and where dispute and defiance had failed humility might succeed. In 1648 the "Humble Petitions of the Souldiours of Hingham" were submitted to the General Court, thanking this honored body for many undeserved favors that they had received "from the

79. Peter Hobart, 15 Mar. 1645/6, diary, Mass. Hist. Soc. By mid-April Otis had rehoused his family by buying out Thomas Turner, his house, lot, "Two Acres meddow in the Broad Cove . . . and twelve Acres of land beyond Crooked Meddow," *Suffolk Deeds*, I, 70.

80. Hosmer, ed., *Winthrop's Journal*, II, 264, 321.

81. 17 Nov. 1645, Mass. Archives, LIX, 8; as well as both signing a local petition, *ibid*., CXII, 17.

Lord, or you his instruments" and requesting the privilege "which we take to be our due, to chouse our owne offesors." They were allowed to elect the lieutenant and ensign; these posts went to none other than Bozoun Allen and Joshua Hobart.[82] It was not till 1651 that they had authority to elect the captain. This time Bozoun Allen received his coveted prize, and upon his retirement the following year, the post went to Joshua Hobart, thereby completing that family's monopoly of local offices. However, the Boston magistrates, determined not to increase the Hobart influence, refused their consent in 1660 to Joshua's application as Hingham's official notary.[83]

By the 1650's Hingham had succeeded in preserving its autonomy. Part of the price of this was the control of its political life by the old guard from St. Andrew's in Norfolk. As expected, its pastor and its deputies opposed the Congregational tenets of the "Cambridge Platform," even when this meant a split in the East Anglian ranks.[84] Economically the plantation had prospered. While the major part of the extant documents confirm the general agricultural nature of Hingham, there are a handful of commercial references showing that it supplied boards, masts, planks, and small boats for the Boston market. Its mariners found steady work as carriers.[85] Significantly, the personnel was mostly from old Hingham. One surviving indenture indicates a high cost for servants. Dermondt Matthew's contract called for £4, a suit of clothing, and a pig *per annum*, while at its conclusion he was to receive "three suits of apparel and six shirts" as well as a "convenient lott." And his son's required two years of formal schooling at its conclusion.[86] For the

82. *Ibid.*, LXVII, 42; Shurtleff, ed., *Mass. Bay Recs.*, II, 252.

83. Upon the request that "Capt. Hubbard be empowered to give oath in all Civil Causes according to Law in Hingham," which would have made him the official notary, the legend is recorded, "Consented not by the Magistrates," 25 Oct. 1660, Mass. Archives, CXII, 129a.

84. Shurtleff, ed., *Mass. Bay Recs.*, III, 16; Thomas Hammond, a Suffolk man, had threatened schism in 1647 but was persuaded against it by John Allin, see Dexter, ed., *Itineraries of Stiles*, 359–360.

85. *Aspinwall Notarial Records* (Boston, 1903), 100, 124, 233–234; Lechford, *Note-book*, 304; Hosmer, ed., *Winthrop's Journal*, II, 321–322; and for occupational classifications, the "Inventory of Debts," Estate of Capt. Allen, Suffolk Court Files, 16: 31 (No. 1389), Suffolk County Court House.

86. Lechford, *Note-book*, 251. At the time of the elder Matthew's death in 1661 he was worth £112, Suffolk Registry of Probate, IV, 88.

Matthews, Hingham meant economic mobility. More typical of town life was the bickering over cows, broken fences, trampled grain, and land.[87] In the Tucker-Otis court case Anna Tucker sued for recovery of meadow land which had been assigned to her first husband, then exchanged to Nicholas Jacob, who gave it to John Otis, Jr. Edmund Hobart favored the Tucker claim, as did the jury, but the General Court after examining the evidence, including a deathbed statement of Jacob, reversed the judgment and found for Otis.[88] Young Otis thus retained this land which had come to him when he had married Mary, the daughter of Nicholas Jacob, formerly of old Hingham. He also had the extensive properties of his father as of May 10, 1649, although the latter was in "consideration of Tenn Pownds p. anno."[89] This is but one example of how well-to-do Hinghamites married each other regardless of their parents' different English backgrounds and past disagreements over policy.[90]

While John Otis, Sr.'s part in new Hingham's first quarter of a century was a minor one compared with the dominating roles of Eames and the Hobarts, it was essential in reconstructing the West Country-East Anglian conflict. Even in his old age the elder Otis retained some of the energy which in the past enabled him to pull up roots three times and to settle in America in his fiftieth year. Now, twenty-five years later in 1655, after being a widower for two years, he married the widow Elizabeth Streame of Weymouth, who was a competent woman in her own right.[91] In his new dwelling at Weymouth, with his Bible, feather beds, chests, two rugs, linen and pewterware, he must have been reasonably comfortable,

87. Lechford, *Note-book*, 80, 83, 175.
88. Mass. Archives, XXXIX, 1–11, 14, and *Aspinwall Notarial Records*, 372.
89. John Otis, Sr., to John Otis, Jr., conveyance, recorded 23 May 1655, in *Suffolk Deeds*, II, 161–162; Nicholas Jacob, will, 18 May 1657, No. 161, Suffolk Registry of Probate; and deposition of Ralph Woodward, Mass. Archives, XXXIX, 9.
90. This was a basic puritan marriage ideal; see Edmund S. Morgan, *The Puritan Family: Essays on Religion and Domestic Relations in Seventeenth-Century New England* (Boston, 1944), 19–20. For the significance of the Hingham marriage pattern, which I hold is the key to reconstructing that society's class structure, see Roland Mousnier, "Problèmes de méthode . . . ," in *Spiegel der Geschichte, Festgabe für Max Braubach* (Münster, Westf., 1964), 552.
91. See Elizabeth Otis's will, 22 Sept. 1672, No. 805, and inventory, Suffolk Registry of Probate.

and there he remained until his death in May of 1657.[92] Resettlement was not unusual in early Hingham, where one-fifth of the first settlers moved. The West Country men proved most mobile with half of the original lot-holders departing, while the old Hingham contingent, in which still a sixth left, was least mobile. Thus Otis conformed to his group profile, even to resettling in Weymouth (named and settled by immigrants from Dorset), although few of the first planters matched his continuing mobility. That so much can be found out about Otis and his neighbors, that documents exist, and that they recorded small farmers and tradesmen rather than just lords and clerics, signifies the emergence of the protestant, literate individual and the nuclear family. That there can be a story of the Otises is proof of this new phenomenon in Western history.

92. Peter Hobart recorded Otis's death in his diary, 31 May 1657, Mass. Hist. Soc. The Otis Inventory, 28 July 1657, Suffolk Registry of Probate, III, 100, lists his household items at Weymouth.

## ℋ II.

# PLYMOUTH ROOTS

Founders of successful families are ordinarily revered regardless of their material success, but John Otis II (1621–1684) deserves a more prominent place in the family annals than his father for grasping the opportunities of a new society with a sure hand. Unlike the elder Otis, John, Jr., refused to be content with producing for a market controlled by others. Rather, John II took his father's land, capital lent by his in-laws, and money entrusted by neighbors and entered into trade, industrial activity, and long-term land speculation. Moreover, his earlier political actions in Hingham, in which he challenged the authority of the constable, and later the special status of Pastor Peter Hobart and his brother Joshua, the militia captain, showed that he possessed a forceful style with strong popular appeal. Nor would there be a shortage of causes wanting leaders in Otis's future home at Scituate: in the 1660's the Quakers sought freedom of worship, while in the 1670's the "ancient" settlers joined together to exclude newcomers from sharing in the town commons. If Otis lacked sympathy for the plight of the Quakers, he had a vested interest in a restrictive land policy for he held by purchase the rights of a first settler. Yet John Otis II avoided these conflicts. When he left Hingham in his fortieth year he shook from his shoes the dust of dissension. For his last twenty years he honored the service requirements of the Scituate community by holding a number of local posts, but he did not enter the political life of Plymouth Colony itself. In Scituate John Otis II channeled his talents toward accumulating property and establishing his eight children.

However, before John Otis, Jr., settled down to a peaceful middle age, the Hingham references show a young rebel who fought against the town's 1650 taxes. In his own individualistic and hotheaded way he refused to pay his "rate either for Mr. Hubbard or for other Town charges" and resisted the constable when he came to collect.[1] When fined for his cantankerous actions he appealed the following year to the General Court for a remission; three years later he still argued that he was right. Finally in 1654 the Court proposed a compromise: if Otis would make a "full acknowledgment of his miscarriage" before the Hingham "congregation" the fine would be reduced to a nominal 30s.[2] As we hear no more of this matter the presumption is that Otis made the required confession and paid the 30s., thus saving himself from the punitive fine of £5. This case is an intriguing instance of the church used as an instrument of discipline by the civil authorities. What did Otis think of this settlement which traded a confession for £5? Were the Hobart supporters in the General Court the authors of this unholy compromise? What prompted the representatives who had censured the Hobarts in the past now to back them in this tax rebellion? Were they afraid of this early challenge to the public support of the clergy? What was the connection, if any, between Otis II's actions in 1650 and the 1646–1647 militia dispute? The extant documents answer none of these germane questions. However, the town records show Otis opposed to the 1655 tax exemption granted to the militia leader Joshua Hobart. In this John was joined by his brother-in-law John Jacob, by Henry Chamberlain and William Hersey, who had been fined £10 for signing the Hobart petition during the

1. Hingham Town Records, I, 109.
2. Shurtleff, ed., *Mass. Bay Recs.*, IV, Pt. I, 52, 191–192.

militia dispute, and by the two John Tuckers and seven other townsmen. In 1661 these leading landholders again dissented "from having Captayne Hubbard freed from paying his *rates* to the public charge of the Town, and for the mayntenance of the ministrye."[3] While they failed to convince a majority of the voters to side with them, it is significant that their protest transcended the regional divisions that had marked so much of the early politics of their town. Otis and his friends had objected to the Hobarts' special status and aggrandizement at their expense. In many respects this signaled Hingham's coming of age. At least on the upper level class interest had replaced ethnicity as a behavioral norm. The following year Otis moved to Scituate in the "Old Colony."

Doubtless many factors combined to lead Otis to Satuit, or Scituate—the "Cold Brook" of the Indians. As his past experiences showed, Hingham's small stage was crowded by the Hobarts. It had a limited amount of land and a town ordinance which gave the community a preëmptive right of purchase. He probably had about as much land as he could get in Hingham, for in 1658 he purchased the Cudworth homestead in Scituate. Thus even before his last altercation in 1661 with Peter and Joshua Hobart he had laid the foundations for moving. Scituate itself was less than a morning's walk from the Hingham "Playne" or training field. Many times John Otis must have taken the "old Indian path" over the gentle hills as they rolled down towards its small harbor, then covered by the primeval pine that reached the water's edge. Beyond lay the sandy beach with its daily sweep of shellfish and the massive cliffs that served as landmarks for its fishermen. The soil was loose where it was not rocky; yet it yielded a fair Indian corn as well as the English wheat. The forest easily provided shingles and boards. The seasonal runs of "Bass, shad, alewives, smelts and eels" with the ubiquitous cod that could be caught outside the harbor completed the list of nature's bounty.[4] It was push and pull, a decade of politi-

3. Hingham Town Records, I, 131.

4. [Samuel Davis], "History and Description of Scituate, Mass., 1815," Mass. Hist. Soc., *Colls.*, 2d Ser., IV (1816), 223–224, 228.

cal difficulties in Hingham, and Scituate's promise of larger opportunities that brought this second generation of Otises to resettle.

After his Hingham troubles John Otis II must have carefully
weighed those factors that would favor success in Scituate. A good
starting point was his store of silver shillings, some from Mary's
share of her father's estate.[5] These would find a general welcome.
Then he had the confidence of several well-to-do Hingham farmers, including his brother-in-law John Jacob. Finally, there was the
town itself. Unlike the closely tilled and tightly organized Hingham, Scituate had been wracked by internecine wranglings over
baptism. Its founding father and leading citizen Timothy Hatherly,
Esq., and half the church had favored "total immersion," while the
pastor John Lothrop, who had dropped the "sign of the cross in
baptism" as a popish superstition, and the rest of the congregation
held for the "laying on of hands." Lothrop's desire to cleanse the
baptismal rite from such post-apostolic additions as the cross reflected his larger separatism.[6] Unlike a majority of the first ministers
in the Bay Colony who still claimed a reformed but nonseparating
membership in the Church of England, Lothrop totally rejected
the mother church. The failure of this charismatic pastor to have his
way resulted in his departure with his adherents in 1639; they remained "stedfast in our resolution to remove our tents and pitch
elsewhere, if we cann see Jehovah going before us."[7] As if this were
not enough, the faithful in Scituate split again, with the majority
electing Charles Chauncy, who became Harvard's president in
1654, while the minority, who insisted they were the true first

5. Mary Jacob Otis's share of Nicholas Jacob's estate came to £40–50; see
Jacob's will, 18 May 1657, Suffolk Registry of Probate, I, 296, and inventory, III, 83.
6. For the background of this ritual issue see Marshall M. Knappen, *Tudor
Puritanism: A Chapter in the History of Idealism* (Chicago, 1939), 64–65. For
Lothrop see Harvey H. Pratt, *The Early Planters of Scituate* . . . (Scituate, 1929),
65–67, and the pastor's own record of separatist admissions in "Toutching the
Congregation . . . of Christ collected at Scituate," 330, Ezra Stiles Manuscripts,
Beinecke Library, Yale University, New Haven, Conn. For the nonseparatists of
Massachusetts see Edmund S. Morgan, *Visible Saints, The History of a Puritan
Idea* (Ithaca, 1965), 64–65.
7. John Lothrop to Mr. Prince, Scituate, 28 Sept. 1638, Rev. John Lathrop,
"Biographical Memoir of Rev. John Lothropp," Mass. Hist. Soc., *Colls.*, 2d Ser., I
(1814), 175.

church, formed another congregation under William Witherell.[8] An enterprising individual who could stay clear of such disputations might find being an outsider something of an advantage.

John and Mary Otis's new home in Scituate had formerly belonged to the Quaker sympathizer and Indian fighter James Cudworth, and then to Deacon Thomas Robinson from whom Otis purchased it in 1658.[9] This large house on Colemen Hill, with its lot, farm buildings, twenty acres of upland, an adjoining meadow, and other land near Stony Brook, was just what was needed for their growing family. They had started with Mary in 1653, added John in 1657, Hannah in 1659, and at the end of their first year in Scituate included Stephen. Within a decade's time there would be three more sons, James, Joseph, and Job, and a final daughter, Elizabeth, who was born in 1671. This was a fruitful marriage, with the added blessing that all eight children lived to maturity.[10] One of the strongest drives in Otis's life was to provide well for this large family, as attested by his will. In addition to taking care of his sons, which was standard practice, Otis provided a handsome dowry for his daughters, each one of whom was to receive £50, the price of fifteen head of cattle.[11]

As a result of John Otis II's move to Scituate he was now subject to the jurisdiction of Plymouth Colony rather than the Massachusetts Bay. Thus in 1662 John took the "oath of Fidelity" to the Old Colony. This meant new civic obligations and in that same year at the "Generall Court held att Plymouth" he served the first

8. For the correspondence on this see Samuel Deane, *History of Scituate, Massachusetts* (Boston, 1831), 59–88.

9. Thomas Robinson to John Otis, conveyance, 30 Oct. 1658, and 29 Sept. 1660 (recorded 1663), Deeds, III, 127–128, Old Colony Records, Plymouth Registry of Deeds, and partially reprinted in *Mayflower Descendant*, XVIII (1916), 91–94. By this purchase Otis obtained the land division rights of a first settler, which in the 1685 grant amounted to 50 acres, Scituate Town Vote, 23 Mar. 1684/5, R. T. Paine Papers, Mass. Hist. Soc.

10. William A. Otis, *A Genealogical and Historical Memoir of the Otis Family in America* (Chicago, 1924), 82–83.

11. John Otis, will, 11 Jan. 1683/4, Wills, IV, 78, Old Colony Records, Plymouth Registry of Deeds. The bovine figure follows the 1683 evaluation rates, Viola F. Barnes, *The Dominion of New England: A Study in British Colonial Policy* (New Haven, 1923), 91.

of his many terms on the Grand Jury.[12] Within Scituate itself Otis and his friend John Cushing (also from Hingham) frequently were called upon to take the inventories of deceased neighbors—and once Otis took a cow in for board. Of much greater consequence was the confidence of such townsmen as Thomas Shave and Elizer Clapp who entrusted Otis with their silver money.[13] This is the profile of the successful petit bourgeois.

Just as Scituate's past communal difficulties help to account for John Otis's quick entry into village life, so his interest in its leading jurisdictional curiosity, the Conihasset Partners, gives witness to his business acumen. This partnership's beginnings are interwoven with the forty-two "Merchant Adventurers of London," who held or obtained the English grants that gave legality to the new Plymouth Colony.[14] These were the financial backers of the Plymouth settlers. However, the lack of profits on the one hand, and general dissatisfaction on the other resulted in the Pilgrims' ending this relationship in 1626 when they obtained the rights of Timothy Hatherly and three other men who had succeeded to the full title of the "Merchant Adventurers." This agreement covered those lands "upon which the Plymouth men had actually settled and the patent to which, they had received in association with the London Company" from Sir Ferdinando Gorges's Council for New England.[15] But did this include a private settlement at Scituate (later adjudicated as three square miles) which the planter and undertaker, Timothy Hatherly, and associates held by virtue of their "original grant with and subsequent purchase from Peirce and Weston"—who had held two earlier patents? Timothy Hatherly said no. By 1642 this merchant adventurer—one of the few to settle in America—had by pur-

12. Nathaniel B. Shurtleff, et al., eds., Records of the Colony of New Plymouth in New England (Boston, 1855–1861), IV, 14, 61, 180, V, 196, VIII, 180, hereafter cited as Shurtleff, Plymouth Col. Recs.

13. Mayflower Descendant, XVI (1914), 126, XVII (1915), 24–25, 217. See also Thomas Shave inventories in Wills, Inventories, Etc. 1637 to 1685, 152, 207, Plymouth Registry of Probate; and Shurtleff, ed., Plymouth Col. Recs., V, 228–229.

14. Charles M. Andrews, The Colonial Period of American History (New Haven, 1934–1938), I, 279–283.

15. Pratt, Planters of Scituate, 17–19.

chase become the sole owner of the "tract of land at Conihasset." Hatherly then formed a "tenancy-in-common" of forty shares, some of which he sold to his friends. All the shareholders then formed a "voluntary association" known as the Conihasset Partners.[16] It was into this tidy arrangement that John Otis and four friends joined when on January 28, 1664, they purchased twenty-three out of the forty shares for £69.[17]

The Conihasset Partners, while not a corporation in the formal sense of the term, gave itself all the paraphernalia of a municipality. It had its own clerk, oath, records, way wardens, and committees. After all, was not its "muniment of title only thrice removed in a direct line, through the Council of New England, the London Adventurers and Hatherly, from the royal patent of King James himself"?[18] The question raised was on what basis could the Plymouth Colony Court claim fealty "so far as this land tenure was concerned"? This little enclave in, but not of, Scituate, of which John Otis II now owned almost a fifth with another fifth going to his son Stephen through marriage, proceeded to maintain a *de facto* independence of the Plymouth Colony until the consolidation of the Dominion of New England.[19] The profit would be in delaying division of the holdings among the owners until the land appreciated in value.[20] This was an investment in the future—and one that would multiply a hundredfold. That June, John Otis and Thomas Woodward took care of the present by buying sixty acres of "upland and meddow land" in Scituate.[21] In the following years John added to his holdings in Scituate as well as in Barnstable, where in 1667 he

16. *Ibid.*, 42–47.

17. Thomas Hatherly, conveyance to Otis, Cushing, Thaxter, Jacob, and Wilder, 28 Jan. 1663/4, Deeds, III (Pt. I), 11, Old Colony Records, Plymouth Registry of Deeds, and partially reprinted in *Mayflower Descendant*, XXVI (1924), 101–103.

18. Pratt, *Planters of Scituate*, 50.

19. *Ibid.*, 51–57.

20. This was made quite clear by John Williams in his 1686 action against the other 17 proprietors, Stephen Otis included, claiming damages of £200, Shurtleff, ed., *Plymouth Col. Recs.*, VII, 301–302.

21. Gowin White to John Otis and Thomas Woodward, conveyance, 1 Jan. 1664, Deeds, III (Pt. I), 12, Old Colony Records, Plymouth Registry of Deeds, partially reprinted in *Mayflower Descendant*, XXVI (1924), 102–103.

purchased a second homestead from John Smith for £150.[22] These activities place Otis in that small group of landholders in the Old Colony whose properties were valued at over £1,000. What is more to the point, they made him the richest man in that small community of 145 householders.[23]

As a large farmer who owned land scattered throughout Hingham, Scituate, and Barnstable, John Otis spent considerable time marketing the produce from his fields, marshes, orchards, and woodlands. We know that he visited Boston. There he had his clothes tailored as befitted a man of his station (and true to fashion, he was late in paying the bill).[24] John frequently attended Plymouth Court, which was the seat of many of his civic responsibilities, and while en route he stopped at many of the smaller towns in the Old Colony. These trips undoubtedly provided useful contacts. John had a major asset in the friendship of his brother-in-law, John Jacob. He owned Hingham's sawmill and supplied Otis with ten cords of wood for the elder John Gorum of Barnstable. Although Gorum had to be sued for payment, this relationship eventually led to the marriage of John Gorum, Jr., to Mary Otis in 1674.[25] And from John's orchards flowed the cider which must have evoked memories of the West Country. He sold it without a li-

22. John Smith to John Otis, conveyance, 25 Oct. 1667, Deeds, III (Pt. I), 148; and for other land transactions, Isaac Stedman to John Otis, 14 Nov. 1670, *ibid.,* III (Pt. I), 184; John Hanmore to John Otis, 4 Apr. 1672, *ibid.,* III (Pt. II), 259; the only recorded sale of land by Otis was in 1668 to Joseph Woodworth of Scituate, who purchased some meadow land for £30, *ibid.,* III (Pt. II), 272, Old Colony Records, Plymouth Registry of Deeds.

23. Based upon an analysis of probate documents, Wills, I–IV, Old Colony Records, Plymouth Registry of Deeds. For the number of householders, I have relied on the hitherto unused list of "Allowed and Approved Inhabitants of the Town of Scituate," *ca.* 1673, which lists 130 householders with a right to division of planting land, and 14 with only "a Common Priviledge Belonging to them." This would give an estimated population of about 900. See Suffolk Court Files, 12: 125 (No. 1183), Suffolk County Court House.

24. Jarret and Ashton Account, Sept. 1672, Suffolk Court Files, 12: 33 (No. 1135), Suffolk County Court House.

25. John Otis and Encrease Clapp *v.* John Gorum, 29 Oct. 1670, Shurtleff, ed., *Plymouth Col. Recs.,* VII, 162, for the details. John Jacob came to most of his wealth through the inheritance of Anthony Eames's only daughter, Margaret, whom he married in 1653, George Lincoln, ed., *Hist. of Hingham,* II, 372.

cense. This brought about his second recorded brush with the law when in 1671 John was fined 40s. for the offense.[26] His nineteenth-century descendent Amos Otis apologized for this departure from propriety. However, we might note that in seventeenth-century Scituate this was something of an upper-class prerogative which Otis shared with his distinguished neighbors, James Cudworth and John Williams.[27] One thing is obvious—the Otises did not take well to restrictions on their moneymaking proclivities.

Yet outside of these heterodox activities, or perhaps because of them, Otis prospered. He avoided the internal squabbles of 1671–1672 in which the first settlers declared the "towne to be full and that they would Receive Noe more inhabitants soe as to have Right in [the] Towne Commons." They were opposed by the more recent arrivals.[28] Otis had learned the advantages of not taking sides in this in-fighting. Moreover, his increasing wealth, which enabled him to build another home overlooking the beaver dam on what is now Otis Hill, obviated concern over the handful of acres involved. John II was also fortunate in that none of the devastations that visited Plymouth Colony in the wake of King Philip's War from 1675 to 1679 touched his lands, while more than a dozen households were burned and a score of his Scituate neighbors killed or wounded in the Indian attack of January 1677. A family tradition has it that John saw service in this war, and this is correct, for his name is found on the summer rolls for 1675 and 1676.[29] Finally in 1677 John Otis was elected constable. Could this have been because of the shortage of available talent? Otis thus ended his public life as the chief law-enforcing official in Scituate.[30] One wonders if he

26. Shurtleff, ed., *Plymouth Col. Recs.*, V, 81, VIII, 135. For the fame of West Country cider, see Wallace T. MacCaffrey, *Exeter, 1540–1640: The Growth of an English County Town* (Cambridge, Mass., 1958), 8.

27. Amos Otis, *Genealogical Notes of Barnstable Families . . .* (Barnstable, 1888–1890), II, 222; Pratt, *Planters of Scituate*, 370.

28. Scituate petitions to Governor Thomas Prince, 1 Jan. 1671/2 and 29 Feb. 1671/2, J. Davis Papers, Mass. Hist. Soc.

29. Scituate Selectmen to Gov. Josiah Winslow, 26 Jan. 1676/7, in Deane, *History of Scituate*, 401; George Madison Badge, *Soldiers of King Philip's War*, 3d ed. (Boston, 1906), 52, 75.

30. Shurtleff, ed., *Plymouth Col. Recs.*, VI, 11.

reflected upon his fighting Hingham's constable in the 1650's. *Mu-tatis mutandis!*

John Otis II's prosperity was most evident in what he did for his children. Specifically, this meant providing for his namesake and heir John Otis III in much the same form as his father had provided for him when he had married Mary Jacob, as well as marrying off his daughters. His eldest daughter Mary was married in 1674. Her husband, John Gorum, Jr., was the son of the elder Gorum, who had been Yarmouth's leading farmer, a tanner, the owner of the gristmill, as well as deputy to the Plymouth Court of April 1654. Gorum, Senior, had seen service as a Barnstable selectman and captain of the militia.[31] John Otis must have considered this a good match. The marriage of his son to Mary Bacon was an even better one. Her father, Nathaniel Bacon, was likewise a tanner. He had served as a deputy for thirteen years and as a Plymouth Colony assistant from 1657 to his death in 1673.[32] Nathaniel's Barnstable properties went *in toto* to John III. Father Otis helped with setting up the farm for the nuptials which took place on July 18, 1683. The governor officiated. But the father was "sick of body" and barely lasted out the year. On January 11, 1684, mindful of what "God hath graciously given me," John Otis II made his last will and testament. Disposing of an estate worth almost £1,500, he yielded his soul to his Maker and his property to his heirs.[33]

During his life the second Otis had been consumed by two objectives: the accumulation of property and the settlement of his

31. Otis, *Genealogical Notes*, I, 408–410, which notes that in one Barnstable rate list, John, Jr., was listed as the second most wealthy man in the town, after his brother, James. This rate, probably before 1710, is unfortunately no longer in the tax records of Barnstable, Office of the Town Clerk, Hyannis. The elder Gorum's estate was valued at £710.04.03, and included plate and a gold watch, "1 negro man" (no value given), as well as 100 acres of land that the Plymouth government gave to his heirs and which also was not valued. Thus the real value was close to £900, with the mill given to John, Jr.; in *Mayflower Descendant*, IV (1902), 153–158, from Wills, III (Pt. I), 162–164, Old Colony Records, Plymouth Registry of Deeds.

32. Otis, *Genealogical Notes*, I, 23–26; Bacon's estate came to £632.10.02. As there was no will, the estate was settled by court-ordered letters of administration.

33. John Otis, will, 11 Jan. 1683/4, Wills, IV, 78–80, Old Colony Records, Plymouth Registry of Deeds.

family. The first object was certainly realized, considering that in the three decades of his stewardship, he had at least tripled the family assets. The role he played within this society was that of the Elizabethan yeoman. The soil and its fruits, his many head of cattle, the wheat in his barns, the tallow, flax, and yarn in his kitchen all tell the same story, while his tailored clothes, table linen, brass and pewter (but no plate or Negro slaves) bespeak a point of comfort on the level of the minor English gentry.[34] While Otis was a member of the Scituate Church, he did not contribute to its parish building fund. His unwillingness to part with his shillings was an omission that could not have been overlooked in Scituate.[35] Even granting the built-in limitations of Old Colony politics, Otis, while active on the local scene, never entered the select ranks of the deputies or assistants as did his boyhood friend and neighbor John Cushing, whose background was almost identical. In short, John Otis like his father before him was a parochialist, partaking little of Aristotle's *zoon politikon*. But what of the settlement of his family? He undoubtedly had a hand in the marriages of Mary and John. Both the Gorum and Bacon families were active in politics, trade, and as their tanneries indicate, industrial enterprise. Otis himself had at least an indirect interest in this, as he supplied the Gorums and perhaps the Bacons with the bark for their vats. These three families were part of a small minority in the Old Colony who participated in a market economy. They were tied into the Boston export market rather than the barter home markets of the past. But this is just a tendency. John Otis II's real provision was a £1,500 patrimony. His son would use his share to obtain ends which his father either did not want or could not obtain.

34. Inventory, *ibid.*, 80.
35. See List of Contributions, 25 July 1681, R. T. Paine Papers, Mass. Hist. Soc. The case against Otis is *ab silentio*.

## 𝕊 III.

## THE BARNSTABLE
## HOMESTEAD

Although John Otis III's (1657–1727) public life started when he served with the Barnstable militia during King Philip's War in the 1670's, his political career did not commence until after the Glorious Revolution of 1689. His real opportunities came only after the disintegration of the "Plymouth Establishment." Before then he had followed the family tradition of piling up stones into fences, planting crops, and holding minor town posts. Now in 1692 John served as Barnstable's first representative under the new charter government. Later he became his county's treasurer, an expert on Indian affairs, and finally one of the four Council members from the Old Colony. On the local scene John headed the West Parish militia, frequently moderated town meetings, and held the probate judgeship and the office of chief justice of the Inferior Court of Common Pleas for Barnstable County.[1] Hand in hand, if not preceding these preferments, lay achievement in trade, commerce, and shipping which by 1720 made Otis Barnstable's leading merchant.

1. Otis, *Genealogical Notes*, II, 223; Barnstable Town Records, I, 51–130, and Probate Index, I, 2, *ca.* 1714, Barnstable Registry of Probate, III, 155, Barnstable, Mass.; *Journals of the House of Representatives of Massachusetts* (Boston, 1715) (reprinted by the Massachusetts Historical Society, [Boston, 1919]), *1715–1717*, 34; and for Scituate, Scituate Town Records, II, 23, Office of the Town Clerk, Scituate.

In his advance Otis tapped the resources of relations in Plymouth and Scituate. In turn he aided them and passed on to his own family an increased and extended nexus of connections, influence, and wealth. He sent John IV (1687–1758) and Solomon (1698–1778) to Harvard and helped them, as well as his son James Otis I (1702–1778), into commerce, the militia, law, and provincial politics. He was the founder of a most remarkable political dynasty.

John III knew that the ownership of land formed the basis of almost all activities in the world in which he lived. Especially in Barnstable, land constituted the basic respectability, that proof of solidity, as it were, the outward sign that marked those who took part in community affairs. Thanks to his marriage arrangements John Otis III, who was twenty-six at the time of his father's death in 1684, had this outward sign in his substantial farm. We are fortunate in possessing plans of this Barnstable property. Here John and Mary Otis spent the days of their life, and here their six children were born. As John came down the country road which bisected the farm along its horizontal axis he could see on his right the first field, which on its lower level adjoined a marsh, then Lane's "Small garden" bordered by some outhouses, next his own upper garden, which also touched the marsh and faced Sandy Creek, and his solid two-story "manshion house." Behind the house was a little field with the swamp in it, next his orchard, and then a small field to the rear of the house. Running the whole length of the road on the other side were his three long fields. The one nearest to his house held the barn with its yard, as well as a hay square.[2] In addition to managing this, John took care of the family properties in which he held a double share, as was the right of the first-born son, for in the distribution of estates, New England followed the law of Moses. An added proviso of his father's will allowed him the first fifth while his mother still lived.[3]

While the assets and family connections of John Otis III are

2. Charles Otis, "Description of Otis Estate," Gay-Otis Papers, Special Collections, Butler Library, Columbia University, New York City.

3. Wills, IV, 78–80, Old Colony Records, Plymouth Registry of Deeds. The double share probably followed Deut. 21:17; cf. Richard B. Morris, *Studies in the History of American Law . . .* (New York, 1930), 111–120.

indubitably respectable, they do not greatly differ from those of his father in 1662. But the political scenery was changing. When John III inherited his estate, Plymouth existed as an autonomous commonwealth. In the next ten years it became part of that experiment in imperial control, the Dominion of New England, next a silent witness to the Revolution of 1689, and finally a part of Massachusetts—having been merged into the enlarged charter government. The key to John Otis's success was his ability to adjust, exploit, and profit from vastly altering political arrangements.

The earlier Plymouth scene had been dominated by a handful of men who served as deputies, or reigned as assistants and governors. Between 1621 and 1686 only twenty-nine men became assistants. John Alden held his office for over forty years, William Collier served for more than twenty-five years, Miles Standish for eighteen out of twenty-five years, and Nathaniel Bacon (Mary Bacon Otis's father) after many years as a deputy graduated into this body in 1667 and served until his death in 1673. These men formed the backbone of the Plymouth Court. Their shared tenure meant that they acted more as a college than as an elective assembly. In Plymouth, provided one maintained the proper degree of religious orthodoxy, one's first election was tantamount to the conferring of a freehold for life. The governors' *cursus honorum* required long service as an assistant as seen in the careers of Thomas Prence, Josiah Winslow, and Thomas Hinckley. It was expected that the incumbent should die in office. With but rare exceptions the governorship itself was limited to the founding fathers and their sons, as was the role of assistants.[4] It should be remembered that it had taken John Otis II's friend and neighbor John Cushing, a member of a most gifted family, a lifetime of local service before his election as an assistant in 1690 to what was the last Court.[5] The

4. See Ebenezer W. Peirce, *Peirce's Colonial Lists, Civil, Military and Professional Lists of Plymouth . . . 1621–1700* (Boston, 1881), 3–4; Jacob B. Moore, *Lives of the Governors of New Plymouth and Massachusetts Bay* (Boston, 1851), 11–232; and for the orthodoxy requirement, John A. Goodwin, *The Pilgrim Republic . . .* (Boston, 1920), 501–504.

5. Shurtleff, ed., *Plymouth Col. Recs.*, VII, 306. As expected, John Cushing was one of the important landlords. The 1708 inventory of his estate records more than £1,200 worth of land, Plymouth Registry of Probate, II, 135.

Plymouth freehold, which at best took in 30 per cent of the house-holders, sustained this establishment without protest.[6] Under normal circumstances, these structural limitations would have operated against John Otis III, even with his enormous energy.

It was the crisis situation of the 1680's which upset this structure. Internally the Old Colony found itself buffeted by Quaker agitation, which in spite of, or more accurately, because of the proscriptions of this authoritarian state, brought about an undermining of "religion and all civil order."[7] Fiscally, the government staggered under the debts incurred during King Philip's War. The extensive desolation and destruction of property during that war now meant a larger tax on a smaller base. By 1690 the after-costs resulted in a tax of 17.5 per cent of the value of the Old Colony ratable estates (figured at £35,900).[8] The real loss, however, was in confidence. Many were convinced that "our sins" now caused the Lord God "to pour out upon us of the cup of trembling."[9] Had not the divines of the first generation predicted "a sweeping scourge" for the New England churches if they turned worldly? It was asked, "Who gave Jacob for a spoil, and Israel to the robbers? did not the lord,—he against whom we have sinned?" The wise saw the obvious conclusion: "God is spitting in our faces."[10]

If left alone the old leaders might possibly have restored the system. This was not to be, however. First there came Governor

6. As Samuel E. Morison noted concerning William Bradford, he had "urged rotation in office in 1624, but the freemen would not let him off," in *DAB* s. v. "Bradford, William." In 1643 the number of freemen was 232 out of 634 men bearing arms, or 34 per cent, based on Shurtleff, ed., *Plymouth Col. Recs.*, VIII, 173–177, 187–196. An analysis of the 1673 list of "Allowed and Approved Inhabitants of the Town of Scituate," gives 40 freemen out of a possible 136 eligible males or 30 per cent, Suffolk Court Files, 12: 125 (No. 1183), Suffolk County Court House; cf. George D. Langdon, Jr., *Pilgrim Colony, A History of New Plymouth, 1620–1691* (New Haven, 1966), 79–99.

7. Thomas Hinckley to William Blathwayt, Barnstable, 22 Nov. 1683, "The Hinckley Papers . . .," Mass. Hist. Soc., *Colls.*, 4th Ser., V (1861), 95–96.

8. See Richard Le Baron Bowen, *Early Rehoboth* . . . (Rehoboth, 1945–1950), I, 12, for table of taxes and number of soldiers drafted.

9. Thomas Cooper, *et al.*, to Thomas Hinckley, Bridgewater, 17 Apr. 1676, "Hinckley Papers," Mass. Hist. Soc., *Colls.*, 4th Ser., V (1861), 3, 7.

10. Peter Tillton to Simon Bradstreet, Hadley, 23 Aug. 1690, *ibid.*, 268–270; Roland G. Usher, *The Pilgrims and Their History* (New York, 1918), 266–268.

Edmund Andros and his Dominion of New England which turned its attention toward Plymouth in 1686. Governor Thomas Hinckley became a member of the Council, claiming that there he could best protect Plymouth's interest. Yet Barnstable soon had cause to note the change when its constable received a preemptory order to return the goods taken from the Quakers "on pretence of paying the minister without any Legall proceedings or Authority for the Same and contrary to his Majesties Gracious Indulgence to all his Loveing Subjects."[11] For Barnstable the Glorious Revolution hardly came soon enough. But the relief was lost in anxiety over the future mode of government. As Increase Mather realized, charters cost money. He warned Governor Thomas Hinckley (who had re-assumed his former place) that if Plymouth expected anything she must pay for it. But, Hinckley wrote resignedly, "the awful and righteous hand of God" had brought a "great drought" upon the land. He doubted that funds could be raised.[12] Nevertheless the towns throughout the Old Colony set about raising funds. John Otis was on the local Barnstable committee to sell "40 or 50 pounds worth of the Commons towards defraying expenses of sending to England for a charter"—but this was too little and too late.[13] The fabric of government had been rent. Authority was not resisted, but denied. Thomas Hinckley reported that in Barnstable a group of "young rebels" refused "to pay the Rates" even for the cost of troops fighting the Indians.[14]

The old leaders of Plymouth Colony now faced the possibility either of being "annexed unto the Government of New York," or of petitioning, as Cotton Mather so nicely put it, "that you may yet become a Province, united unto a Colony which you may find

11. At a Council at Boston to William Bestoe, 1 June 1687, Mass. Archives, XI, 40. This followed James II's "Declaration of Indulgence," Barnes, *Dominion of New England*, 125–127. See also Goodwin, *Pilgrim Republic*, 570.

12. Increase Mather to Thomas Hinckley, Deal [Kent], 12 Sept. 1689, and Hinckley to Mather, Boston, 4 Feb. 1689/90, "Hinckley Papers," Mass. Hist. Soc., *Colls.*, 4th Ser., V (1861), 211, 227–229.

13. 25 Feb. 1690/1, Barnstable Town Records, I, 63.

14. Hinckley to the governor, Barnstable, 13 Dec. 1691, Mass. Archives, XXXVII, 208.

it more advantageous for you to belong unto."[15] The result was obvious: the Old Colony became part of the Massachusetts charter government with a guarantee of four seats in the Council and representation in the Assembly. The currents of change washed away Andros, former Governor Hinckley, and the other remnants of the old order. John Otis, captain of the Barnstable militia, now received election as the town's first representative under the charter of William and Mary. He had witnessed the collapse of Plymouth's leadership before the Stuart rulers, and doubtless he had his thoughts about the Lord's anointed. John III gladly signed the oath of loyalty to the persons of the new monarchs (he did it twice),[16] but this did not mean that he or his fellow signatories yielded long-held beliefs on their rights.

As a representative, John Otis III placed his faith in neither kings nor men. As he saw it, he was subject to the royal charter and the laws of Massachusetts. Behind this attitude lay the theory of the king's two bodies. This had backboned John Winthrop's corporate commonwealth. It would serve the same purpose in John Adams's *Novanglus*, which declared that the colonies owed no allegiance to an imperial crown that included "in it a house of lords and a house of commons," but only "to the person of His Majesty."[17] Massachusetts had held this position in 1682 with its refusal to admit that it was subject to a parliamentary navigation act. Affirming allegiance to "our Soveraine Lord the King," it proceeded to pass its own navigation law as befitted its concept of itself as an autonomous realm.[18] In 1692 the representatives summed up these experiences in the first session of the General Assembly with their resolve that "the said house may use and exercise such Powers and Privileges

15. Cotton Mather to Thomas Hinckley, Boston, 26 [Apr.] 1690, "Hinckley Papers," Mass. Hist. Soc., *Colls.*, 4th Ser., V (1861), 248–249.

16. Simeon L. Deyo, ed., *History of Barnstable County, Massachusetts, 1620–1890* (New York, 1890), 381; oaths before William Stoughton, 31 May 1693 and Nov. 1693, Mass. Archives, XLVIII, 213[2] and 222[2].

17. Charles F. Adams, ed., *The Works of John Adams . . .* (Boston, 1850–1856), IV, 114.

18. Michael G. Hall, *et al.*, eds., *The Glorious Revolution in America: Documents on the Colonial Crisis of 1689* (Chapel Hill, 1964), 20–22.

here as the house of comons in England may and have usually done there allways having Respect to their Majesties Roy[al] charter and the Laws of this Province." They had declared that they should be considered the equivalent of the House of Commons, and as the manuscript journal reads, they expected this "as their due."[19] The royal governor witnessed an example of this Massachusetts independency when in November of 1693 the speaker of the House adjourned it without his consent. This clearly violated the charter. Major Penn Townshend, Dr. Daniel Allen of Marblehead, Mr. William Screven of Kittery, Mr. Nehemiah Jewet of Ipswich, and John Otis of Barnstable, the five leaders of the Assembly, who in all probability authored the 1692 resolve, were forced to acknowledge this mistake. They promised "they should be cautious for future of any such practice."[20] Yet these representatives did not yield in their loyalty to their province, nor did they cease in their desire to see Massachusetts governed by its own institutions. This is what John Otis argued for in 1698 when he attempted to persuade the governor and Council of the "need of opening forthwith a High Court of Chancery."[21] Here was the patriot, the man of vision, the provincial politician. The other side of Otis, the parochialist in action, is seen in the score of local tasks he undertook for Barnstable—settling its accounts with the treasurer, studying the feasibility of a Cape Cod canal, doing favors for his constituents, and working on boundary disputes.[22]

The depth of Otis's identity with Barnstable received its initial testimony when in 1686 he was admitted as a townsman, while his partnership with the Hinckleys, Bacons, Lothrops, Pains, and Crockers in the "fulling Mill" venture of 1689 confirmed his mem-

19. *Acts and Resolves, Public and Private, of the Province of the Massachusetts Bay* [1692–1786] (Boston, 1869–1922), VII, 34, 390–391, hereafter cited as *Mass. Acts and Resolves.*

20. *Ibid.*, VII, 29, 30, 36, and 391, following Council Records, VI, 309, Legislative Archives, State House, Boston.

21. 22 Nov. 1698, Mass. Archives, XL, 530.

22. *Mass. Acts and Resolves*, VII, 171; Mass. Archives, CCXLIV, 179, Docs. 287–289, XXXI, 17–19, XL, 954, XLV, 356, and CXIII, 439, 440, 505–507, 534, 534a; Survey of Tisbury, Dukes County, 1709, Suffolk Court Files, 558: 45 (No. 73), Suffolk County Court House.

bership in the local gentry. Along with this admission went service on local committees, involvement in the inevitable land disputes, and in 1690 the constableship.[23] The following year Mary took membership in Barnstable's Congregational Church. However, it was two more years before John ate with her at the "Table of the Lord," when he declared "in the Name of our Lord Jesus Christ, In the presence of God, and his Holy Angels, and with all possible Solemnity" that he covenanted himself with the people of God. John and Mary thus joined the "Visible Saints," waiting with them "for pardon and Remission, Beseeching him to make our Spirits Stedfast in his Covenant, and to Owne Us as his Church and Covenant People, forever, Amen."[24] The Otises now stood as part of the very marrow of their community.

Exactly what was this Barnstable like that John Otis III represented? We have noted the difficulties it faced in the 1680's from nature, the war debt, and the Quakers. A more serious problem for the Old Colony as a whole, and Barnstable County in particular, which held an almost constant one-third of the population, was the silent but ever visible demographic explosion of the seventeenth century. This quadrupled its people from roughly 2,500 in 1653 to slightly more than 10,000 in 1690. And while in this same period the number of towns increased from ten to twenty-nine, these new settlements, which occupied the less fertile and the uncleared lands, only partially alleviated the various tensions caused by a rapid increase of people in a nonexpanding economy.[25] Barnstable town provides four priceless documents for this era. First is the decision to divide the commons in 1692, which was quickly followed by the repossession of meadowland granted to Hinckley in 1659 (for that grant had the limiting clause "till ye Town Cause to order it otherways"). This could be the action of some of the young men whom

23. Barnstable Town Records, I, 51, 59, 64–65, 68.

24. Records of the West Parish of Barnstable, I, [11], Mass. Hist. Soc. As the covenant of the West Parish is not extant, the text follows that of the First Church of Scituate, *Mayflower Descendant*, X (1908), 90–96.

25. Bowen, "Population Estimates," in *Early Rehoboth*, I, 11–20. For the importance of cleared Indian fields in the early settlements, see Ralph H. Brown, *Historical Geography of the United States* (New York, 1948), 15–16.

Hinckley had denounced previously for not paying their rates, or perhaps it reflected the community's bitterness over his participation in the Royal Council established by James II's Dominion of New England. At any rate the former governor lost land he had held for over thirty years. However, it is to the actual divisions of the commons of January 12, 1697, and February 19, 1703 (along with the rejected proposal of January 30, 1694) that we must turn for our knowledge of those tensions as reflected in Barnstable's land distribution.[26]

This society believed that a man's station mirrored the design of Providence. The manner of dividing the commons in Barnstable, as in the frontier town of Northampton in western Massachusetts, testifies to the belief in a hierarchical social order. This is in marked contrast to the egalitarianism posited by Wertenbaker and Brown as the dynamic force within seventeenth-century Virginia and eighteenth-century Massachusetts.[27] In John Otis's Barnstable the ancient rule held "that the Lands within this plantation, both meddows and upland shall be divided . . . one third part to every house Lot Equally, one third to the Number of Names that are immovable and the other third according to Men's Estates." The first proviso favored the original settlers' successors, by either blood or purchase, while the third discriminated on the basis of the total wealth held. Only the second provision called for an equal division and that for but a third of the land to be distributed. Hence a study of these allotments outlines the diverse stations of the freemen, for they reflect in two out of three categories existing property concentrations.[28]

26. Barnstable Town Records, I, 64, 84–91, 127–128. The 1702/3 division list is in James F. McLaughlin, ed., *Records of the Proprietors of the Common Lands in the Town of Barnstable . . . 1702–1795* (1935), 16–22.

27. See Thomas J. Wertenbaker, *The Planters of Colonial Virginia* (Princeton, 1922), 38–59; and Robert E. Brown, *Middle-Class Democracy and the Revolution in Massachusetts, 1691–1780* (Ithaca, 1955), 401–403. Northampton's 1663 rule for dividing the commons gave 15 acres to each family head, 3 acres to each son, and 20 acres to every £100 estate, in Judd Manuscripts, I, 460, Forbes Library, Northampton, Mass.

28. This rule was first recorded in the 1640 records. It was reaffirmed in 1703. This issue received extensive debate on 11 Mar. 1701, when the Rev. Mr. Russell moderated the town meeting. Six items were on the agenda: "1 . . . whether the

An analysis of these proposals reveals a clearly defined property structure. At the top, 40 per cent of the land rested in the hands of about one-fifth of the farmers. This group included James Gorum, Nathaniel Bacon, Deacon Job Crocker, Captain Lothrop, John Hamblin, and John Otis. These interrelated families constituted the office-holding and ruling elite of the town. At the other end of the scale, less than one-fifth of the land was in the hands of almost 40 per cent of the population. To this group an acre of land, worth approximately £6, was of vital import. It comes as no surprise that this bottom stratum was the most vociferous in rejecting the 1694 division proposal. Better than half of this group registered disapproval, twice the average for all other strata. The 1703 share-division figures indicate that one out of every seven males participated only in the freemen allotment of land. This figure can be refined by removing from it the sons of the well-to-do. This then leaves a hard core of a dozen men, about 7 per cent of the town's adults, who constituted the relatively impoverished of this rural society. These are usually Barnstable's unknowns, including Ralph and Sam Jones, Sam Phiney, and George and Joseph Lewes. These men left no probate records. Presumably they either departed from the county or held no property at the time of death. A middle sector nested in between these two extremes. It represented a little better than 40 per cent of the males and held slightly less than half of the land.[29] Perhaps the most interesting point about these recipients of

---

bare admission of a person to be a Townsman gives him a Right to the Commons under our Circumstances; 2 . . . whether there be any Right of Commons belonging to the Commons already Divided?; 3 . . . Whether their be any Right of Commons to Personal Estates?; 4 . . . Whether any Right of Commons belongeth to house Lotts as such?; 5 . . . Whether any Respect Shall be had to the number of Male Children in each family?; 6 . . . Whether the Right to Commons heretofore granted to any Doth extend to his and their heirs and Successors." While these questions show some of the tensions within this community, they also reflect the views of the "old" established inhabitants. See Barnstable Town Records, I, 3, 121–125.

29. See John J. Waters, The Otis Family in Provincial and Revolutionary Massachusetts (unpubl. Ph.D. diss., Columbia University, 1965), Appendix 1, Table 1, for the 1694 proposal. Table 2 outlines the 1697 schema, while Table 3 represents the final 1703 division. If the distribution of the commons had been based solely on the freeman factor the average allotment would have been 28 shares. Almost one-third (57 out of 177) of the grantees received less than that.

the 1703 division is their stability within their geographical setting. Slightly more than 80 per cent of those receiving the 177 grants continued to reside in Barnstable County until the time of death.[30]

While the land distribution shows that the rich and poor existed in this New England town, the concentration of property in an upper-class group is less marked than in either Wertenbaker's "Nansemond County" for 1704 in which 45 per cent of the farmers held 80 per cent of the land, or the Boston of 1689, in which a gentry class, comprising 15 per cent of the polls, controlled 58 per cent of the wealth.[31] All things considered, the average man in this society probably enjoyed more of the things of this world than his peers in any other contemporary Western society. However, this widely held property does not necessarily equate with a belief in an egalitarian social order, just as an economically classifiable proletariat does not mean that a political proletariat exists. All modern theories aside, these men of Barnstable viewed themselves as part of an organic hierarchical community headed by the gentlemen "of much piety and worth." The real import of the Barnstable protests was that they cut across all property groups. This indicates the general stress of population upon a stagnant agrarian economy. Barnstable's failure in 1698 to maintain a schoolmaster gives additional testimony to this fact, while the presence of prostitution is but another sign of crisis.[32]

For Otis this period of stress in Barnstable, beginning with the collapse of the old Plymouth leadership, an event paralleled by conditions in the Massachusetts Bay, provided the ideal framework for a "new man." The crucial decade of the 1690's witnessed the unseat-

30. Barnstable Registry of Probate, III–X, XII, XIII, XVII, XX.

31. Rent Roll for Nansemond County, 1704, in Wertenbaker, *Planters of Virginia*, 197–201. I have followed the curve pattern and computed large farms at 200 or more acres. For Boston in 1689 see James A. Henretta, "Economic Development and Social Structure in Colonial Boston," *Wm. and Mary Qtly.*, 3d Ser., XX (1965), 79–80.

32. "Grand Jury Presentment," 1698, Suffolk Court Files, 31: 90 (No. 3725), Suffolk County Court House; and Presentments Made and Agreed Upon by the Grand Jury Inquest and Given in at the Quarter Sesions Holden at Barnstable . . . April 1708, Mass. Hist. Soc., Manuscripts, L.

ing of the old order on the one hand, and on the other, a period of dynamic experimentation and social mobility that brought with it the advent of a political and economic *nouveau riche*. Bernard Bailyn called attention to this in his analysis of the Belcher and Wentworth families, while a preliminary study of the "Harvard Graduates" reinforces this interpretation.[33] John Otis willingly assumed political leadership and at the same time pioneered in novel economic ventures both within and without his community. In this he received aid from his brothers in Scituate (where as early as 1690 he supplied glass for its meeting house),[34] as well as from those Boston merchants who extended him credit, and finally from associates in Barnstable. In 1696 he obtained the town's permission to erect the first warehouse on Barnstable Harbor at Rendezvous Creek. Thus began an era of expansion that increased the Barnstable fleet from one sloop of 10 tons to seven vessels totaling 170 tons in 1713. These ships, built at Middletown, Hingham, Bristol, and Plymouth (which nicely describes the Otis family activities) were two-thirds owned by John's townsmen. He himself had a part interest in the sloop *Elizabeth*. This was an exceptional performance for a provincial center. It marks Barnstable as one of the few outports in this period after 1700 to resist the trend of Boston consolidation and dominance.[35] John could consider himself fortunate in that his self-interest had combined with his community's needs. Trading, shipping, and whaling—these propelled Barnstable out of its depression. They also guaranteed Otis's preeminence. He was the transmitting agent for the missionary works of the New England Company, which gave him additional control of trade goods enter-

33. Bernard Bailyn, *The New England Merchants in the Seventeenth Century* (Cambridge, Mass., 1955), 196–197. The remark on the Harvard men is based upon an analysis of family backgrounds as found in Clifford K. Shipton, *et al.*, *Sibley's Harvard Graduates* . . . (Boston, 1873——), IV, V, which indicates a decline in students coming from first settlers and Harvard fathers, a steady increase from the skilled workers category (10 per cent), as well as 10 per cent unknowns.

34. "Letter-Book of Samuel Sewall," 3 Dec. 1690, Mass. Hist. Soc., *Colls.*, 6th Ser., I (1886), 113.

35. For the *Elizabeth*, see Register of All Such Ships . . . , Mass. Archives, VII, 472. The collected data come from Bernard Bailyn's *Massachusetts Shipping, 1697–1714; A Statistical Study* (Cambridge, Mass., 1959), 68, 79, 88, 96, 112.

ing the Cape area, while his notes circulated as a recognized medium.[36] By 1715 Otis stood as the leading merchant of his port.

We know a great deal about how John Otis III carried on his mercantile activities. The goods he dealt in fall into three classes. First are general materials such as box iron, flints, and nails; then finished consumer items such as brass skillets, pewter dishes, warming pans, chamber pots, alchemy spoons, frying pans, and "large new fashioned porringers" at 2s. each. And finally, there were luxury goods such as buckles, fine cutlery, men's hose, broadcloth, and "mohair" at 20s. for those who could afford it.[37] One does not know where to include rum in this list although Otis took care to go to Bristol and taste that universal solvent before purchasing it.[38] In short, we have what another generation would recognize as the stock of a general store.

Thanks to John Otis's tendency to delay payment (a talent he shared with the majority of his fellow merchants and litigants) we know a good deal as to the financing of this trade, which brought him into the world of such Boston men as James Oliver, Jonathan Sewall, Philip Hedman, and Job Lewis. Most of his goods came from Boston jobbers, who had imported them from England—assuming that Otis did not smuggle, which was a point Wait Winthrop would not concede, and once again assuming that the jobbers did not deal in illegally imported Holland ware.[39] John Otis usually

36. For the New England Company and its effects on the Cape economy, see George P. Winship, "Samuel Sewall and the New England Company," Mass. Hist. Soc., *Proceedings*, LXVII (1941–1944), 84–98. One note on Otis for £ 100 is preserved in Suffolk Court Files, 209: 124 (No. 24912), Suffolk County Court House. See also "A short Accot of the Present Stat of NE. Anno Domine [16]90," Miscellaneous Bound MSS, IV, Mass. Hist. Soc.

37. William Man and Phillip Hedman, accounts, Suffolk Court Files, 102: 80–83, (No. 10705), and 111: 18–19 (No. 11803), Suffolk County Court House.

38. Deposition of Joseph Sturgis, 9 July 1717, Suffolk Court Files, 119: 64–68 (No. 12931), Suffolk County Court House.

39. Wait Winthrop to John Winthrop, Boston, 8 July 1717, thought something was fishy when Otis's cousin told his story of a pirate ship that overtook a conveniently located boat, with provisions and an essential pilot, who after his service was landed safely between Cape Sable and Cape Cod. Winthrop wrote, "this story he told to the Governor and Councill today. He is a Barnstable man, Coll. Otis cousin, who was then present at the Councill; yet some suspect him, for he remembers not the masters name well, nor the ships name he was going in, but thinks they

received these goods on credit, entering them in his ledger under the merchant's name. Across the page would be listed the barrels of turpentine and whale oil, as well as the herring and other fish which he put up himself or received as payment from one of his own customers. All this he shipped to his Boston creditors who then entered credits on their ledgers. Only now and then would they strike a balance or perhaps receive a small cash payment.[40] Liquidity was at a minimum in this bartering operation sustained by sophisticated bookkeeping.[41] Mary Otis, as the wife of this prospering merchant, was conscious of her place in society. She wore the best Irish linen as well as imported calico and sought the "newest fashion patterns for Caps and bonets."[42]

So far we have looked at the mechanics and structure of John Otis III's business ventures. But what do we know about the man himself? Was he honest, was he ethical, was he solvent? With the best of evidence, these questions would be hard to answer definitively, and answers must come from what partial truths one can gather out of court dockets. The first thing to note is the large number of his creditors who sued him for payment. Representative of this group are such merchants as William Mann, who acted in 1715 to collect on merchandise consigned to Otis in 1711, and Jonathan Waldo, a specialist in dealing with "Country Customers," who brought a successful action against him in 1717. In these cases he did not deny the obligations and met judgment when called for by the law.[43] His delay was part of the custom of the times, when it was often cheaper to postpone paying a debt than to borrow at

---

called them by such names, he being a stranger to the master when he shipt himselfe just upon their going away," *Winthrop Papers*, Pt. VI (Mass. Hist. Soc., *Colls.*, 6th Ser., V [1892]), 346.

40. Suffolk Court Files, 102: 80–83 (No. 10705), Suffolk County Court House; and Jonathan Sewall to John Otis, Boston, 20 Sept. 1723, Otis Papers, I, 2, Mass. Hist. Soc.

41. For another example of this common practice, see the "Account Books" of Josiah Winslow of Bristol, 1690–1730, Special Collections, Butler Lib., Columbia.

42. Family Minite, *ca.* 1717, Harrison Gray Otis Papers, Box I, Mass. Hist. Soc.

43. Suffolk Court Files, 102: 80–83 (No. 10705); 111: 18–19 (No. 11803); 114: 20 (No. 12232), Suffolk County Court House; Carl Bridenbaugh, *Cities in the Wilderness: The First Century of Urban Life in America* (New York, 1964), 333.

interest. Otis doubtless claimed that his payments were in turn dependent upon his own customers' paying him or his family. Their debtors included such New England types as Samuel Jenkins of Falmouth. He sold "all his Cattle" to his father so that "Capt. John Otis [IV] might not sue him and take them from him for that he was in Capt. Otis's debt, and daily Expected to be sued."[44] Underlying this continuous litigation over debts, in which Otis became a legal expert with an extensive law practice,[45] was the chronic shortage of a circulating medium. As far back as 1690, Cotton Mather had pointed out in his election day sermon that the balance of trade ran against the Bay Colony, which meant that it was drained of every form of credit to the detriment of the people.[46] The need for a medium formed a constant theme in the politics of that time, with the General Assembly continuously seeking "proper Ways and Methods to facilitate Payments both publick and in Trade."[47]

So much for giving John Otis III the benefit of the doubt. Even if one's chivalry is offended by his treatment of such women as Sarah Martyn, the widow of a sea captain, who had to sue for the recovery of a debt of £114, or of Sussanah Jacobs, the Boston shopkeeper, who had a bond that Otis delayed meeting, this is no proof of fraud—although the reader might not want to have been an Otis creditor.[48] A somewhat dubious case dealt with the Reverend

44. John Brown, deposition, Nov. 1722, Suffolk Court Files, 169: 18 (No. 19244), Suffolk County Court House.

45. Unfortunately, the 1822 Barnstable County Courthouse fire destroyed most of its records up to that time, thus making it difficult to gauge the exact extent of Otis's legal practice. However, the Plymouth Minute Books for the Superior Court of Judicature give ample evidence on this point; see Minute Book I (Plymouth), No. 1719, 1723, etc., Superior Court of Judicature, Suffolk Court Files, Suffolk County Court House. See also John's action against his client John Blackmore for nonpayment of fees, Otis v. Blackmore, 1725/6, Suffolk Court Files, 168: 116 (No. 19183), ibid.

46. See Joseph Dorfman, The Economic Mind in American Civilization, 1606–1933 (New York, 1946–1959), I, 105–106.

47. Mass. Acts and Resolves, IX, 351 (ch. 9, 1717).

48. Martyn v. Otis for debt, 15 Oct. 1715, writ issued 22 July 1718, Suffolk Court Files, 114: 113 (No. 12568); Sussanah Jacobs, debt action for June 1723 obligation, writ issued 27 Aug. 1726, Suffolk Court Files, 172: 83 (No. 19674), Suffolk County Court House; however, she again lent money to him as seen in his obligation of 25 June 1725, Gay-Otis Papers, Butler Lib., Columbia.

Daniel Greenleaf, who claimed to have paid Otis £20 he owed him and was supported by several witnesses. Otis, backed by his brother Nathaniel, as well as his wife and son, denied this. The jury decided that Greenleaf had paid and the Superior Court affirmed judgment notwithstanding Otis's technical objection that no written proof of payment existed.[49] Still this leaves James Oliver's suit charging fraud against John Otis. Oliver claimed that Otis "on the 17th day of June Anno. Dom. 1714 . . . [did] sell Bargain and deliver unto the said plaintiff Eighty Six barrels of fish affirming the Same to be Herring at Eighteen shillings a barrell" and which Oliver found out much to his loss were "not Herring but ailwives and not good for anything." The jury found for Oliver.[50] Otis had probably received the misgraded fish from one of his clients and passed this offensive merchandise along to Oliver. Yet Otis, who at a later date helped pass an *Act for the better Curring and Culling of Fish*, certainly must have known what he was doing.[51] One question that can be answered with certainty was that of John Otis III's solvency. Unlike many of the leading Boston merchants, he left assets totaling £5,000 when he died in 1727.

John Otis III was indeed a "new man." He came to the fore by his skills, his ability to tap the capital of others, and his opportunism. He made the most of the chances offered by the new regime and charter government in Massachusetts. His entry as a representative in 1692, the same year in which he took the covenant oath, together with his continuing leadership in the West Parish militia (his brother-in-law headed the East Parish contingent) and active role in the town meeting, ultimately rested upon his performance.[52] He delivered on the political scene just as he innovated in the economic.

49. Otis *v.* Greenleaf, Apr. 1717, Suffolk Court Files, 119: 64–68 (No. 12931), Suffolk County Court House.

50. Oliver *v.* Otis, Feb. 1715, Suffolk Court Files, 103: 123 (No. 10865), and recovery, June 1716, Suffolk Court Files, 104: 81 (No. 10957), *ibid.*

51. 18 June 1726, *Mass. House of Reps. Jours.*, 1726–1727, 71, 76, 84.

52. Otis was the captain of the Barnstable militia, until its division into two companies in 1701, following the orders of the Earl of Bellomont, at which time the first foot went to Capt. Gorham and the second to Capt. Otis. The dividing line was later utilized as the bounds for the two parishes, Barnstable Town Records, II, 10.

His townsmen annually reelected him to the House until his elevation to the Council. And as a member of that honored body he served on the prime committee in charge of instructing the London agent, along with such notables as Elisha Hutchinson and Samuel Sewall in 1710 and 1711.[53] A decade later he joined forces with such old friends as Penn Townshend, Thomas Hutchinson I (1676–1739), John Cushing, and of course Sewall, insisting that the paper money emitted by Massachusetts have safeguards "so always that the value of the Publick Bills be not Depretiated."[54] Otis must thus be ranked as a monetary conservative. However, his continuing interest in the Council concerned the Indians, in which matter he was the acknowledged expert.[55] Although he traveled in the circles of the powerful he never really occupied any of the positions of provincial influence. Arrival sufficed. Such was the career of John Otis the Third.

John Otis's relatives aided him, and he returned the favor by helping them whenever possible. While mutual aid contributed to success, individual accomplishment was the necessary starting point. John's brothers and sisters illustrate this key combination in colonial mobility. Mary was the wife of John Gorum, whose role in Barnstable has been noted already. Sister Hannah, after what she described as a "long and lingering illness," died in 1676.[56] Elizabeth was the first of her clan to marry into the Allyne family of Old Colony fame. The larger part of the family property at Scituate went to brother Stephen, who had married Hannah Ensign, the mother of his seven children and the only daughter of an only son.[57] This was certainly a nice consolidation of property ending with Stephen as a director of the Conihasset Partners. He was also captain of the

53. See committees, 10 Nov. 1710, and 22 Oct. 1711, Mass. Archives, XX, 151, 176.
54. 21 Mar. 1720, *Mass. House of Reps. Jours., 1718–1720*, 371–372.
55. *Mass. House of Reps. Jours., 1715–1717*, 245; *1718–1720*, 314; *1722–1723*, 92–95; *1723–1724*, 132; *1724–1726*, 345; *1726–1727*, 84–85.
56. Hannah Otis, will, 2 July 1685, Plymouth Registry of Probate, I, 15.
57. Thomas Ensign, will, 3 July 1663, Wills, III (Pt. II), 18–20, and John Ensign, will, 5 July 1676, made as he went forth against the "barbareous Nations," Wills, III (Pt. II), 16, Old Colony Records, Plymouth Registry of Deeds. As there was only one heir in each case only goods and chattels were inventoried. For the family see *Mayflower Descendant*, X (1908), 175–180, 225–230.

local militia company and took part in the disastrous Nova Scotia expedition of 1710.[58] James the bachelor was somewhat of a dandy if we might judge from his fine sword and silver buttons. He had the distinction of being the first of his family to participate in a foreign expedition, that of Governor Sir William Phips against Quebec in 1690, where he perished before its walls. While one might be tempted to rate this as participation in an imperial project, James, in a manner characteristic of his family, interpreted it in purely parochial terms. These might be the battles of Britannia, but he was fighting "against the bloudy Salvage Heathen and Roman Catholick enemys of the people and Churches of God in New England."[59]

Of the two other brothers, only Joseph served in a political post above the town level. Like the rest of his family, he married well. His wife was his cousin, Dorothy Jacob Thomas, the daughter of the Plymouth judge. Joseph sat on the same bench as his father-in-law when he also became judge of the Court of Common Pleas for Plymouth, a post he held from 1703 to 1714. In addition, Joseph was a representative in the Assembly in 1710 and 1713.[60] There can be little doubt that his listing on the Scituate church rolls directly after the pastor and the two deacons is a correct estimation of his status.[61] The father of twelve children, he moved to New London in 1721, but not before his name had been dragged through the courts in connection with land fraud.[62] Lastly, there was Job, the father of seven. He married Mercy Little, a descendent of the Warrens of Plymouth Plantation. Job operated one of the first tanneries in Scituate, kept a store, and was a shipwright of some local fame.[63] The ketch *Little Otis* was his, and he probably worked on the

58. Pratt, *Planters of Scituate*, 53, 56, 62, 370–371; Stephen Otis left lands in excess of £2,200, will, 16 May 1729, Plymouth Registry of Probate, VI, 401–402.

59. James Otis, will, 1690, Suffolk Registry of Probate, Misc. Dockets No. 1790.

60. Pratt, *Planters of Scituate*, 53, 56, 62, 370–371.

61. "Records of the First Church at Scituate," *Mayflower Descendant*, X (1908), 90–96.

62. Court of Assize and General Goal Delivery . . . Holden at Plymouth . . . , Mar. 1716, Suffolk Court Files, 108: 2 (No. 11363), Suffolk County Court House.

63. Job Otis, "Petition," 1719, Suffolk Court Files, 119: 70 (No. 12934), *ibid.* However, he was not beyond delaying on his own bonds, as the successful action of Sarah Briggs for £200 indicates, Suffolk Court Files, 214: 44 (No. 27672), *ibid.*

*Sarah's Adventure* which belonged to brother Joseph, and perhaps on the *Elizabeth*—John's ship (and thus these three brothers belong in that broad group of capitalists whom Bernard Bailyn has studied in *Massachusetts Shipping*).[64] In 1721 he purchased six hundred acres at Pembroke for £900. For the remainder of his eighty years, he continued to accumulate the goods of this world.[65] All in all, a useful group who in their own way were leading to family dominance in the Old Colony.

John III's immediate family of six is illustrative of the same tendency. His first daughter Mary married her cousin, Isaac Little, who was approved for Council membership by Governor William Shirley in 1743. Mercy married Jonathan Russell, the minister's son, who would inherit his father's office. Son John IV, the heir of one of the richest men in the Old Colony, went to Harvard (a sure sign that the Otises belonged), and he married a woman from a very wealthy family. His father's will indicates that he received a marriage settlement of about £2,000.[66] John followed his father's footsteps in trade and in the local militia where he was captain. In the 1740's, along with Isaac Little, he ended up on the Council. This long delay was probably due to the hostility of Governor Jonathan Belcher, who steadily opposed the Otises during the 1730's. However, when Belcher was displaced by William Shirley, John's public life opened up again, and he crowned his legal career with appointment as king's attorney for Barnstable.[67] John IV's and Isaac Little's contacts were primary factors in James's career. Brother Nathaniel married Abigail Russell (thus doubling the connection with that family), was town clerk in 1726–1727 and a shipwright. His early death in 1729, before his fortieth year, cut short what might have been a profitable life. He seems to have had

64. Under dates 7 Oct. 1700 and 2 Jan. 1700/1, Mass. Archives, VII, 171–179, 472.
65. See sale of Baker estate to Job Otis, 1721, Suffolk Court Files, 141: 74 (No. 15749), and 158: 92 (No. 17881), Suffolk County Court House.
66. John Otis, will, 3 Apr. [1724], Barnstable Registry of Probate, IV, 472.
67. See John J. Waters and John A. Schutz, "Patterns of Massachusetts Colonial Politics: The Writs of Assistance and the Rivalry between the Otis and Hutchinson Families," *Wm. and Mary Qtly.*, 3d Ser., XXIV (1967), 545–546.

no trouble in obtaining creditors although his death found him insolvent.[68] He had also served as register of probate for Barnstable in his father's court.[69] The third son, Solomon, married Jane Turner of Scituate, a granddaughter of the Elder Brewster. Solomon graduated from Harvard in 1717. He is depicted by Shipton as the last of a breed whose life was occupied in filling well a number of small offices within his community, all of which, it should be noted, had fees attached to them. His most lucrative post was register of deeds for Barnstable, a post which his son, Solomon, also occupied.[70] Old Solomon remained on good terms with all the members of his family. His eldest brother John backed him in several ventures, one of which involved £500.[71] However, in 1766 his nephew Samuel Allyne had grave doubts about his integrity. Uncle Solomon could not resist the temptation to use the Otis name and pass bills for which he did not have credit. This placed the nephew in the unenviable position of either redeeming them or else seeing his own credit suffer.[72] The last son, his father's executor and probable favorite, was James, who fell heir to the family responsibilities in Barnstable.

Having lived the Biblical three score and ten years, John Otis III departed this life in 1727 respected, solvent, the father of a multitude, an honored member of the Council, and Barnstable's leading citizen. Like his father before him, he had tripled the family assets in his lifetime, ending up as one of the three richest men in the county. He had also moved his family into the stream of commerce; merchants and shipowners his sons would remain. Wherever one turned and found a political office, it must have seemed that there was an Otis. John was captain of the militia, Nathaniel register of

68. See Nathaniel Otis, inventory and settlement, 18 Feb. 1729/30, Barnstable Registry of Probate, IV, 497a–498, V, 117, 154.

69. Probate Index, I, 2, *ibid.*

70. Shipton, *et al.*, *Sibley's Harvard Graduates*, VI, 200–201. At Harvard Solomon "won distinction as either the ringleader or the best marksman in three destructive riots."

71. "Bond," 22 Sept. 1719, Misc. Bound MSS, VIII, Mass. Hist. Soc.

72. Samuel A. Otis to Joseph Otis, Boston, 7 Feb. 1766, Gay-Otis Papers, Butler Lib., Columbia; and Samuel A. Otis to Joseph Otis, 13 Feb. 1766, Otis Papers, II, 125, Mass. Hist. Soc.

probate and town clerk, Solomon was register of deeds for Barnstable. Only James had not transferred his flair for accounts to office. In addition, Otis's in-laws and the families of his brothers had their own secure niches in their local power structures. In Barnstable even the ministry in the person of his son-in-law Jonathan Russell was part of this influence pattern. John Otis III could rest secure in the knowledge that the family tree was well rooted in Plymouth soil.

# BARNSTABLE BAILIWICKS

By the beginning of the eighteenth century when John IV (1687–1758) and James Otis (1702–1778), entered public life, the profile of a Barnstable politician had taken a fairly set form. Availability, to use a modern expression, was the prerogative of a limited number of first families. The list is small: the Bacons, Bourns, Gorhams, Lothrops, Thatchers, and the Otises were its mainstays. It need hardly be added that most of these families already were closely connected by marriage, although this in itself did not insure political unanimity. They shared something else in common—property; this society did not entrust the conduct of public affairs to those who lacked competence in managing their own estates. Their stage was the town meeting. It was here that those who aspired to office were heard, while their mettle was tested in committee work. If the initial assay was favorable, the next step would be to serve as hogreeve (an official who keeps track of the hogs), way warden, surveyor, and ultimately selectman. Somewhere along the line one would become a justice of the peace and perhaps obtain a rank in the local militia. Only after this proven service might one move on to the lucrative plums, such as county sheriff which Governor Shirley in 1741 estimated to be worth four or five hundred pounds a year, registrar of deeds, or even better, a judge of probate, posts in the giving of the governor which required county connections.[1] Assuming one had cornered such a position and was still moving up, the next step would be taken as an elected representative to the General Court, where with luck and longevity a Council seat awaited before retirement with dignity. In Barnstable this process took the better part of thirty years.

Yet such a simple outline hides as much as it reveals. Always there would be more aspirants than offices, more politicians than political plums. The fields would be winnowed by the winds of time, while personality and nepotism were factors of real import. The careers of John Otis III's sons illustrate this pattern. John IV, the firstborn, had been groomed to assume his rightful place in society. John received his A.B. from Harvard in 1707, then in course took the second degree in medicine, and in 1711 married Grace Hayman of the wealthy Rhode Island mercantile family. In Barnstable he practiced medicine, entered trade, served on various town committees, and acquired a captaincy in the local militia. In the 1720's he shifted his interest to the law and built up a local practice in the Barnstable Court where his father sat as chief justice.[2] In the next decade his practice became quite extensive. It probably was not hurt by the charge that he had fixed a jury to win a case for a hard-pressed client.[3] John IV never pushed any of his various activities, be it medicine, trade, or law, so as to dominate the Barnstable scene, nor does he seem to have given offense to his colleagues, for then he had no need to achieve wealth and status in his community. In fact, in 1747 John was elected directly to the Massachusetts Council, bypassing the traditional apprenticeship in the lower house. This was made possible by his impeccable local and

1. William Shirley to Newcastle, Boston, 23 Aug. 1741, Charles H. Lincoln, ed., *Correspondence of William Shirley* . . . (New York, 1912), I, 42.

2. Shipton, *et al., Sibley's Harvard Graduates*, V, 339–340.

3. John Norton, deposition, 29 Mar. 1734, in which he noted that as the jury was going out "I heard Capt. John Otis who was one of the case for the defendants say Capt. Jenkins stand to it." Suffolk Court Files, 268: 24 (No. 39023), Suffolk County Court House.

provincial connections and by the advent of Governor William Shirley. John Otis was a gentleman born and so died in 1758 after experiencing a political life of effortless success. The career of James, the youngest son, is the contrasting story of a man with a genius for organization. As a merchant, lawyer, politician, and speculator, James was the master of endless details in a drive for success which left him the first man of Barnstable.

For three generations "prudent marriages and careful husbandry" had been characteristics of the Otis family. James Otis's marriage in 1724 to Mary Allyne, when they were both twenty-two, was no exception to the rule. Joseph Allyne, the bride's father, although a native of Plymouth, had moved to Wethersfield, Connecticut. James probably met Mary while there on his father's business. On her mother's side Mary counted as an ancestor Edward Dotey, whose singular claim to fame is his signature on the Mayflower Compact.[4] While property did accrue to her, it certainly did not approach that of John IV's wife.[5] James, however, was the youngest son. Mary's Copley portrait, although painted after her family had been reared, reveals a somewhat square, plain face, while the plump figure indicates that this must have been a full-bosomed young woman.[6] The marriage of Mary and James was based upon more than property consolidation. Unlike John's delicate spouse who successfully mothered but a single child, Mary became pregnant on an average of once every eighteen months for a stretch of twenty years. All told, Mary presented James with thirteen children, although two epidemics took their toll in life and health. Six of this large brood did not survive infancy, the highest mortality rate since the family's coming to Hingham in 1631.[7] Their first child was a boy, born on February 5, 1725, and they named him after his father. James, Jr., was followed the next March by Joseph, and during the next six years three daughters were added to this growing family.

4. Otis, *Memoir of Otis Family*, 83.
5. Nathaniel Stillman to James Otis, Sr., Weathersfield, 25 Apr. 1743, Otis Family Manuscripts, I, 15, Butler Lib., Columbia.
6. Otis, *Memoir of Otis Family*, 85.
7. *Ibid.*, 99–106.

First was the famous Mercy in September 1728; then in 1730 sister Mary, who would marry the wealthy Boston merchant and future loyalist, John Gray; and Hannah in 1732, destined to be the family old maid. The following years introduced a heavy note of sadness, for the next three children, Nathaniel, Martha, and Abigail, all died in infancy. With Elizabeth in 1739 and Samuel Allyne in 1740 all went well. However, neither Sarah, born in 1742, nor another Nathaniel in 1743 would survive, while the last child, an unnamed girl, died the following year. Mary's constant gracing of the "borning room" near the large chimney on the first floor of the family house undoubtedly weakened her health, while the deaths of so many children produced a certain melancholy cast to her disposition.[8]

James inherited the family homestead by the terms of his father's will, along with its large old chests, three fine mirrors, and one of the first clocks in the county. James and Mary would live all their lives in that "high double house with a gambrel roof and three dormer windows." However, they embellished it with more fashionable cabinets and damask-covered tables and added to the collection of plate that showed to advantage on the sideboard, perhaps to remind themselves as well as others of the solidity of its owners.[9] It was here that Otis played the role of a country squire, eased by good rum, standing ribs and mutton chops, as well as by fine pipes of Madeira for which he kept an open eye.[10] Summer would find the house shaded by its "great buttonwood trees" while in winter it was warmed by its immense fireplaces which consumed more than fifty cords of wood.[11] Yet these signs of gentility should not disguise the fact that this house was the center of a large farm. Neither London the Negro slave, the earthy servants, nor the girls as their

8. [James Otis, Sr.] to [James Otis, Jr.], Weathersfield, 14 Apr. 1740, Gay-Otis Papers, Butler Lib., Columbia.

9. John Otis, will, 1727/8, Barnstable Registry of Probate, IV, 472; Gustavus Hinckley, sketch, in Trayser, ed., *Barnstable*, 445; Otis Family MSS, IV, 309, Butler Lib., Columbia.

10. James Otis, Jr., to James Otis, Sr., Boston, July 1745, Otis Papers, I, 56, Mass. Hist. Soc.

11. Katharine S. Anthony, *First Lady of the Revolution: The Life of Mercy Otis Warren* (Garden City, N. Y., 1958), 27.

mother trained them in soap-making and embroidery would be permitted an idle moment. And as James's work took more and more of his time, Mary Otis became the mistress in fact and name.[12] No small part of the family's increasing prosperity must be credited to the competence of this hardworking New England wife. Yet there were moments of recognition. When Barnstable came to celebrate its centennial in 1739, it was held on this and the neighboring Hinckley farm.[13]

James had served a long apprenticeship in his father's store. He had clerked, argued with debtors, shipped goods, traveled for bargains, and come to know how to turn a penny on every transaction. This was a going enterprise. The large number of memoranda, orders, dunning letters, lists, and ship instructions departs but little from those of the 1720's.[14] Neighbors such as Gabie Goodspeed and relatives such as Uncle Solomon would still bring in bed tick at 8d. a yard, or the finer worsted for which Otis posted a credit or made an exchange in butter, cheese, or some other commodity.[15] Exactly how extensive the family's part in the local weaving industry was is unclear, although James was the major supplier of wool to artisans such as Sam Richards. He was also a large purchaser of mohair and other materials.[16] In addition Otis dealt in onions, produce, and the more important exchange articles of pickled fish and pork.[17] In his turn he purchased boards, rum, manufactured goods, and an increasing number of luxury items such as silks, satins, fine linens, and ribbons.[18] While James did engage in some coastal trade

12. For a surviving example of Mercy Otis Warren's needlework, see display in the Pilgrim Museum, Plymouth.

13. Trayser, ed., *Barnstable*, 445.

14. Itemized lists (n.d.), Otis Legal Memoranda, 118, Suffolk County Court House.

15. Memo with 1731 entry, "Received of Solomon Otis Esq. weaving 27 yards of worst" and from "Goodspeed 13 yards ½ of bed tick at 8d per yard," *ibid.*, 145.

16. Memo, and account, Otis Legal Memoranda, 142, 151, Suffolk County Court House; Eliot Tyler to James Otis, Sr., Boston, 30 June 1737, Otis Papers, I, 12, Mass. Hist. Soc.

17. Antipas Hathaway to James Otis, Sr., 29 Aug. 1740, Otis Papers, I, 81, Mass. Hist. Soc.

18. Receipt, Benjamin Crocker to James Otis, Sr., 1 May 1742, Gay-Otis Papers, Butler Lib., Columbia; and order lists (James Otis, Jr.?), Otis Legal Memoranda, 68, Suffolk County Court House.

and would ship two or three hundred bushels of grain for Freeman Parker, Ebenezer Crocker, and himself, his business was mostly within the Cape and was subsidiary to Boston.[19] In the absence of a bank or clearing house he exchanged local notes for his Barnstable neighbors as well as for such merchants as Josiah Quincy of Boston.[20] These various activities formed and maintained relationships that would be of value in the future. The great difference between James's management of the business in the 1730's and his father's twenty years earlier is the absence of lawsuits from suppliers for nonpayment. This was a solvent enterprise marked by increasing prosperity.

If James's roles as family man and merchant were traditional, so were his duties as a leading citizen in the third decade of the eighteenth century. Otis was a member of the town's committee of thirteen which sought to police the conduct of "Indians negroes and other disorderly persons" who formed the lowest sector of his society.[21] This was usually the servant group. In the Old Colony, drinking, bastardy, and miscegenation amongst the lower-class whites, the Negro slaves, and the indentured Indians (with occasional assistance from the "Saints") were social problems that the ruling class considered not only as immoral, but also as involving a loss in time and service to the masters. (Historically this amalgamation into the lower white servant class explains in large part the

19. William Newcomb to Isaac Lothrop, Jr., Sandwich, 14 Dec. 1734, contains the earliest reference located on a shipping venture, Suffolk Court Files, 1236: 39 (No. 166241), Suffolk County Court House. See also invoices, Sam Sturgis to James Otis, Sr., 14 Jan. 1742/3, Otis Papers, I, 47, Mass. Hist. Soc.; and James Otis, Sr., to Mr. Howland, 22 Sept. 1755, Suffolk Court Files, 1269: 76 (No. 171516), Suffolk County Court House. For additional products, reverse side, Port of Boston pass for the *Ranger*, 9 Nov. 1750, Otis Family MSS, I, 26, Butler Lib., Columbia. For grain shipments see order for "Corn to go on Board Nye at the Deep hole," which included a mixed cargo of corn and rye, and which concluded with the instructions, "you will Put some Rum and Sugar and some coffee and a Little Molasses to Receive the money when the Company is Paid off" (n.d.), Otis Legal Memoranda, 144, Suffolk County Court House.

20. Josiah Quincy to James Otis, Sr., Boston, 29 Sept. 1737, Otis Family MSS, I, 8, and John Miller to James Otis, Sr., Middleborough, 22 Dec. 1736, Gay-Otis Papers, all Butler Lib., Columbia.

21. Barnstable Town Records, II, 59.

disappearance of the Cape Indian and Negro.)[22] Petty larceny of a scarf and a few rags, even when the goods were returned, called for threefold damages and court costs as "James Robin an Indian man of Sandwich" found out to his dismay when he was sentenced to service for "One Year and Six months and Twenty-four days."[23] As a justice of the peace, for which he was commissioned in February 1734, James would join with his brother John in enforcing the letter of the law on indentures.[24] Nor was this a disinterested

22. Lorenzo J. Greene, while recognizing this trend in his *Negro in Colonial New England, 1620–1776* (New York, 1942), 96, 198–210, only supplied statistics for mulattoes in Rhode Island for the year 1782, at which time they constituted one-eighth of the total (464 out of 3806). His earliest figures, at least for Barnstable, underestimate the Negro totals; see Barnstable Registry of Probate, I–III. While the material on miscegenation is fragmentary, due in large part to the loss, deletion, or destruction of church confessional records, Emil Oberholzer's *Delinquent Saints: Disciplinary Action in the Early Congregational Churches of Massachusetts* (New York, 1956), 134–144, lends substance to this point. For Barnstable see the confessions of Tamor, a Negro Woman, and Experience Peter, an Indian Woman, 27 May 1739, and 6 Feb. 1742/3, Records of the East Parish Congregational Church, 1725–1816, I, 77, 79, in Office of Barnstable Treasurer (custodian), Barnstable; and Joseph Otis *v.* Isaac Hinckley, July 1746, Suffolk Court Files, 387: 108–16 (No. 62026), Suffolk County Court House. Nathaniel Freeman in a letter to the Mass. Hist. Soc. in 1792 stated that of the almost three hundred local Mashpee Indians "at least two-thirds are mixed" with Negroes, Mass. Hist. Soc., *Colls.*, 1st Ser., I (1792), 230. R. L. Bowen in his study of "warning out notices" in *Early Rehoboth*, II, 140, 142, 152, records the cases of four Negroes, and two mulattoes—one of whom was from Newport. One unused documentary source is the private list of Pastor Ebenezer Gay, The Death of Blacks, entries 1749 to 1778, which if representative shows a mulatto to Negro ratio of one to three, in Vital Records (Gay Pastorate), First Church Records, Hingham, Box 8, Mass. Hist. Soc. See also "Records of the First Church of Scituate," *ca.* 1730, *Mayflower Descendant*, XI (1909), 138–142. That this was not always *déclassé* may be seen in the marriage of Mary White, granddaughter of Gowin White, the Conihasset Partner, to her African slave, James Newell, in 1690. Their son, James, Jr., married into the Nichols family, in Deane, *History of Scituate*, 314, 382–383.

23. "Sentence," 19 Mar. 1740, Court of General Sessions, Barnstable, John Sturgis, clerk, as in Otis Family MSS, I, 9, Butler Lib., Columbia. On 25 Mar. 1742 Robin changed masters, entering into a new indenture with John Fuller of Barnstable for a term of two years in consideration of £36 which was paid to Consider Howland of Plymouth County, *ibid.*, I, 12 (as witnessed by John and James Otis, justices of the peace).

24. For the commission see William H. Whitmore, *The Massachusetts Civil List for the Colonial and Provincial Periods, 1630–1774* (Albany, 1870), 145. Outside of the Robin indenture, see also indenture between Joseph Freeman "an Indian Boy" and Benjamin Lothrop, 20 July 1753, Gay-Otis Papers, Butler Lib., Columbia, once again witnessed by John and James Otis as justices of the peace. For execution of a writ of attachment, see John Sturgis *v.* Robin Sunkason, "Indian," 29 Nov. 1743, before James Otis, and executed by John Otis, deputy sheriff, 5 Jan. 1743/4, Suffolk Court Files, 1254: 113 (No. 169125), Suffolk County Court House.

action, for besides his slaves, he held at least three Indian servants by indenture in this period.[25]

James Otis's involvement in the values of his community is best seen in his legal practice. A nineteenth-century tradition has it that Otis became a lawyer by chance when a neighbor, finding himself without counsel, asked James to defend him. James is reputed to have won the case and thus entered law.[26] The first case record we have of Otis's legal work is dated 1730. The following year he took the oath as attorney before Justice Benjamin Lynde of the Superior Court.[27] James's practice mirrors the Barnstable community. Almost without exception the routine crimes of theft, violence, and murder that came to the attention of the court originated with the impoverished whites, the Negroes, and the depressed Indian groups. Yet the Barnstable juries had their own interpretation as to how the law should be enforced. The notation, "Both partys agreed that Eleven Jurors shall try this Case one of the twelve not being Indifferent," is not uncommon and illustrates the procedural flexibility of country justice.[28] In matters of substance, juries, when asked to convict women such as Mehitable Will for the killing of "her Female Bastard," continually brought in verdicts of not guilty.[29] Perhaps they counted upon the solemn terror of the court proceedings in which the accused was charged with not "having the fear of God before her eyes but being thereto instigated by the Devil" to have a reforming effect. In the case of Jeremiah Ralph, indicted for the death of Jacob Jacob, James Otis was successful in having the charge reduced to manslaughter, as "premeditated Malice" could

25. See indentures, Thomas Ames "indian man," 10 Feb. 1733/4, James Paump, a literate "Indian Boy," 24 Jan. 1737/8, and Solomon Pepeno "Indian man," 25 Dec. 1740, all to James Otis, Suffolk Court Files, 1234: 11 (No. 165980); 1242: 100 (No. 167168); and 1249: 54 (No. 168134), Suffolk County Court House.

26. Emory Washburn, *Sketches of the Judicial History of Massachusetts from 1630 to the Revolution in 1775* (Boston, 1840), 213–214. The opportunity might have been provided by James Otis (as executor) *v.* John Savell, Apr. 1730, Suffolk Court Files, 218: 22 (No. 29184), Suffolk County Court House.

27. Barnstable, 23 Apr. 1731, Minute Book, 1729–1736, Superior Court of Judicature, Suffolk County Court House.

28. Barnstable, Apr. 1737, No. 7, 11, Minute Book, 1733–1741, *ibid.*

29. List of Prisoners, Barnstable, 17 Apr. 1733, 16 July 1745, Suffolk Court Files, 249: 28 (No. 35139); 381: 12 (No. 60778), Suffolk County Court House.

not be proven. Ralph pleaded benefit of clergy. He was released after a branding "with the Letter T on the Brawn of his left Thumb." Flexibility, however, can work both ways. The Indians Solomon Nautompon and Philip Wepequish, who had stolen £15 from Shubal Gorham, the town's representative to the General Court, were not so fortunate in their punishment. It was ordered that "Each of them be Whipped ~~Fifteen~~ Twenty Stripes on his Naked Back at the Public Whipping Post" and pay triple damages. (Presumably they merited five extra stripes because their crime was against a magistrate.) If unable to pay, they were to be sold into servitude for six years.[30] Only rarely did James handle a paternity suit such as that of the lad bound to Christopher Stuart of Provincetown. Stuart's niece claimed that the lad had "gitton her with Child in the Last week in May" although the uncle added, "I think I can prove that he was than out a whalon."[31]

The vast bulk of James Otis's legal work, however, reflected an upper and middle class concern over property. Not an untypical client was Nathaniel Staple, who in a dispute over land thought his antagonist "more Dishonest than Ahab was with Naboth."[32] In processing land titles, Otis was a careful craftsman who researched seventeenth-century deeds and town records. His everyday work dealt with an unending series of debt actions on notes, bonds, and accounts due. Otis was himself a constant litigant against his customers and debtors.[33] In addition, he had to protect such clients as

30. Barnstable, 21 Apr. 1733, Minute Book, 1732–1735, Superior Court of Judicature, Suffolk County Court House.

31. Christopher Stuart to James Otis, Sr., Provincetown, 12 Mar. 1735/6, Otis Papers, I, 11, Mass. Hist. Soc.

32. Nathaniel Staple, Jr., to James Otis, Sr., Taunton, 22 Mar. 1749, Suffolk Court Files, 1232: 137 (No. 170518), Suffolk County Court House; see also Bethiah Child to James Otis, Sr., Rochester, 13 Apr. 1741, Misc. MSS, Box 4, Mass. Hist. Soc.

33. James Otis, Sr., deposition concerning nonpayment of legal fees by Dr. Solomon Bacon, 21 Mar. 1732, Suffolk Court Files, 248: 22 (No. 34875), Suffolk County Court House; James Otis, Sr., *v.* Cornelius and Peter Drew, ship carpenters, for nonpayment of bond, 21 Jan. 1734/5, *ibid.*, 269: 48–49 (No. 39228); James Otis, Sr., *v.* Benj. Quincy of Middleborough for a debt of £5, *ibid.*, 380: 50 (No. 60579); and James Otis, Sr., judgment against Eleazer Metcalf, Bristol trader, 21 Nov. 1745, for £4.4.8, not executed, with notation of Charles Church, sheriff: he "is dead and I cannot find aney of his Estate," 23 June 1746, *ibid.*, 387: 37 (No. 61928).

Jonathan Bourn, who had been caught catching fish at ebb-tide with "Loop nets" and wanted Otis to challenge the town's ordinance.[34] There would be quarrels between neighbors that defied solutions. What could poor Ebenezer Finney of Middleborough do with neighbors who had twice pulled down his fence and stated "they will pull it down as often as I put it up"?[35] These cases are standard for any lawyer who has ever hung up a shingle. The real importance of Otis's legal career is to be found in the money he made, the nature of his clientele, his legal contacts, and the geographical distribution of his practice.

In his home town James Otis's clients included his fellow merchant Samuel Sturgis, Captain John Gorham who shipped his goods, Peter Thatcher who wanted Otis to think of the next world and at the same time save him sixpence in this, Ebenezer Lewis, Sylvanus Bourn a political confidant, Joseph Lothrop, Roland Cotton, and Thomas Winslow, to cite but a few. In Barnstable these were the merchants, shipbuilders, traders, and substantial farmers of the community. Most of them were justices of the peace and formed or would form by 1760 the backbone of the County Court of Common Pleas.[36] This influence pattern was repeated for the Cape Cod area in general. John Turner, of Scituate's leading family, who insisted that lawyer Otis stay at his home if he returned from Boston that way, John Marshall a member of the famous legal family, the Rev. Othniel Campbell of Plimpton, sea captains Abajah White and Ebenezer Clapp, Christopher Stuart the whaler from Provincetown, and the Indian property owner Elisha Sachem all stood for important interests within their own bailiwicks.[37] They spoke not only

34. Jonathan Bourn to James Otis, Sr., 24 Apr. 1742, Otis Papers, I, 41, Mass. Hist. Soc.

35. Ebenezer Finney to James Otis, Sr., Middleborough, 13 Apr. 1741, Gay-Otis Papers, Butler Lib., Columbia.

36. Whitmore, *Massachusetts Civil List*, 104, 145–146.

37. John Turner to James Otis, Sr., Scituate, 11 Apr. 1748, Otis Papers, I, 83, Mass. Hist. Soc.; James Otis, Sr., to John Marshall, legal account, Sept. 1744, for £68 15s, Suffolk Court Files, 1255: 131 (No. 169332), Suffolk County Court House; James Otis, Sr., statement, as attorney for the Rev. Mr. Campbell of Plimpton, May 1744, Mass. Archives, XII, 517; Abajah White to James Otis, Sr., Marshfield, 24

for Bristol, Scituate, and Plymouth, but also for hamlets such as Pembroke, Windham, Sandwich, Taunton, Eastham, Truro, Attleborough, and Chatham Harbor.[38] Of even greater importance were the friends and legal contacts James made as he went up and down the dusty Cape roads. James Warren of Plymouth was a close associate as early as 1734, while Otis had working relationships with John Winslow and James Bowdoin.[39] When the case demanded it, James Otis, William Bollan, Robert Auchmuty, and Jeremiah Gridley could pool their talents; they worked together to purchase a potentially profitable milling works in 1744.[40] That Otis could consider such a venture is testimony to both his thrift and his success.

In July of 1744 James Otis represented almost half of all the liti-

---

Sept. 1741, Otis Papers, I, 35, Mass. Hist. Soc., who delayed payment as the province had not yet paid him for the use of his sloop; and Ebenezer Clapp, Rochester, 1742, who stated simply, "I go a boating and cannot come to pay you now," *ibid.*, I, 45; Christopher Stuart to James Otis, Sr., Provincetown, 12 Mar. 1735/6, *ibid.*, I, 11, with reference to past legal work; and Elisha Sachem, power of attorney to James Otis, Sr., Barnstable, 29 Oct. 1728, Suffolk Court Files, 1224: 80 (No. 164620), Suffolk County Court House.

38. See letters, orders, bonds, etc., to James Otis, Sr., from: Moses Mandell, Bristol, 8 Mar. 1744, Gay-Otis Papers, Butler Lib., Columbia; John Turner, Scituate, 11 Apr. 1748, Otis Papers, I, 83, Mass. Hist. Soc.; Robert Covey, Plymouth, 1737, *ibid.*, I, 13; Isaac Little, Pembroke, 16 Apr. 1734, *ibid.*, I, 4; B. (?), Windham, 16 June 1742, *ibid.*, I, 43; Joseph Pearse, Sandwich, 1730, Gay-Otis Papers, Butler Lib., Columbia; James Walker, Taunton, 1743, Suffolk Court Files, 1254: 69 (No. 169047), Suffolk County Court House; Godfrey Alfrey, Eastham, 1 Nov. 1740, Gay-Otis Papers, Butler Lib., Columbia; Michoh Gross, 14 Jan. 1742/3, Truro, *ibid.*; John Foster, Attleborough, 8 Sept. 1747, *ibid.*; Benj. Godfrey, Chatham Harbor, 26 Oct. 1743, Otis Papers, I, 50, Mass. Hist. Soc.

39. The relationship with James Warren is evident from Warren's testimony on Otis's behalf in Otis *v.* Cornelius and Peter Drew, 21 Jan. 1734/5, Suffolk Court Files, 269: 48–49 (No. 39228), as well as the fact that Warren continued to witness Otis's paper, as did brother John; see Jabish Wadsworth, bond, Kingston, 26 Apr. 1735, Suffolk Court Files, 270: 20 (No. 39392), Suffolk County Court House. See also James Otis, Sr., account and receipt, to John Winslow, Plymouth, 22 Sept. 1733, Suffolk Court Files, 1233: 4 (No. 165860), *ibid.*; same to same, 27 Dec. 1735, Gay-Otis Papers, Butler Lib., Columbia; as well as James Otis, Sr., to James Otis, Jr., 10 June 1748, enclosing Bowdoin's execution, Otis Family MSS, I, 19, *ibid.*

40. See Thomas Cobb to James Otis, Sr., Taunton, 24 Oct. 1744, "pray use your Best skill" in our behalf for which you will receive £10 and "if you think proper call in Mr. Bollan to assist you if you care," in Otis Papers, I, 60, Mass. Hist. Soc.; (?) Shulburne to [James Otis], 11 July 1747, noting Mr. Auchmuty desires to "be with him one hour or two before the Court," *ibid.*, I, 79; Jeremiah Gridley to James Otis, Sr., 5 Dec. 1743, requesting speedy enquiry, *ibid.*, I, 51; and Gridley to Otis, Jan. 1743, in which Oliver and Warren are mentioned in the mill venture involving £2,500, *ibid.*, I, 52.

gants in the Barnstable Court.[41] He had extended his local practice to its maximum possibility as he could hardly speak for both sides in an action. "Learned he is not" was the academic comment of John Adams in the 1760's, though most of Otis's contemporaries were more realistic in evaluating his talents.[42] Isaac Doane, when he wrote "I'll give you Dubel for Coming" to Eastham, knew he would get his money's worth.[43] In fact, Otis became so successful that Sam Willis of Dartmouth begged Otis not to take up any case against him.[44] Samuel White, a Harvard man and able lawyer in his own right, shared that sentiment when he insisted that Otis defend his client at Taunton.[45] While James's local practice was large, he constantly rode the court circuit to extend it and increase his income. In the law, Otis averaged 15 to 20s. an action. The only way to make a living with such low fees was to establish an extensive practice. One can get some idea of the money Otis made from his list of fees for a 1737 March Court. It involved 40 actions that came to £30, while at the June Court for Bristol in 1741, Otis had 113 charges, and for the April and September Courts for 1741 at Plymouth, the case load was 52 and 108 respectively.[46] His long list of bonds and other paper for 1737 to 1748 comes to £4,681 old tenor. By 1745 Colonel Otis (for he had picked up the militia title) was making close to £1,200 a year from his legal work.[47] As one of his nineteenth-century descendents observed, this was the key by which "he accumulated a large part of his ample estate."[48]

41. Barnstable, July 1744, Minute Book, 1740–1746, Superior Court of Judicature, Suffolk County Court House.

42. 8 June 1762, Lyman Butterfield, et al., eds., The Diary and Autobiography of John Adams (Cambridge, Mass., 1961), I, 227.

43. Isaac Doane to James Otis, Sr., 20 Feb. 1737/8, Otis Papers, I, 16, Mass. Hist. Soc.

44. Sam Willis to James Otis, Sr., 19 Aug. 1741, ibid., I, 33.

45. Samuel White to James Otis, Sr., Taunton, 29 May 1741, Misc. Bound MSS, XI, Mass. Hist. Soc.

46. For the account of fees, Mar. Court 1737, see Otis Legal Memoranda, 88, Suffolk County Court House. The Bristol Court list for 1741, and Plymouth for Apr. and Sept. 1741 are in the Gay-Otis Papers, Butler Lib., Columbia.

47. Otis Legal Memoranda, 101, Suffolk County Court House; and accounts, Gay-Otis Papers, Butler Lib., Columbia.

48. John Otis, Otis Family Genealogy, [ca. 1833], 3, Gay-Otis Papers, Butler Lib., Columbia.

This was a society of fundamental values which were reechoed in its conservative church. In Barnstable, James was a pillar of the West Parish, while his brother John IV was one of the founding fathers of the Second Church in the East Parish. James's pastor, as well as the private tutor for his children, was his brother-in-law Jonathan Russell, a clergyman of orthodox views befitting his Yale education.[49] His parish remained almost untouched by the Great Awakening. While it is true that Nathaniel Ewer and family defected to establish a "separate" church in 1750, this defection developed from a doctrinal rather than a "new light" dispute, which involved a marginal group from Yarmouth and Hyannis.[50] The Great Awakening served as an occasion, not a cause, for Ewer's separation. For twenty years Ewer had been objecting to lax discipline, changes in hymn singing, and dancing by the young folk.[51] Pastor Russell, however, saw no need to join with his county colleagues in denouncing the itinerant preaching and the revivalism of the 1740's.[52] His ship was not tossed by the emotional currents of Enthusiasm. Yet this congregation was mindful of its Christian obligations and empowered its deacons to relieve the "poor out of the Churchs Stock," which it entrusted to Otis to manage.[53] If James had any doubts about the faith, as did his cousin Job, they remained unrecorded.[54] The West Parish was an unshaken rock.

Barnstable, that little self-contained world of unshifting values, did not favor an unstable currency. "The Diminution of the value of the Bills of Public Credit, is the Cause of much Oppression in

49. Franklin B. Dexter, *Biographical Sketches of the Graduates of Yale College* ... (New York, 1885), I, 77–78.

50. C. C. Goen, *Revivalism and Separatism in New England, 1740–1800* (New Haven, 1962), 94–95, 230–231, 347.

51. "Reasons for N. Ewer's Separatism," Records of the West Parish of Barnstable, 1668–1807, 211, Mass. Hist. Soc.

52. See *The Declaration of Ministers in Barnstable County, Relating to the Late Practice of Itinerant Preaching* (Boston, 1745), 8.

53. Church order, 24 Apr. 1745, Records of the West Parish of Barnstable, Mass. Hist. Soc.

54. "The Reason in Job Otis and Joshua Youngs Letter of 10 march 1734. voted insufficient to justifie their withdrawing from our Communion and a Committee Chosen to tell them So and discourse with them to Solve their Doubt etc," in "Records of the First Church of Scituate," *Mayflower Descendant*, XI (1909), 142.

the Province And I dare not have a Hand in adding to the heavy Weight of this Oppression, which is already become insupportable" was a sentiment that the first Colonel Otis supported in 1724.[55] As might be expected, the land bank scheme of 1740 made no appeal to the propertied elite of Barnstable town. In fact that town held the unique position of not having a single subscriber, while the county mustered only ten supporters of the "manufactory Bills." No other region in Massachusetts stood so firm against a land-backed medium.[56] Barnstable remained outside of the main currents of provincial life. Old ways held sway.

There could be no doubt that James and Mary Otis had prospered in Barnstable and that they upheld its values. They had gained wealth and status, and they intended that their children would inherit their places. To this end they employed Pastor Russell as a private tutor to teach their sons the necessary Latin and Greek for admission to Harvard. James, Jr., showed himself a good student and entered the class of 1743. Joseph was another case. He lacked the aptitude for Uncle Russell's books. His one asset was a legible hand and his father put him to work on the ledgers of the family store. Scandal touched Joseph when Isaac Hinckley, Jr., hinted that he was responsible for getting the Hinckleys' colored "nanny" pregnant.[57] Isaac showed haste in placing the blame elsewhere for he realized "People on Such Occassions were apt to Lay such things to the Masters Sons . . . [and] this could not but give him some uneasiness." From the very first, the Hinckley case was weakened by the admission that both David Manning and Joseph Otis "had Carnal knowledge of the said Nannys Body."[58] Aunt Russell sought to stop the gossip, stating that "if Joseph Otis wanted a Negro they had one at home." The Hinckleys quickly rejoined, "There was a

55. "Diary of Samuel Sewall," Mass. Hist. Soc., *Colls.*, 5th Ser., VII (1882), 345–346; *Mass. House of Reps. Jours.*, 1718–1720, 371–372.

56. "Land Bank Papers," Barnstable, 30 Dec. 1740, Mass. Archives, CII, 120, for town identification of owners. While Barnstable had 10 backers, Plymouth had 42, Essex 115, Middlesex 119, Suffolk 122, and Worcester 165, pp. 9–16, and Andrew McFarland Davis, "List of Partners in the Land Bank of 1740," Col. Soc. of Mass., *Pubs.*, IV (1910), 169–194.

57. Suffolk Court Files, 387: 108–116 (No. 62026), Suffolk County Court House.

58. John Crocker, deposition, *ibid.*, 111.

Difference between a Clean whore and a Durty one."[59] The decision of the court was in Joseph's favor.[60] If this episode sounds like a tale from the Old South, it but reflects the common conditions that exist in a society of unequals, of masters and slaves. (Years later the tories would circulate a garbled version of this story with James Otis, Jr., as the culprit.) Sister Mercy was now in her teens. The future held for her a marriage to James Warren, Jr., son of her father's friend and colleague at the bar. It was obvious that the Otis children would be closely connected to the aspirations of their parents.

Barnstable knew that James Otis stood for its way of life, with all of its pettiness and provincialism. He had served his town on innumerable committees, had moderated its meetings, and was elected hogreeve in 1739 (along with his brother John) and a selectman in 1744. In 1745 James Otis received the ultimate approval of his bailiwick when the seventy-odd voters who constituted the Barnstable electorate made him their representative to the General Court.[61] This was the political community's ratification of his long apprenticeship. He was the successful merchant and townsman.

This Barnstable, resting securely in a fertile plain hedged by a thin rim of hills, presents a picture of remarkable stability. Its society was homogeneous. It was not rocked by serious religious, economic, or political conflict. No immigrant group entered its society to change it. Nor was it receptive to the Great Awakening or the land-bank experiment. The fundamental values of its church epitomize the mores of its inhabitants. In the period of James Otis's ascent to power it remained impervious to the larger world beyond its hills. James's apprenticeship had schooled him in these values. His business had made him the familiar of the Cape's local leaders from Scituate to Provincetown. He now would represent the Barnstable bailiwick in Boston, where he intended to serve his town as well as himself on a larger stage.

59. William Bassell, Jr., deposition, *ibid.*, 110.
60. Midwife Mary Annable, evidence, *ibid.*, 110, and Mary O'Reilley, who asked Nanny "whether Joseph Otis had any thing to do with her. She said yes but She never Said he had got her with Child," *ibid.*, 114.
61. Barnstable Town Records, II, 59–103.

## V.

# *JAMES OTIS, SR.*
## *COLONIAL POLITICIAN*

By the time James Otis, Sr. (1702–1778) was elected to the Massachusetts House of Representatives in 1745 it had come close to substantiating its 1692 belief that it "may use and exercise such Powers and Privileges here as the house of comons in England." Its charter required it to meet on the last Wednesday of May but gave little other direction as to how the House should proceed. In its ritual, such as the administering of the "Oath of Adjuration" to newly elected representatives, it followed English usage. The occasion offered a perfect opportunity for this protestant state to reaffirm loyalty to the Hanoverian Succession and the charter government. After this formality the House proceeded to examine the writs and precepts of the last election, for it was the judge of its own members. Only then did it choose its speaker and present him to the governor for his approbation. Once the governor gave his expected approval the House considered itself organized. It then formed the various committees that would control its activities.[1]

1. *Mass. House of Reps. Jours., 1745–1746*, 3–5. For a copy of an election writ, see precept of the sheriff of Middlesex to Lexington Selectmen, Charlestown, 24 Apr. 1756, Mass. Archives, CXVII, 137–138.

If the House's formal structure with its oaths, methods of voting, precepts, speaker, and committees reflected its English heritage, it was also shaped by its own evolution under the Charter of 1691. This covenant in its ambiguities and silences called forth many interpretative clashes. In general, the House favored resolving such clashes in the light of its own precedents while prerogative-minded governors relied upon crown rights and royal orders. A primary example of this conflict dealt with Boston as the capital city. Although the charter did not specify a meeting place, the General Court considered Boston its normal habitation. It consistently held that only fire, invasion, plague, or necessity provided sufficient grounds for convening elsewhere. In 1737 some of the representatives even questioned Governor Jonathan Belcher's royal instructions which called for holding the Court at Salisbury for a special meeting to settle the boundary between Massachusetts and New Hampshire. What the General Court deeply resented was political interference such as William Burnet's expressed intent of freeing the representatives from the influence of the Boston "Town-meeting" when in 1728 he held Court at Salem. It is no surprise that Thomas Hutchinson's similar exercise of the prerogative in 1770, when the Court met at Cambridge, was viewed as a subversion of Massachusetts liberty.[2]

The charter was also silent on how long the House should sit, how many sessions a Court would have, and the remuneration for representatives. Hence these points were resolved by either circumstances or provincial laws. In the critical war year of 1745–1746, during which colonial forces took the French-Canadian fortress of Louisbourg, the House sat for 180 days in five sessions. However, in 1751–1752 a nervous governor and the presence of smallpox combined to make an unusually short Court of 63 days. During James Otis's first decade of service the General Court averaged slightly more than a hundred meetings a year. Even when the pay was raised from 3 shillings to 7 shillings 6 pence *per diem* in 1748–

---

2. *Mass. House of Reps. Jours., 1737–1738,* 132–133, *1727–1729,* 362–363; Thomas Hutchinson, *The History of the Colony and Province of Massachusetts-Bay,* ed. Lawrence S. Mayo (Cambridge, Mass., 1936), III, 377–394.

1749 it was still miserly, scarcely enough to pay boarding costs for the representatives.[3] It was the other perquisites of office that interested Otis. These included the guardianship of the Mashpee Indians (the family store sold them blankets), farming out the "excise on tea, coffee, arrack, coaches, etc." for Barnstable County, a say in the granting of the liquor license, and a hand in naming the local justices of the peace. It was expected that Uncle Solomon would continue to collect his fees as Barnstable's notary public, that Otis himself would hold the liquor license, that in 1750 his son Joseph would become collector of the excise, and that his friends would continue in commission as justices of the peace.[4] In time of war there were government contracts if one had reached a proper understanding with the governor. Yet this list, to be complete, must include the intangibles of office—honor, status, and the satisfaction of political action itself.

The legal provisions for eligibility were minimal, the charter requiring only that a representative possess a freehold and the 1694 electoral law adding residency.[5] Thus Otis by owning property worth £40 sterling within Barnstable was qualified to sit in the General Court. But that he held his post without interruption until 1757 shows that Otis conformed to the mores of his society. He benefited from his town's ethos which held property to be sacred and considered political election as a kind of freehold.

Fortunately for James Otis's ambitions his term of office coincided with that of a most remarkable colonial governor, William Shirley, under whose administration Massachusetts enjoyed an unprecedented political stability. The sure hand of this brilliant governor, an adept at court intrigue, flattery, and patronage distribution, gave this era direction. He guided the province through King

---

3. For sittings and sessions see *Mass. House of Reps. Jours., 1745–1755, passim*; for the salary see *Mass. Acts and Resolves*, III, 285, and *Mass. House of Reps. Jours., 1748–1749*, 189.

4. For Solomon Otis, *Mass. House of Reps. Jours., 1749–1750*, 38; James Otis, Sr., petition, 10 Dec. 1753, praying that his license to sell liquor might be transferred to his son Joseph (granted), *Mass. House of Reps. Jours., 1753–1754*, 107–108, and as excise collector, *ibid., 1750–1751*, 41, *1751–1752*, 43.

5. Brown, *Middle-Class Democracy*, 63–64.

George's War (known in Europe as the War of the Austrian Succession) and helped bring about the final British victory over the
French for the possession of North America in the French and Indian War. His tenure also witnessed the first call for colonial union,
the adoption of the Gregorian calendar, and the institution of a
stable silver-based currency for the province. To achieve these
aims Shirley enlisted in his cause John Choate and Robert Hale,
who had backed the land bank, as well as such hard-money men as
Thomas Hutchinson, Chambers Russell, and James Otis. However,
his greatest achievement was forging a vehicle for his grand design
of a British North America out of the discordant elements and
shifting cliques that constituted that *terra incognita*, the Massachusetts House of Representatives.[6]

It is one of the oddities of colonial historiography that no study
exists on the composition and functioning of the General Court
comparable to Jack P. Greene's analysis of the Virginia burgesses.[7]
At best, this tentative outline, starting with James Otis's Barnstable,
moving on to other politicians, towns, and regional groupings, may
provide a rough framework for an understanding of the politics of
this era. James Otis's Barnstable was but one town out of forty in
the Old Colony, which in its turn took in about a fourth of the 160-
odd towns in Massachusetts. The first observation is that Barnstable's political stability, as seen in its "no contest" elections and
the constant attendance of its representatives at the General Court,
is exceptional. A preliminary examination of the 110 towns that
sent representatives to Court during Shirley's administration indicates that only 10 per cent shared a political structure similar to the
"Barnstable Bailiwick." Half of such seats were located in the "old"
county of Middlesex: they included Framingham, the seat of power
of Colonel Joseph Buckminister; William Lawrence's Groton; as

6. George A. Wood, *William Shirley, Governor of Massachusetts, 1741–1756: A History* (New York, 1920), is solid on imperial policy and military movements up to and including Louisbourg, while John A. Schutz, *William Shirley, King's Governor of Massachusetts* (Chapel Hill, 1961), is a superb study of the political factors during Shirley's tenure.

7. See Jack P. Greene, "Foundations of Political Power in the Virginia House of Burgesses, 1720–1776," *Wm. and Mary Qtly.*, 3d Ser., XVI (1959), 485–492.

well as Medford and Lexington, which for political purposes belonged to the Hall and Read families. These men were Otis's fellow committee members.

In Barnstable County the town of Sandwich came under James's sphere of influence. Until 1752 it elected his fellow barrister Timothy Ruggles, and after that date his old friend, Roland Cotton, the perennial clerk of the House.[8] Sandwich was representative of a larger block of about forty seats which were held by politically conscious towns. First among these was Boston, which had the privilege of returning four men to the House. Usually the speakers came from this group—the wealthy Thomas Cushing from 1742 to 1745, Thomas Hutchinson, a *realpolitiker* if ever there was one, for 1746 to 1748, and that man of many charities, Thomas Hubbard, who served from 1750 until elevated to the Council in 1759.[9] Such men as Harrison Gray, the conservative merchant and sometime treasurer of the province, and Benjamin Prat, that crippled, cynical giant of the bar who called the species "the ape-kind" and held that man's chief aim was "to provide food etc. for other Animals," lent a special lustre to the Boston delegation.[10] It is because of the talents of such men that the reputation of the "seaboard merchant aristocracy" has loomed so large in historical annals. The port towns of Charlestown, Salem, Ipswich, and Newbury were unique in exercising their option of electing two representatives. As the towns paid the salary costs through a local assessment this indicates both political leadership and community consciousness. Salem is typical. She chose the rich and socially prominent Samuel Gardner in 1749 and Henry Gibbs from 1753 to 1756 to be her representatives. Both men represented commercial interests and championed the belief that the farmer-dominated assembly continually overtaxed Salem's trading stock, and they were right.[11] The town of Berwick in York

8. Shipton, *et al.*, *Sibley's Harvard Graduates*, VI, 298–304, IX, 200–201.

9. *Ibid.*, V, 572–574, VI, 492–493, VIII, 157.

10. Samuel E. Morison, "The Property of Harrison Gray, Loyalist," Col. Soc. of Mass., *Pubs.*, XIV (1913), 320–333; Shipton, *et al.*, *Sibley's Harvard Graduates*, X, 230–231.

11. For Gibbs's protests see Mass. Archives, CXV, 579, and CXVII, 432. The

County met its obligation by rotating its selectmen as representatives. Milton usually alternated between two candidates, Samuel Miller and Samuel Swift. This procedure was utilized by almost a dozen other towns such as Marlborough and Billerica in Middlesex, Bradford in Essex, Lancaster, Harvard, and Westborough in Worcester, as well as Dartmouth in Bristol.[12] On the other side of Massachusetts, the political process was usually controlled by such "River Gods" as John Stoddard of Northampton and Israel Williams of Hatfield.[13]

In his political career Otis had great difficulty in dealing with what the eighteenth century called the "Independent Gentlemen." During James's tenure ten members, whose seats and motives for serving were usually outside of political arrangements, were in this group. Cambridge town supplied a goodly quota of these men of fixed opinions. First there was Andrew Boardman, the fifth of his line to be college steward. He held his seat almost continuously from 1742 to 1769. He only yielded it in 1750–1752 to Edmund Trowbridge, one of the peers of the Massachusetts bar, who was elected by the simple expedient of giving notice that he would serve without pay.[14] In 1754 and 1755 William Brattle, the scion of a most distinguished family, returned to the House where as an expert on military matters he served on several committees with James Otis.[15] Two independents who went out looking for their seats were Will Bowdoin and Jeremiah Allen. Bowdoin enjoyed being a big fish in Needham's little pond. He served without pay from 1752 to

Gardner family was now in its fifth generation and supplied three of Salem's representatives in this period, Capt. John for 1741–1743, and 1747–1748, Samuel—who however did not take his seat, and Daniel, the "Gentleman" and farmer of the tax records, for 1750. The estates of these three men were respectively £2,000 (1784), £20,000 (1769), and £1,800 (1760), Frank A. Gardner, *Thomas Gardner Planter and Some of His Descendants* (Salem, 1907), 163–177. There is a brief sketch of Daniel Epes, who represented the town six times during Shirley's governorship, in James D. Phillips, *Salem in the Eighteenth Century* (Boston, 1937).

12. *Mass. House of Reps. Jours., 1742–1748*, 4; see petition signatures, 16 June 1751, Mass. Archives, CXVI, 43–45.

13. Shipton, *et al.*, *Sibley's Harvard Graduates*, V, 96–118, VIII, 301–332.

14. *Ibid.*, VI, 295–296, VIII, 510–511.

15. *Ibid.*, VII, 11–17; *Mass. House of Reps. Jours., 1754–1755*, 51, 59, 180, 228, 275.

1756, although he hoped to profit from connections in the House. Allen intentionally settled in Stoneham in 1741, where he had himself elected the better to lobby for bills favorable to his business. Both men had limited influence.[16] On the other hand, the town of Taunton gained from the residence of that old Otis client, Samuel White, its first lawyer in a hundred-year history, as well as a representative from 1749 to 1759. And in 1755 Brookline obtained a gifted moderator and representative when Jeremiah Gridley settled within its bounds. He was a friend of Otis and the recognized dean of the Boston bar.[17] This is but a sampling of a group: many of these men were public servants of the highest caliber, but some of them could be bought or bribed. Under ordinary circumstances they all held their seats for indefinite tenure.

Although Barnstable never provided a contested election, James Otis had friends involved in one or two of them. Two classics of the genre were the Brunswick election of 1743 and that of Haverhill in 1748. In Brunswick one party insured a favorable although limited poll by posting up the election notice "on the Inner Side [of] the meeting house door." The General Court decided in this case that a new election was required. In Haverhill there had been a difference of opinion between the two parishes when newcomers moved into the West Parish. When election day came accompanied by a heavy snow, the West Parish saw an opportunity for swamping the polls. One of the selectmen possessed wits enough to take the opposition "votes out of his hatt," which served as the ballot box, "and cast them away."[18] The selectmen held that the votes thrown out belonged to unqualified electors—although only from the West Parish—and justified their position by a list of seventy-seven true voters (their supporters) and a petition of twenty-six others who would have voted had the weather not kept them at home. Added together, these certainly gave the seat to Nathaniel

16. Shipton, *et al.*, *Sibley's Harvard Graduates*, VIII, 540–545, IX, 474.

17. *Ibid.*, VII, 525, IX, 110–111.

18. Benjamin Larrabee, *et al.*, Brunswick, 25 May 1743, Mass. Archives, CXV, 50–53; deposition of Thomas Hayes, Haverhill, 30 Mar. 1748, *ibid.*, 301.

Peaslee, who incidentally served as moderator and his own floor manager in that affair. Strange as it may seem, he was allowed by the House to occupy his seat.[19]

The difficulty of making generalizations about democracy and the electorate may be seen in Upton's 1746 dispute. In the past its "poor Freeholders were allowed Liberty to vote . . . although not qualified by Law." This is but another example of the autonomous nature of town government. This frontier settlement in Worcester dispensed with voting regulations because it seemed just that everyone should vote for the local officials who would have to defend the town in case of attack. Added to that was the practical consideration that the greater part of the tax money came from the lower ranks. However, in 1746 several of the selectmen attempted to "enforce" the provincial law and limit the ballot to "ten qualified voters." Forty Upton petitioners protested this move. The General Court decided against the selectmen, holding that they had overcalculated the property requirements. Thus, the disputed electors would vote.[20] Natick in 1748 and Needham in 1749 also had contests that hinged upon the qualifications of voters.[21]

Towns such as Brunswick and Haverhill, as well as Upton, Natick, and Needham, because of the very fluidity of their politics, could not be counted on to supply the backbone of a political grouping. The same held true for Wells in York, Almsby in Essex, Luenburgh in Worcester, and Swanzey in Bristol, all of which sent six different representatives to the Court during Shirley's administration. A dozen other towns were almost as active, and each year would find six to eight members who had been dragooned into serving. These representatives usually showed no interest in politics

19. Petition of John Sanders and Other Freeholders and Inhabitants of Haverhill, 3 Mar. 1747/8, Mass. Archives, CXV, 288–290, and reply of the Selectmen, 28 Mar. 1748, *ibid.*, 305–308, with memorial of the twenty-six, 29 Mar. 1748, *ibid.*, 309. On 24 Dec. 1748 the "Question was put, *Whether* Mr. Peaslee *be directed to withdraw from his Seat?* It pass'd in the Negative." *Mass. House of Reps. Jours., 1748–1749*, 153.

20. Petition, presented by John Hazeltine of Upton, 2 Apr. 1746, Mass. Archives, CXV, 319–320. For the House action, *ibid.*, CXV, 706–706a.

21. Natick Petition, 1748, *ibid.*, CXV, 411, and Needham Petition, 12 Mar. 1749/50, *ibid.*, CXV, 624.

and hence their influence would be minimal. Most of the single-term men were in this category.[22]

Some of the problems facing the "House managers" Choate, Otis, Williams, and Speaker Joseph Dwight as they attempted to carry a supply bill in the 1749 January session can best be understood when House membership figures are collated with regional and county data.[23] The first consideration is that the province of Massachusetts was an agricultural society in which a good 70 per cent of the membership of the General Court would list farming as a primary occupation. Then as now, the apportionment laws favored such a status. The statute of 1731, the disallowance of which by the crown was *de facto* ignored by Massachusetts, specified that every town could send one representative, while towns with 80 qualified voters must be represented. If a town had 120 voters, it could send two members. Boston was in a class by itself. It held a tenth of the province's population and was granted four seats, thus giving it the same weight in the legislature as four Hampshire towns with a population of barely 320 freeholders.[24] A full third or about fifty towns did not send representatives. Forty of these probably were not required to do so under the law and thus saved themselves the assessment. After all it was the town that paid the salary cost. Usually ten towns were absent and subject to a fine, although special circumstances, such as Grafton's settling a minister in 1750, or Uxbridge's great expense in maintaining its nine bridges of which three were over county roads, generally brought a remission.[25]

For the counties this meant that Worcester, Hampshire, and

<hr/>

22. *Mass. House of Reps. Jours., 1742–1758*, p. 4 of each volume.

23. *Mass. House of Reps. Jours., 1749–1750*, 154.

24. *Mass. Acts and Resolves*, II, 592–593, and Brown, *Middle-Class Democracy*, 64–66. However, the document cited for the case of Raynham, Petition of the Selectmen, 27 Dec. 1760, Mass. Archives, CXVII, 609–610, is not explicit.

25. See Grafton petition, Mar. 1749/50, with House notation of approval, 2 Apr. 1750, Mass. Archives, CXV, 605–606. Hopkinston in its petition of 19 Jan. 1750/1 claimed that the majority of its inhabitants were tenants and that as a new town it was very poor—although this excuse need not be taken at face value, *ibid.*, 791. Poverty was also offered as an excuse by Shrewsbury in its petition of 29 Mar. 1751, *ibid.*, CXVI, 98. Uxbridge's memorial of 6 Jan. 1761 is in *ibid.*, CXVII, 626–627.

York with their forty-eight towns averaged in the period 1742–1758 about 50 per cent representation, as did the Old Colony with nineteen of its forty-one towns returning members. Essex, Suffolk, and Middlesex with a total of seventy-one towns yielded 70 per cent attendance. Even counting these differences in county percentages, it is evident that the so-called merchant aristocracy was lost in a sea of farmers.[26]

As James Otis must have observed by the seasonal return of faces, the three settled counties of Essex, Suffolk, and Middlesex consistently returned their incumbents in two out of every three contests.

COUNTY REPRESENTATION IN THE MASSACHUSETTS GENERAL COURT, 1742–1758*

| County | No. of Towns | Average Absence & Per Cent | Incumbents | Former Members | New Men | Total |
|---|---|---|---|---|---|---|
| Essex | 20 | 6 30% | 152 60% | 27 11% | 72 29% = | 251 100% |
| Suffolk | 18 | 6 33% | 148 63% | 28 12% | 59 25% = | 235 100% |
| Middlesex | 33 | 13 40% | 234 72% | 23 7% | 69 21% = | 326 100% |
| Plymouth | 14 | 5 35% | 85 60% | 15 10% | 42 30% = | 142 100% |
| Bristol | 15 | 7 47% | 59 50% | 12 10% | 49 40% = | 120 100% |
| Barnstable | 9 | 4 45% | 44 60% | 4 5% | 26 35% = | 74 100% |
| Dukes & Nantucket | 4 | 3 75% | 5 62.5% | 1 12.5% | 2 25% = | 8 100% |
| York | 11 | 4 36% | 50 50% | 10 10% | 41 40% = | 101 100% |
| Worcester | 22 | 11 50% | 83 50% | 22 13% | 59 37% = | 164 100% |
| Hampshire | 15 | 8 53% | 56 46% | 22 18% | 43 36% = | 121 100% |

(header rows: "Seats Held by:" spans Incumbents, Former Members, New Men columns)

* Based on an analysis of election returns as printed in the *Mass. House of Reps. Jours., 1742–1758.*

26. See table.

In addition, one out of every ten seats went to a former occupant—which left one out of four seats open to new blood. The Old Colony occupied a middle position. It returned 57 per cent of the previous seatholders but, at the same time, it had a 35 per cent average for freshmen. It remained for York, Worcester, and Hampshire, the most recently settled and perhaps most politically active (which need not be the same thing as most democratic) to average the lowest rate of returns as well as the highest figures for new men. These three counties returned barely half the incumbents while four out of every ten seats went to new members. Frontier Worcester, as might be expected, had the highest ratio of militia officers as representatives—usually a third of that county's delegation. In such towns as Lancaster and Leicester, the two positions were combined in one and the same person much as they had been in Hingham and Scituate in the seventeenth century.[27] A special group within this membership, from which such professionals as existed in this society came, was that "inner community more closely bound than any like group today," the Harvard graduates. If at times they dominated the House, it was not by numbers but by influence.[28]

Thomas Hutchinson had come close to understanding some of the negative points of this system and doubtless William Shirley was aware of its salient features.[29] In fact, when Governor Shirley began putting together a "party" based on support from such bailiwicks as Otis's Barnstable, Buckminister's Framingham, and Lawrence's Groton, while seeking the rank and file in Essex, Suffolk, and Middlesex, he was but following in the footsteps of Elisha Cooke and the "Country Party."[30] In operation, forty members usually were sufficient to guarantee control of the House. And in 1751 James Otis and the other administration men were able to outvote

27. *Mass. House of Reps. Jours., 1742–1748*, 4.

28. Clifford K. Shipton, "Introduction," *New England Life in the 18th Century* . . . (Cambridge, 1963), xxiii.

29. Thomas Hutchinson in his efforts to support the Bernard administration depended upon Israel Williams's getting out the Hampshire delegation, although its representatives either did not show or would not stay to the end of the session, Williams Papers, II, 156–170, Mass. Hist. Soc.

30. Shipton, *et al.*, *Sibley's Harvard Graduates*, IV, 351–356.

the "paper money" lobby with but thirty-one members present. However, that maneuver required the cooperation of a "kept" Council as well as the expedient of waiting for a thin House at the end of the term.[31]

The simple fact is that party structure in the modern sense of the word did not exist. If it had, William Shirley would not have put together his first coalition that supplied the needed forty votes until 1748. It included Samuel Waldo and other Maine proprietors who wanted enforcement of the forest laws, and country farmers who did not. Added to this were the land bank associates such as Robert Hale of Beverly and John Choate of Ipswich, as well as Admiralty Judge Robert Auchmuty, who *ex officio* gained from the strict enforcement of the Navigation Acts, and a string of merchants led by Thomas Hancock who wanted neither. The expected strains in such a relationship were not improved by the demands of Shirley's English friends for both hard money and a strict trade policy. And while the governor might need the merchants—and they were by no means a united group—it was personally profitable to catch the smugglers. It is important to remember that the law gave a third of the seizures to the governor—and money was very important to a man who had left England for the lack of it and then waited ten long years for his main chance.[32] John A. Schutz perceptively noted

31. On Apr. 5, in the 1750–1751 Court, a move was made to make "good Tender in Law" the notes, certificates, and interest bills on the paper being called in under the refunding measures that Otis and Hutchinson had backed. As the bill was framed in the negative, an affirmative vote was against it. The measure was opposed by Speaker Thomas Hubbard, Chambers Russell, Israel Williams, Andrew Boardman, James Otis, and 28 other representatives. Those in favor of the measure totaled 46 and included James Allen, John Tyng, as well as Joseph Buckminister and Benjamin Read (probably under popular pressure as the deflation was hurting their county). The Council defeated the measure and a committee of both the Board and House was appointed to present a new bill. The members included Sylvanus Bourn, Andrew Oliver, and Thomas Hutchinson, while the House provided Hubbard, Otis, Williams, Russell, Tyng, and Harrison Gray. This delayed voting for two weeks and when the measure came up in a slightly different form on 20 Apr., the administration mustered 31 votes against 28 of the Allen-Tyng faction. Benjamin Read moved over to the government side, Buckminister did not show, while the popular support presumably went home. *Mass. House of Reps. Jours., 1750–1751,* 194–195, 199, 224–225.

32. Schutz, *William Shirley,* 64–73.

that this fragile bark was held together by patronage, war "contracts and commissions." Only high profits could constrain the mutual antagonisms within this coalition.[33] Peace might be a blessing; it could be a political disaster. By Otis's third term the governor would be seeking a new working arrangement.

Part of William Shirley's problem was that his imperial vision of an all-British North America depended upon colonial tools for its implementation. His initial message to the first session of the 1745 Assembly dealt with the problems facing the Massachusetts troops in their siege of French-Canadian Louisbourg. Although the province had made heavy sacrifices the previous year, circumstances now forced Shirley to ask for additional efforts.[34] As expected, the prime business of the House during this time of war was defense. Fortunately its "committee of war" mirrored the broad spectrum of Shirley's working coalition: John Choate, Robert Hale, Thomas Hutchinson, Andrew Oliver, Joseph Buckminister, and by the end of the term, James Otis.[35] Yet this was no rubber stamp, as Shirley found out in his attempt to enlist Massachusetts men under "Irish Officers." While the House realized "the Appointment of the Officers is with his Excellency," it knew also that men were needed to serve in the ranks. Would it not be wiser, it asked, to appoint the "Officers in the several Parts of the Province where the men are rais'd"?[36] The House resented the governor's plan of filling up militia posts with the sons of his Irish and English clients and insisted that this local patronage belonged to the Massachusetts politicos who alone could guarantee recruitment.

Of equal import was the annual supply bill which provided the funds to pay for these troops, build the forts on the eastern and western frontiers, maintain Castle William, and cover the ordinary charges of government and the governor's salary. The latter had become an annual ritual, although this year Otis witnessed one of

33. Ibid., 123–133.
34. Mass. House of Reps. Jours., 1745–1746, 8–10.
35. Ibid., 1744–1745, 11–12, 1745–1746, 231.
36. Ibid., 1745–1746, 239.

the rarest of events: on June 12, 1745, the House reconsidered its first offer of £1,450 and taking "leave chearfully to express their Satisfaction in your Excellency's Administration" granted £1,500.[37] Two other functions were the regulation of Indian affairs and correspondence with the colonial agent in London. The latter usually reflected the current state of domestic politics and English policy. To this list of major committees should be added work on the tax, impost, and apportionment, which determined what, how, and where the tax money would be raised. In contrast to the general flux in the House rolls, these committees were unusually stable in their personnel, as James Otis's service illustrates.

When James Otis started his provincial career in 1745, Massachusetts was waging King George's War. The first bill Otis moved placed a bounty on Indian scalps of £100 for males "twelve Years or upwards" and £50 for females, and a premium of £5 if the Indian "shall be taken Captive and delivered to the Order" of the governor.[38] This was indicative of the strong military line that became a key feature of Otis's leadership in the House. As a country man Otis was both distrustful and suspicious of Boston, which always seemed to present special problems. He was shocked by the conduct of the Boston bakers when they defied the weight regulations set for the sale of bread by the selectmen and entered "into a Combination not to bake any more Bread unless the Assize can be set as they desire it." He approved of the House's action when on that very day it ordered a bill brought in to curb this evil "of a very pernicious Nature." It disqualified those who entered such an illegal combination from "ever exercising the Trade or business of a Baker afterwards."[39] Otis was much more sympathetic to the colonial protests against impressment of seamen off local ships, an

37. *Ibid.*, 44.
38. *Ibid.*, 78.
39. "A Memorial of the Select-Men of the Town of *Boston*," 28 June 1745, *Mass. House of Reps. Jours.*, *1745–1746*, 55–56. While the intent of the House is clear, no bill was brought in as there is nothing in *Mass. Acts and Resolves*, III, 223–276, or XIII, 466–485. The Council Records, XI, 432–438, are likewise silent as are the Legislative Records of the Council, XVII, 610–624, Legislative Archives, State House, Boston.

offence which vitally concerned Barnstable's trade.[40] However, it was the town of Boston which made the major complaint against impressment, a practice which, it was declared, forced its inhabitants to "labour under insupportable Grievances." These were aggravated by the "Behaviour of the [English] officers, who with their lawless Rabble like Russians enter the Houses of the Inhabitants in the Night." The Council, after carefully reading this petition, rejected it. Did it not charge the government with "Breach of Magna Charta, and the Charter of this Province, and an Act of Parliament"?[41] Clearly the issues James Otis, Jr., defended in the 1760's were deeply rooted in the history of Massachusetts.

In contrast to these headline activities Otis and his colleagues spent most of their time serving on dozens of minor committees. The routine of a representative's life involved counting ballots, preparing thanksgiving and fast proclamations, running the lottery, judging disputed elections, hearing protests from underpaid Harvard tutors, signing currency notes, and above all, examining countless petitions.[42] In point of space the petitions occupy close to a fourth of the *Journals* for this period. After all, this was the chief way in which a representative demonstrated his support of home interests. Such 1747 petitions as those of Jabez Fox, Plymouth's representative, who sought liberty to sell the small estate of his ward "*Benjamin Wright* a Minor" to pay debts, or of "*Sarah Sepit* and *Hannah Shanks*, Indians, Widows praying Liberty to sell a Tract of Land in *Plymouth*" are typical.[43] When William Bassett of Barnstable lost £42.10s. old tenor in a fire, James Otis was instrumental in obtaining favorable action and personally handed him the new notes.[44] Nor could such veterans as Benjamin Lovell be ignored. He claimed compensation for a wound in his right foot received while serving on the eastern frontier.[45] Of much greater

40. *Mass. House of Reps. Jours., 1746–1747*, 75–76.
41. *Ibid.*, 205–206, 210–212, 221–222.
42. *Ibid.*, 5, 15; *1747–1748*, 86, 235.
43. *Ibid., 1747–1748*, 23, 64.
44. *Ibid.*, 245.
45. *Ibid., 1752–1753*, 245.

service to Otis's town was his sponsorship of "an act to prevent the destruction of the Meadow called Sandy-Neck . . . and for the Better preservation of the Harbour there." This act preserved the wild grass for the town by ending free foliage for farmers who let out their horses and cattle in the open meadow.[46] Now and then there would be a rare special act such as the one dissolving the "Marriage Contract" of Mary Clapham with William Clapham, who left her and "stands convicted of committing Adultery with Another Woman." Judge Saltonstall, James Otis, and John Choate were the fathers of the bill.[47] And there was the even more unusual naturalization act for John Amiel who had prospered in Boston's mercantile life, which received Otis's backing. Earlier he had served on the committee to encourage the "importation of foreign protestants."[48] Nor would New England have been true to its puritan past if Representative Otis had not had a hand in legislation seeking to limit the extravagance of funerals, and naturally, an act "to encourage the Codd and Whale Fishery."[49]

The most striking aspect of James Otis's career in the House is the rapidity of his ascent. Usually the first term of any newly elected member is given to watchful waiting. Yet by April of the 1745–1746 Court, Otis was a member of committees considering the governor's message, dealing with Indian policy for the Six Nations, prohibiting Rhode Island money in Massachusetts, and providing for defense.[50] In the 1746 Court, James became a member of the all-important supply committee, while in 1747 he continued in these posts, and in the 1748 House he concluded his garnering of capital

46. *Mass. Acts and Resolves*, III, 339–340, 361–362.

47. *Ibid.*, VI (Private Acts), 169 (No. 82); *Mass. House of Reps. Jours., 1754–1755*, 163.

48. James Otis's action on John Amiel's petition was first submitted to committee on 14 Dec. 1753, read a third time, and sent up for concurrence on 21 Dec. 1753, *Mass. House of Reps. Jours., 1753–1754*, 121, 135, 194. There is no record of the Council acting upon this bill. However, on 11 Dec. 1755 John Amiel affixed his signature to the petition of the "Inhabitants of Boston" who were protesting the overtaxing of that town by the province. Thus while there is no record of naturalization, the supposition is that Amiel was naturalized, Mass. Archives, CXVII, 53.

49. *Mass. House of Reps. Jours., 1748–1749*, 25, *1750–1751*, 147.

50. *Ibid., 1745–1746*, 86, 110, 154, 231.

assignments by appointment to the committee corresponding with the colonial agent in London.[51]

How had it come about that within the space of four years James Otis had become a major figure in the Assembly? Leaving obvious talent aside, Otis's initial advantage lay with relatives and friends who shared in the inner workings of the Shirley administration. In 1743 his brother-in-law Isaac Little and his neighbor Sylvanus Bourn both obtained at-large Council seats. It is likely that they, along with James's eldest brother John IV, engineered Otis's election as the Barnstable representative in 1745. Hence it was no accident that James Otis came on the scene as a Shirley supporter. With James in the House and Bourn working in the Council, along with Shirley's support, John Otis IV collected his due as an anti-Belcher man when he received reelection to the Council in 1747.[52] In addition, Otis was on familiar terms with many of the Old Colony representatives. He was at least on speaking terms with the Boston merchant James Allen, who in 1745 offered to sell him "good Claret [and] Sugar" cheap (either Shirley had appeased the merchants by relaxing trade enforcement or they had improved their evasion techniques).[53] Otis on his part showed the most important of virtues for a newcomer in the House: the 1745–1746 General Court was in session for 180 days and Otis was there for all but 10.

The 1748–1749 sessions of the Court showed that Otis had arrived at precisely the right time to profit by Governor Shirley's reshuffling of the political cards. It was the merchant sector, already badly split by Thomas Hancock's efforts to dominate the war trade by a ruthless exclusion of such fellow merchants as James Allen, that indicated that this was the opportune time to draw a new hand.[54]

51. *Ibid.*, *1746–1747*, 20, *1747–1748*, 12, 26–27, 65, *1748–1749*, 129.

52. Schutz, *William Shirley*, 282.

53. James Otis, Jr., to James Otis, Sr., Boston, July 1745, Otis Papers, I, 56, Mass. Hist. Soc.

54. On 4 June 1745 Thomas Hancock wrote John Bastide, "We have keept James Allen out of the house of Representatives and Council this Year" a theme which he repeated in his 27 May 1746 letter to Christopher Kilby, "Tomorrow is our Election of Counsellors, and all I Desire and push is to keep Allen out" as had just been done in the Boston elections to the House. By keeping Allen out of the

The end of hostilities meant the termination of those profitable bonds that had guaranteed the support of Samuel Waldo and friends. In fact, it was a squabble over fees and Waldo's conviction that he was too well connected for the governor not to depend upon him that led to Waldo's undoing.[55]

The thought occurred to Governor Shirley that he might find an alternate base for support in the House by turning to the hard-money men. That past February Thomas Hutchinson, in a brilliant "Memorial" submitted to the governor and legislature, suggested that the expected parliamentary reimbursement for the province's support of the successful Louisbourg campaign "be the means of sinking the present variable paper Medium of Trade and substituting a fix'd unalterable Currency in the room of it."[56] In short, Hutchinson was suggesting that the dizzy spiral of paper money emissions that had exceeded £700,000 during the past four years be ended. William Shirley believed in hard money and knew that the ministry was unlikely to support him in allowing more cheap paper.[57] To make Hutchinson's memorial an administration measure, minus the ten-year redemption period, would allow the governor to form a new coalition, satisfy his conscience, and please those English merchants and politicians who sustained him in London.[58] His speech of October 17, 1748, informed the General Court that Parliament intended that the reimbursement be used in "such Manner as will put an End to the Paper Currency in New England." It

administration, Hancock hoped to frustrate his attempts in exchanging bills, as well as "any further Attempt for the Annapolis Supplys," see Thomas Hancock to Kilby, 15 July 1745, and to Bourryau, 27 July 1745. The final blow was intended in Hancock's 26 July 1745 letter to Kilby in which he stated that whatever Allen bid he would offer 10 per cent more. See Hancock Letter Books, III, Mass. Hist. Soc.

55. William Shirley to Newcastle, London, 23 Jan. 1749/50, Lincoln, ed., *Correspondence of Shirley*, I, 493–498.

56. Thomas Hutchinson, "Memorial," 3 Feb. 1747/8, Mass. Archives, CII, 366–369.

57. William Shirley in his 22 Feb. 1741/2 letter to the Lords of Trade gave his early critique against the paper money situation. See Seligman MSS, Special Collections, Butler Lib., Columbia.

58. William Shirley to the Duke of Bedford, 31 Jan. 1748/9, Lincoln, ed., *Correspondence of Shirley*, I, 462–468, which gives Hutchinson special credit "in concert with whom alone this act was originally plann'd."

was now the task of the House to decide how it would achieve this end.[59] The committee in charge of the currency issue was heavily loaded in favor of Shirley's proposal. It was headed by Speaker Thomas Hutchinson, the co-author of the silver redemption plan, and included Thomas Hubbard, Isaac Little, and colonels Otis, Choate, and Hale, as well as James Allen of Boston, the committee's one dissenter. Yet the measure was not popular in the House. It took almost four months before a "compromise" bill received the final third reading from this miniature Commons. James Otis had the honor of sending it up to the Council for its concurrence.[60] Massachusetts could now enter upon "a happy Silver age" of financial stability,[61] when a pound sterling equalled one and a third pounds Massachusetts money in place of the fluctuating currency of the past. Yet this proved a politically expensive measure, costing Thomas Hutchinson his Boston seat in the next election and placing John Tyng in the growing ranks of the opposition headed by Samuel Waldo and James Allen.[62]

James Otis's new role as an administration champion received quick acknowledgment from Roland Cotton, the clerk of the House, who wrote in a July note, "I shall Esteem it an addition to my Obligations to you if you will use your Interest among my Friends in the House . . . that I may continue on the Committee for Signing Bills" of credit.[63] In that 1748–1749 Court the position that faced Shirley's party was far from pleasant. The skills of Robert Hale and Thomas Hutchinson had been removed by their defeat at the polls, and the administration's popularity had suffered from the return of conquered Louisbourg to France under the terms of

59. *Mass. House of Reps. Jours., 1748–1749*, 81–82.

60. *Ibid.*, 84, 180. See also Thomas Hutchinson to Israel Williams, 1 Feb. 1748/9, Williams Papers, II, 139, Mass. Hist. Soc. For the opposition see roll call on supplementary legislation, 5 Apr. 1751, *Mass. House of Reps. Jours., 1750–1751*, 194–195 (also see above, n. 29).

61. Sam Sturgis to James Otis, Sr., Barnstable, 10 Mar. 1749/50, Otis Papers, I, 100, Mass. Hist. Soc.

62. Schutz, *William Shirley*, 144–146.

63. Roland Cotton to James Otis, Sr., Boston, 7 July 1749, Otis Papers, I, 91, Mass. Hist. Soc. There was a special remuneration allowed for service on this committee.

the Treaty of Aix-la-Chapelle. The feeling in Massachusetts was
that the fortress was necessary to the security of the province. It
had been conquered by colonial troops, and the shock of seeing it
bartered away by Britain for her own advantage went deep and left
a lasting doubt about the benevolence of the mother country. All of
these factors aided Samuel Waldo, John Tyng, and James Allen as
they continued their vendetta against Shirley.[64] The first sign of
this was a £200 cut in the salary grant, which the governor prudently accepted considering the distressed state of the province.[65]

The economic retrenchment that followed the peace proved
doubly crippling when coupled with a summer drought. James
Otis's second son, Joseph, who was now running the Barnstable
store, wished he were out of business, characteristically concluding
that the "world is filled with fools and madmen."[66] As Thomas
Hancock saw it, the trouble in trade was that "nobody buys any
thing, nor pays Debts but in bills of the other Governments."[67]
James Otis, Jr., who had learned to discount the crisis hyperbole,
wrote his father that he had "No news but of Invasions without and
Civil Commotion within—Scarcity of money, Ruin of trade etc. etc.
—according to the Customs of Boston." In a serious vein he reported
that Andrew Oliver would confer with him within a week about
problems that faced the administration.[68] The most pressing issue
concerned currency reform, for the anticipated refunding of Massachusetts paper for silver, which in turn would be convertible into
sterling, had made the paper a much desired and hoarded medium.
Shirley realized that if this continued, the Massachusetts bills would
be driven out of circulation by the cheap emissions of the other
provinces. A day before young Otis wrote his father, Shirley in-

64. James Otis, Jr., to James Otis, Sr., 10 Sept. 1750, *ibid.*, I, 107.

65. *Mass. House of Reps. Jours., 1748–1749*, 130, and for the reduction, *ibid.,
1749–1750*, 18, 41.

66. Joseph Otis to James Otis, Sr., Barnstable, 8 Jan. 1749/50, Otis Family MSS, I,
21, Butler Lib., Columbia.

67. Hancock to Kilby, Boston, 31 Jan. 1750, Hancock Letter Books, III, Mass.
Hist. Soc.

68. James Otis, Jr., to James Otis, Sr., Boston, 3 Aug. 1750, copy in Gay-Otis
Papers, Butler Lib., Columbia.

formed the House that he was leaving for England. There he successfully lobbied to put "an End to the paper currency in the other three Colonies of New England."[69] Shirley left Lieutenant-Governor Spencer Phips strict instructions to block the inflationists.[70]

The important question of choosing the colonial agent, Massachusetts's special lobbyist at Westminster, was yet unresolved. Shirley counted on James Otis and Thomas Hutchinson to obtain the post for his son-in-law, William Bollan. The position had been held by that adroit master of power politics, Christopher Kilby, who when faced with opposition confidently wrote, "I do not apprehend that in their circumstances the General Court, or the Major part of its members will be inclined to dismiss me."[71] As Shirley saw it, this confidant of Thomas Hancock, spokesman for the Boston trading interests and special friend of his bitter opponent, Samuel Waldo, had too many other masters to serve him well. Shirley knew that he had helped the opposition in "Attempts to make me uneasy in my Government."[72] On the other hand, there was William Bollan, who had acted as temporary agent and had been effective in obtaining parliamentary reimbursement for Massachusetts's war expenditures. Under the rules of eighteenth-century politics, the choice was an elementary matter—Bollan was the governor's son-in-law. However, with Shirley out of the Bay Colony, success would depend upon the efforts of Otis in the House and

69. See William Shirley to Josiah Willard, London, 28 Nov. 1749, Mass. Archives, VI, 80–84, on the threat of R. I. money to the medium, while his letter of 13 Feb. 1749/50 concerns ending the other paper currencies, *ibid.*, VI, 87–88. Shirley's message to the House is in *Mass. House of Reps. Jours., 1749–1750*, 57.

70. William Shirley to Spencer Phips, [11] Sept. 1749, Lincoln, ed., *Correspondence of Shirley*, I, 491.

71. Kilby to Hancock, [London], 17 Sept. 1748, Domestic Letters, I, Hancock Papers, Baker Library, Harvard University.

72. Shirley to Newcastle, London, 23 Jan. 1749/50, Lincoln, ed., *Correspondence of Shirley*, I, 496–497. Hancock realized that Kilby's attitude was ruining his agency—which had been so helpful to business—and warned him to change course, but Kilby did not listen, 10 Feb. 1746/7, Hancock Letter Books, III, Mass. Hist. Soc.

Hutchinson in the Council, for these were times when they "used to think alike."[73] It proved hard work. Otis not only had to round up votes but also had to keep Bollan steady as to the advantages of the agency. Colonel William Williams of Deerfield thought James would come through in spite of formidable opposition, "as your advantage is double to your antagonists, viz., ability and right. I can't doubt Success."[74] If we give full credence to John Tyng's report of the voting, the majority of the House was for Dr. Benjamin Avery, but as the vote was by joint ballot with the Council, which was packed with administration men, Bollan squeezed by with a narrow margin.[75] No matter what the vote, another government measure had been sustained. James Otis was well on his way to earning the sobriquet, "Shirley's henchman."

It would be incorrect to think that James Otis's activities during this time were limited to what the governor wanted, or for that matter that he did not sail an independent course. He undoubtedly considered himself a successful lawyer. His interest in the "Committee for Laws," which examined the temporary acts to decide which would be retained, is not at all surprising.[76] James relished his October 1750 assignment "to prepare the Draft for the settlement and Distribution of Intestate Estates, so far as relates to half Blood." Not only would the legal points be abstruse, but his co-workers were distinguished lawyers, Edmund Trowbridge and Thomas Foster.[77] Otis undoubtedly enjoyed hobnobbing with the elite of the legal profession, and the House proved willing enough to go along with

73. Wood, *William Shirley*, 336–337, 400–401, for Bollan's service. The quote is from Thomas Hutchinson's letter to Israel Williams, Boston, 15 Apr. 1763, Williams Papers, II, 157, Mass. Hist. Soc. A good deal of the politics of this era was arranged in private dinner parties. See Fitch E. Oliver, ed., *The Diaries of Benjamin Lynde and Benjamin Lynde, Jr.* (Boston, 1880), 168, for the Otis-Hutchinson alliance.

74. William Williams to James Otis, Sr., Weston, 21 Jan. 1749/50, Otis Family MSS, I, 22, Butler Lib., Columbia.

75. John Tyng to Samuel Waldo, Boston, 31 Jan. 1749/50, Mass. Archives, LIII, 485–493.

76. *Mass. House of Reps. Jours.*, 1750–1751, 9.

77. *Ibid.*, 91.

his vanity. In both 1748 and 1749 it voted him the attorney-generalship, a position which was not its to give and election to which every governor since 1730 had refused consent *pro forma*.[78] The House had done this only once successfully, but by the middle of the eighteenth century it was as much a part of its tradition to keep on trying as it was to snipe at the Council for minor violations of the charter.[79] Both sides realized what the rhetoric of the occasion required. Otis backed the House in its actions and was probably flattered by the attention, but he was also a strong supporter of its rights.

James Otis considered himself an expert on Indian affairs. In Barnstable he and Sylvanus Bourn shared the guardianship of the local Mashpee tribe for whose welfare both showed genuine concern. This was not a sentimental, or as we understand it a humanitarian attitude. Rather it was the obligation that a superior owes to an inferior, the moral rule of the elite. And while Otis would do what he could to help these natives, he would be under pressure from the white community of Barnstable, which with an increasing poor list of its own, chafed at supporting the indigent Indians.[80] Many of these Indians worked on the local farms. It is to the credit of both John and James Otis that, as justices of the peace, their indentures were legal and that they attempted to protect their wards from sexual abuse by the "English." Yet one wonders if Otis understood the Indians' point of view about their land which embraced both communality and inalienability. This is the substance of the 1748 and 1753 Indian complaints against guardians Sylvanus Bourn and James Otis. They admitted "that said Gentlemen are Good

78. Mass. Archives, XLII, 706, 851.

79. Stewart Mitchell, "Introduction," *Mass. House of Reps. Jours., 1750–1751*, viii–x. For a criticism of the Council on a point of law, see the note sent up by James Otis and others, 24 July 1746, *ibid., 1751–1752*, 114.

80. From 1715 to 1732—the last year for a separate entry—the cost of providing for the poor increased from £20 to £65. The protest of the inhabitants against being "put to for the Indians and praying that we may be Reimbursed the same as also that some measures may be taken to prevent further Charges to this Town from Sick and Indigent Indians" was entered in the minutes of the 11 Mar. 1741/2 meeting, Barnstable Town Records, II, 5, 46, 86.

Honest Men" but complained that they rented out Indian land to
some of the "English."[81] What Otis and Bourn had done was to
lease land that had belonged to Indians who died without heirs or
that was not under cultivation. They used the revenue to pay for
the blankets and other necessaries that the natives picked up almost
daily from the Otis store, an action which the General Court agreed
was proper.[82] As a representative, Otis had his hand in many matters touching Indian life, whether bringing "in a Bill further to
provide for poor Indians" or serving as one of the commissioners at
the Treaty of Falmouth in 1749.[83]

The next four years saw a continuation of James Otis's committee
work in the House. This had settled down to a fairly routine procedure of supplying the treasury, working on tax bills, curbing the
paper-money men, rounding up votes to make gold a legal tender,
and writing to Agent Bollan.[84] During this interval Otis became one
of the inner directors of the House. Peter Oliver, who was related
to Thomas Hutchinson by marriage, was quick to inform Otis of a
French-Canadian Indian attack on the frontier in 1750. He hoped
that a war would provide the means to take the province out of its
economic doldrums. "Pray set your Head and Heart on making
Paper Money next Session. . . . Blessed Times! The Golden Age is
returning! We shall all be Kings, Priests and any Thing else we
incline to."[85] Otis also found a friend in James Russell, representative from Charlestown, who was a fellow committee member, a

81. See complaint of Zacheus Hatch against Silvanus Parker for holding that
Mercy Hatch had "Carnal knowledge" with a male Indian "which is Contrary to
law," May 1745, Suffolk Court Files, 1256: 60 (No. 169448), Suffolk County Court
House.

82. A True Translation of an Indian Petition, Mashpee, 29 Mar. 1748, Mass.
Archives, XXXI, 576, and The Petition of the Indian Proprietors of Mashpee,
(n.d.) but presented to Otis on 10 Dec. 1753, *ibid.*, XXXII, 424–425. The reply of
Bourn and Otis, 27 Dec. 1753, with the resolution of the Court continuing the
guardianship, is in *ibid.*, XXXII, 449–451, 453.

83. *Mass. House of Reps. Jours., 1753–1754,* 128; Hutchinson, *Hist. Mass.,* ed.
Mayo, II, 329.

84. *Mass. House of Reps. Jours., 1749–1750,* 9, 16, 59, 95, 154, *1750–1751,* 69, 120,
140, 195, *1751–1752,* 20, 43, 53, *1752–1753,* 22, 35, 64, 160.

85. Peter Oliver to James Otis, Sr., Boston, 3 Aug. 1750, Otis Papers, I, 105, Mass.
Hist. Soc.

reporter of political news, and a purchaser of Barnstable produce
from Otis.[86] James's relationship with Harrison Gray started with
a common interest in politics, expanded to trade, and finally to
marriage between the two families. Harrison was a source of information on Governor Shirley's stay in England. Along with
Oliver, he rejoiced in the new bills of credit that would take care
of current expenses and possible "invasion." This was "[c]alculated
exactly to ease the Debtors to the no small Mortification of some
of our Usurious Creditors."[87] Gray was particularly critical of the
province's treasurer, William Foye, and outlined his objections in
detail in his letter of June 23, 1752, to Otis. Emphatically, Massachusetts needed a new treasurer of absolute propriety who understood the workings of public credit.[88] Harrison Gray's letter was
transparently a notice of his availability. Undoubtedly Otis was
instrumental in Gray's election at the next session to a post that paid
£200 a year, no small sum in these depression years.[89] Joseph Otis
in Barnstable spent the better part of 1751 dunning old creditors,
while Thomas Hancock was caught with £10,000 sterling worth
of goods.[90] Otis had his own reasons for wanting a limited amount
of paper currency. He wrote Joseph in 1754 that "money grows
short and unless We can command some I Don't see How we carry
on trade longer."[91]

These hard times greeted William Shirley upon his return in
August of 1753. The old supporters were still there—James Bowdoin, Joseph Buckminister, Benjamin Read, and James Otis, but in

86. James Russell to James Otis, Sr., Charlestown, 8 Sept. 1750, Otis Family
MSS, I, 25, Butler Lib., Columbia.

87. Harrison Gray to James Otis, Sr., Boston, 16 Sept. 1751, *ibid.*, I, 28.

88. Harrison Gray to James Otis, Sr., Boston, 23 June 1752, Otis Papers, I, 114,
Mass. Hist. Soc.

89. *Mass. House of Reps. Jours., 1753–1754*, 59.

90. More than a dozen letters were sent out in Jan. 1750/1, some of which referred to debts dating back to 1740. All of these letters are from James Otis to the
parties concerned, but the copies are in the hand of Joseph Otis, Otis Papers, I,
110–114, Mass. Hist. Soc. For Thomas Hancock see his letter of 24 Aug. 1752 to
Robert Turner, Hancock Letter Books, IV, Baker Lib., Harvard.

91. James Otis, Sr., to Joseph Otis, Boston, 18 Dec. 1754, Otis Papers, I, 128,
Mass. Hist. Soc.

spite of their efforts the Shirley men failed on January 3, by a vote of forty-one to forty-four, to obtain a special grant for the governor's services while he was in England. The opposition was led by none other than James Allen.[92] What patronage Shirley had—and it was never enough to go around—was spent in the 1754 election, but success only resulted in a hopeless split among administration men over raising additional revenue, while the lack of funds caused a cut in defense expenditures for the western areas.[93] A combination of hard times, a deficit in the budget, and old enemies together with restive new members of the House, was too much for an administration that had barely enough jobs to take care of the old reliables. While the House voted down an additional salary grant, effective control over Shirley lay in frustrating his program. The House cut back funds for western defense and then defeated the Albany Plan of Union.[94] What might have happened to William Shirley's reputation if the 1754 skirmishes in the backwoods of Pennsylvania had not developed into the Seven Years' War is a question well worth speculation. The waging of this war, combined with Shirley's policy of land grants in Maine, provided the means for reforming political ranks. Patronage and patriotism now joined forces. For Barnstable's representative this meant profit, influence, and power for himself and his family—at least as long as William Shirley was governor.

"We shall be supported in a Great Measure by the Crown with ships and money," the elder Otis noted as he directed son Joseph to go about discreetly buying up the available supply of whaleboats. He warned, "Make no noise and Dont tell any Body what you are about."[95] Obviously, Otis was not in a position to be a major supplier of powder, shot, and money, as was Thomas Hancock, but he realized that a series of inland battles in the New York lake country would require small boats for transport and landing. He knew most of the local boat-builders such as Zacheus Macy of Nantucket; and

92. *Mass. House of Reps. Jours.*, *1753–1754*, 154–155.
93. Schutz, *William Shirley*, 171–177.
94. *Mass. House of Reps. Jours.*, *1754–1755*, 153, 182.
95. James Otis, Sr., to Joseph Otis, 13 Feb. 1756, Otis Family MSS, I, 34, Butler Lib., Columbia.

he dealt in the necessary naval goods, purchasing as much as thirteen thousand feet of timber at a time.[96] In 1757 he secured seventy-eight boats for £380, then arranged carting, transport, freight, and delivery to New York which brought the bill to £772. He concluded by adding on a 5 per cent commission or an additional £38 sterling.[97] Otis's whaleboat business was now in the process of radical expansion. It reached its high point in 1758 when General James Abercromby placed an order with him for two hundred boats, fifty times as many boats as he had supplied to Thomas Hancock just four years before.[98] Undoubtedly there were commissions and profits for Otis as whaleboat victualer in Massachusetts. What was even more important was the patronage this business placed at his disposal, for it insured his preeminence throughout his Barnstable bailiwick and the lower Cape area.

As a colonel in the provincial militia, as well as a strong backer of Shirley's military program and a supplier of whaleboats, James Otis was in a position to mobilize Barnstable behind the war effort. There was gain here too, for the soldiers he enlisted were outfitted from his Barnstable store. It was more than military efficiency that made Otis prompt in submitting his muster rolls and accounts.[99] He knew that he was expected to get results, and from his point of view the Quakers, who refused to show up for militia musters, were deliberately frustrating his military preparations. He refused to recognize that they were acting in good conscience. In fact, it took an order from the Council to restrain the overzealous Barn-

96. Credit invoice, Joshua Freeman to James Otis, Sr., Falmouth, 5 Aug. 1752, Harrison Gray Otis Papers, Box 1, Mass. Hist. Soc.

97. James Otis, Sr., copy of account sent to James Campbell, 1757, Otis Family MSS, I, 43, Butler Lib., Columbia. Partial tallies of Aug. 1757 in Suffolk Court Files, 1271: 40, 43 (No. 171782, 171787), Suffolk County Court House; while the Macy invoice, Nantucket, 29 Aug. 1757, is in Otis Papers, Box 1, Mass. Hist. Soc.

98. James Otis, Sr., to Thomas Hancock, Barnstable, 11 Apr. 1755, Domestic Letters, I, Hancock Papers, Baker Lib., Harvard.

99. Daniel Lewis to James Otis, Sr. (1757/8?), Gay-Otis Papers, Butler Lib., Columbia; James Otis, Sr., account, Province of the Massachusetts Bay, 1750, *ibid.*; James Otis, Sr., to William Brattle, Barnstable, 17 Apr. 1758, muster return, Otis Family MSS, I, 56, *ibid.*

stable authorities.[100] Otis rarely saw the merits of an opposition, and he could see no reason for refusing to coerce the local Quakers. James Otis was not the only politician to profit from war contracts. His friend Major James Warren of Plymouth supplied pork for the troops while Thomas Hutchinson made the arrangements for shipping matériel.[101] Within the Barnstable militia Otis, Sr., was colonel, while both his son Joseph and his nephew John Otis V (1714–1792) were captains. For what he termed "the familys Sake" he obtained a captaincy for his brother-in-law, James Allyne.[102] Otis also used his influence with Shirley to obtain the promise of a major's rank for his political protégé and cousin, Edward Bacon. He considered this as a proper act of "friendship to my Relations, especially the Bacons side who I shall always value for my mothers Sake."[103] Although Otis saw nothing wrong in filling Barnstable's civil and military posts with his relatives, Shirley told young James Otis in July of 1756 that he found the elder Otis's first nominee for an administrative post unacceptable "by reason of the near connection —and appearance of partiality."[104]

Governor Shirley did not intend to open himself up to any criticism which might interfere with the war effort. All his energies were now bent toward gaining control of the continent. His plans called for a major offensive against the French forts at Frontenac, La Galette, and Niagara, which controlled the Great Lakes and the Ohio Valley. Then he would take Quebec. Unfortunately Shirley's heavy dependence upon his Massachusetts suppliers antagonized a handful of influential New York merchants. Led by the De Lancey

100. See Richard Baxter to James Otis, Sr., 4 May 1758, Otis Family MSS, I, 58, *ibid.*; and return of Captain Silas Bourn, Sandwich, 8 May 1758, listing 62 male Quakers over 16 years of age, in Misc. Bound MSS, XII, Mass. Hist. Soc. The "Petition" of Joseph Wing, *et al.*, to the Council, Barnstable, 8 Jan. 1757, with the Council's stay of execution and order releasing Wing, is in Mass. Archives, XIV, 2, 22, 30.
101. Thomas Hutchinson to James Otis, Sr., Plymouth, 9 Aug. 1758, Otis Family MSS, I, 66, Butler Lib., Columbia.
102. James Otis, Sr., to Joseph Otis, 13 Feb. 1756, *ibid.*, I, 34.
103. James Otis, Sr., to Edward Bacon, Boston, 1 Mar. 1756, *ibid.*, I, 36.
104. James Otis, Jr., to James Otis, Sr., Boston, 24 July 1756, *ibid.*, I, 39.

brothers, who were eager to gain control of the war for their own benefit, they formed a cabal including Thomas Pownall and the Indian expert William Johnson. The right moment for them to strike came in the fall of 1756 when the French took Fort Oswego, and rumors spread linking Shirley with treason. Shirley, now in an exposed position, was called home, the official reason being to give advice "upon measures for carrying on the war."[105] In fact, however, British politicians were looking for a scapegoat for the defeats of the English army. Thomas Pownall, who had returned to London and had the confidence of Lord Halifax as well as the friendship of the Duke of Cumberland, skillfully exploited the situation. Just as Shirley had obtained the governorship upon the ruins of Governor Belcher's career, so now Pownall turned the trick on Shirley.[106]

Shirley's sudden fall was an unexpected blow to his Massachusetts supporters, and their future fortunes were the source of much speculation at Boston. James Otis, Jr., whose information to his father was ordinarily accurate, wrote in August of 1756 that Shirley would "Remain Governor as long as he pleaseth" and expected to see Otis at the next Court.[107] Otis thought for some time that he could salvage some of his war business, for Shirley's military successor, Lord Loudoun, treated him in a "gentlemanly manner,"[108] and the elder Otis evidently believed that if he acted fast enough he might achieve his ambition and obtain a seat in the Council. He relinquished his Barnstable post in the House to Edward Bacon, who campaigned for him. Otis himself lobbied among old associates for his election to the Council. Benjamin Lynde laconically

105. Hutchinson, *Hist. Mass.*, ed. Mayo, III, 34; John S. Barry, *The History of Massachusetts*, II (Boston, 1856), 211–212, 220; Schutz, *William Shirley*, 221–224.

106. John A. Schutz, *Thomas Pownall, British Defender of American Liberty: A Study of Anglo-American Relations in the Eighteenth Century* (Glendale, Cal., 1951), 58–70, 82–83. See also William Shirley to Samuel Waldo, Boston, 15 Apr. 1739, ed. Amelia C. Ford, *American Historical Review*, XXXVI (1930–1931), 350–360.

107. James Otis, Jr., to James Otis, Sr., Boston, 9 Aug. 1756, Otis Family MSS, I, 40, Butler Lib., Columbia.

108. James Otis, Sr., to Joseph Otis, Boston, 31 Jan. 1757, Otis Papers, I, 143, Mass. Hist. Soc.

recorded the results: "I, chosen anew. Daniel Russell, Esq., and Otis left out."[109] News of this bitter blow even reached Will Fletcher at St. Eustatius. He wrote Otis of his sorrow "to find, that you are not among the Number of the *Elect*, especially at this Critical juncture."[110] What Otis wanted was not sympathy, but an explanation of why he had been defeated. By August of 1757 he thought he knew the answer, and he did something very unusual for a man of his nature—wrote himself a memo. It followed a reported conversation in the Council. Its point was that:

my Business Would ~~then~~ Be Effectually Done upon the new Governours comeing for Mr T Hutchinson and Mr Olliver would Be his advisers and that they had a Bad opinion of my Conduct and that Mr Hutchinson had said that I never Did Carry things while in the Court By any merit But only By Doing Little Low Dirty things for Governor Shirley such as Persons of ~~merit~~ worth Refused to medle with and that Shirley made use of me only as a Tool for [their?] Purposes.

This document, buried for two hundred years in a family archive, shows the elder Otis's belief that it was Thomas Hutchinson and friends who opposed him.[111] Their cruel appraisal cut James Otis deeply; he wondered now whether his services were not being appropriated for the gratification of others. His bitterness spread to Hutchinson and the Olivers as successors of the Shirley administration, and even to Shirley himself. He viewed his defeat at the hands of the Hutchinson clique as an attempt to deny himself and his family the success they merited. His determination to achieve high honor was intensified.

About the time that Otis wrote his memo, Governor Thomas Pownall arrived in Boston. Although the elder Otis was not sure that the new governor would welcome his services, his son James quickly became Pownall's friend and companion. On August 25, Pownall asked Otis in a polite letter to forward to New York "one

109. Benjamin Lynde, 25 May 1757, Oliver, ed., *Diaries of Lynde*, 186.
110. William Fletcher to James Otis, Sr., St. Eustatius, 6 Nov. 1757, Otis Papers, I, 172, Mass. Hist. Soc.
111. James Otis, Sr., memo, *ca.* 15 Aug. 1757, Otis Family MSS, I, 44, Butler Lib., Columbia.

hundred Whaleboates."[112] As might be expected the governor had some questions about James's business methods. However, he suggested that Otis should meet with him and Lord Loudoun at Plymouth in March of 1758. Pownall seemed to have been willing to reach a settlement, although it would probably have required a compromise on Otis's part. Much to the annoyance of the governor, Otis did not attend, the ostensible reason being an attack of lameness.[113] James, Jr., writing as tactfully as possible, told his father that Pownall considered the invitation to meet him "more than a Compliment and really expected you."[114] Intended or not, offense had been given. The next letter from Governor Thomas Pownall, dated March 13, concluded with the admonition, "Make as much saving to the Crown as possible and transmit your accounts to me for examination and payments."[115] This point was made even clearer by James De Lancey, who received the boats in Albany and audited the various charges. He told Otis that headquarters was convinced that his freight charges were too high. If Otis wanted his higher figures honored, he should get Governor Pownall to write to "General Abercromby on his head."[116] Unfortunately for Otis, the Barnstable troops at Albany were not improving his standing with the army. The remark was made that only Colonel Otis "could have sent" so many sick and lame and that he was "an old Pirate and a Cursed old Rogue."[117] If this opinion was known in Boston, it might explain the coldness of General Amherst who refused to "Look Into any Past Transactions" or to accept Otis's figures. James had been in Boston politics long enough to realize that he had offended Pownall and that it would be unwise to press his inflated freight charges. "I find the Governor is Quite Tired with

112. Thomas Pownall to James Otis, Sr., Boston, 25 Aug. 1757, *ibid.*, I, 45.

113. James Warren to James Otis, Sr., Plymouth, 5 Mar. 1758, Otis Papers, II, 3, Mass. Hist. Soc.

114. James Otis, Jr., to James Otis, Sr., Boston, 3 Mar. 1758, Otis Family MSS, I, 48, Butler Lib., Columbia.

115. Thomas Pownall to James Otis, Sr., 13 Mar. 1758, *ibid.*, I, 49.

116. James De Lancey to James Otis, Sr., New York, 2 June 1758, *ibid.*, I, 61.

117. Examination of Ebenezer Chipman, 8 Aug. 1758, *ibid.*, I, 67.

the affair," James commented in telling his tale.[118] Otis by his own conduct and lack of tact had made himself unpopular with the new administration.

James Otis wanted to be a member of that gentlemen's club, the Massachusetts Council, and realized that he must hold elective office if he expected his supporters to remain loyal to him. Once again James made detailed arrangements with his protégé Edward Bacon, who had replaced him as the Barnstable representative, to work for his election to the Council in May of 1759. A more prudent man would have realized that this was not the best time to seek a seat in the upper chamber. If Otis ran for one of the four area seats reserved specifically for the former Old Colony, he would have to oust an incumbent. Sylvanus Bourn, Otis's old friend and neighbor, who held one of those four territorial seats, did not intend to sacrifice his own political career for Otis's benefit. He also enlisted Edward Bacon to be his campaign manager in the House. Bacon now lined up both Bourn's and Otis's friends, letting it out that "he and the Party he made would vote" for Otis as one of the councilors-at-large "if Coll. Bourn might be saved this year." However, once Bourn was reelected, Otis thought that Bacon did not really work for his success. It was left to two old friends, Benjamin Prat and Samuel White, and his one-time enemy, John Tyng, to maneuver unsuccessfully for James. This second failure unnerved Otis since the impetus for it came from his "own Townsmen." The rallying cry which they used against him was that he already had "too much Power."[119] It is a pity that Otis did not reflect upon that charge. Otis should have realized that his candidacy would be a direct threat to an old friend and ally, Silvanus Bourn, who, as a member of the Council for many years, had a prior claim to the seat. By

118. James Otis, Sr., to [Zacheus Macy], Barnstable, 4 Aug. 1758, Otis Papers, II, 24, Mass. Hist. Soc. It is clear that the Boston authorities at least knew of the turmoil in Barnstable for on 29 July 1758 Thomas Hutchinson sent a warrant to James Otis, Sr., for the arrest of the local rioters and deserters. See J. M. Robbins Papers, *ibid*.

119. James Otis, Sr., to [Joseph Otis], Boston, 13 June 1759, Otis Family MSS, I, 74, Butler Lib., Columbia.

this precipitate bid for power Otis had lost both the election and an influential friend.

It now seemed imperative to Otis that he regain his seat in the House, heretofore the field of his greatest success, where he could obtain political leverage. In the next Barnstable election he displaced Edward Bacon. Otis still wanted to be a councilor, as well as a justice of the Superior Court, but he would now seek these goals from a position of power in the House. In 1760 his friends in the Assembly, after close lobbying on his part, presented him to the governor as their choice for speaker. As almost his last act of office, Governor Pownall signified his approval, thereby leaving the incoming governor, Francis Bernard, to deal with James Otis as the leader of a House of Representatives proud of its independence and marked by factionalism.[120]

What are we to make of these sixteen years? First of all, they reveal a fluid structure of provincial politics, devoid of any fixed or permanent party alignment. The stability of the Shirley administration did not reflect the attitudes of the representatives so much as the governor's skill in mastering them. In fact, it was the very instability of the local groupings that allowed the governor to form and reform his coalitions. Nor was Shirley always successful. For one thing, the parochial sentiments of the towns thwarted his imperial vision, while many representatives felt that the British policies he represented were at times opposed to the best interests of the province. The return of Louisbourg to the French after it had been won by Massachusetts arms was a case in point. The Magna Carta was cited in the 1740's, as it would be in the 1760's, as arguing against unconstitutional acts such as the impressment of Massachusetts sailors. In this period, there were no cries from the back country against oppression by the seacoast towns. In fact the contrary is true. The seaport towns complained constantly against excessive overtaxation that favored the dominant agrarian interests. Yet

120. Thomas Pownall to the House, 28 May 1760, in *Mass. House of Reps. Jours., 1760–1761,* 5; John Chandler to James Otis, Sr., Worcester, 30 May 1760, Otis Family MSS, I, 75, Butler Lib., Columbia.

the House, with its effective membership hovering at slightly under a hundred, was not divided on any clearly regional or economic lines. When all is said, it was broadly representative of Massachusetts. It was conscious above all of its autonomy and it conceived of itself as a miniature House of Commons.

James Otis during this period stood for one of the towns that formed the House. While his liabilities were many, he had demonstrated obvious skills. He was wont to count enemies and insults where they did not exist, as seen in his temperamental outbreaks when he thought Harrison Gray and James, Jr., were not answering his letters. Not everyone would be as understanding as Harrison, who pointed out to James that he should have at least considered the possibility that the mail had not arrived in the first place.[121] Likewise, his early difficulties with Governor Pownall, as well as his defeat for the Council, were probably due more to his failing than to the combinations he saw opposing him. His ideals were limited—"Honour and Interest" and family position.[122] Yet James Otis, Sr., if he stood for anything, stood for Barnstable. He had many friends and valuable allies in his three sons. The careers of James, Jr., who had staked out a claim in the larger world of Boston, and of Joseph, who was in the process of taking over the Barnstable bailiwick, were interconnected with their father's success. A wise politician would realize the folly of attempting to exclude him or them from public office. The Otises were confident that they could handle the future.

121. Harrison Gray to James Otis, Sr., 16 Sept. 1751, Otis Family MSS, I, 28, Butler Lib., Columbia; Joseph Otis to James Otis, Sr., 8 Jan. 1749/50, *ibid.,* I, 21.
122. James Otis, Sr., to [the Harvard Board], Barnstable, 27 June 1750, *ibid.,* I, 27.

## ✖ VI.

# THE FIFTH GENERATION

If the study of the political structure of Barnstable County reveals anything it is a way of life, a set of values, a pattern of interests which connected father, son, and family. Four generations of Otis patriarchs sweated and stored up treasures that their sons might succeed them. Just as the elder Otis had received his father's fine sword and silver-headed cane, so he prayed that his son James might inherit these symbols of status and authority.[1] He intended that Joseph (1726–1810), and Samuel Allyne (1740–1814), as well as James (1725–1783), would help him in realizing his lifelong objectives in trade and politics. He considered their education as an investment, one, however, which he was careful to charge against James's and Samuel Allyne's portions of his estate. He spent his money putting James, Jr., through school in anticipation of the "fine prospects" his son would have to be "useful to himself and family and the world."[2] He counted on Harvard to provide a ready entrance into proper Boston society for his sons. He knew that the diploma gave as a right what it had taken him twenty years of hard

---

1. Preamble, James Otis, Sr., will (attested copy), 21 Apr. 1774, Gay-Otis Papers, Butler Lib., Columbia.
2. James Otis, Sr., to James Otis, Jr., Barnstable, 1 Aug. 1772 (draft copy), *ibid.*

work to achieve. He expected young James's career to embrace both Boston and Barnstable.

Harvard did provide James with the entrance into polite society which his father had expected. It mirrored traditional values of order and hierarchy, and it also gave James a way of viewing reality that separated him from the provincialisms of country life. Cambridge, with its formalities, its carefully regulated fines which ran from two pennies for lateness to a pound for playing cards, and the class lists in which each student was ranked according to his family's "social position," enshrined the traditional values of society.[3] The curriculum, following an even older ideal, sought to give each student a thorough command of Latin, Greek, and Hebrew, as well as a "knowledge of Rhetorick, Logick, Natural Philosophy, Geography, Ethicks, Divinity, Metaphisicks, and . . . the eliments of Mathematicks."[4] James's study of logic centered on the mastery of the dialectical, topical, modal, and indirect syllogisms as expounded by Franconus Burgersdicius, who had been a leader of puritan thought in the seventeenth century. His future political writings show the effects of this training in logic, as well as a general acceptance of the whig interpretation of the classics and of English history. His heroes were Brutus, Cromwell, and the patriots of the Convention Parliament. They had been manful enough to oppose Caesar and the Stuart kings, those subverters of ancient constitutions. History taught him that whenever governors "deviate from truth, justice and equity, they verge towards tyranny, and are to be opposed."[5] As a senior James took the side of Nathan Prince, a Harvard fellow who had been dismissed by the overseers for "Speaking with Contempt of the President and Tutors as to Learning" and a host of other offenses.[6] James carefully read Prince's

3. "College Laws," (1734), II, 6, IV, 11, 13, 16, VIII, 16, Harvard Univ. Archives.
4. *Ibid.*, III, 3, and see "A Particular Account of the Present Stated Exercises . . .," 1 Mar. 1725/6, *Harvard College Records*, III, Col. Soc. of Mass., *Pubs.*, XXXI (1935), 455–456.
5. James Otis, Jr., *Rights of the British Colonies Asserted and Proved* (Boston, 1764), 13.
6. Shipton, *et al.*, *Sibley's Harvard Graduates*, VI, 272–274.

defense, which included long citations from the early charters of Massachusetts Bay. Prince argued that these documents proved that only the General Assembly, which held all power in the province, could fire him. James agreed with Prince's position. He urged his father to read Prince's tract for it showed that the overseers had exceeded their delegated authority. The Harvard administration, James declared, was a "miserable, Despicable and arbitrary Government."[7] This is the first example of a line of argumentation that brought the young Otis political fame in the 1760's. Harvard gave him his texts on natural law, reinforced his belief in contractual rights, and made him familiar with the early laws and charters of the colony.

Otis's letters to his parents during this period reveal a bright, sensitive, somewhat introspective youth who missed the security of his family and the companionship of his brother Joseph.[8] At Harvard he was fortunate in finding a friend and roommate in his cousin Lothrop Russell, whose quietness matched James's youthful ebullience. In the winter of 1740 they found themselves deeply moved by George Whitefield's revival visit to Cambridge. They joined a small coterie which "prayed together Sung Psalms and discourced" on religion while their friend "Roby had a vision of Hel Open, hims[elf] and Others dropping in."[9] The story that the future patriot while home on vacation was dragged out to fiddle a "country dance," which he fled from crying, "So Orpheus fiddled, and so danced the brutes," surely dates from this time.[10] This is the earliest emotional crisis we know of in the life of James, Jr. Whether it shows mental instability at this stage in young Otis's life is a moot point. One could argue that the rest of Otis's career at Harvard,

7. James Otis, Jr., to James Otis, Sr., Cambridge, 4 Apr. 1743, Otis Family MSS, I, 14, Butler Lib., Columbia; Nathan Prince, *The Constitution and Government of Harvard College, from Its Foundations in 1636 to 1742 with Reasons to Prove That the Overseers Have No Independent Power over the Corporation* (Boston, 1742), 15, Amer. Antiq. Soc.

8. James Otis, Jr., to James Otis, Sr., Cambridge, 5 Sept. 1740, Otis Papers, I, 31, Mass. Hist. Soc.

9. Entries, Dec. 1740 and Jan. 1741, Henry Flynt's Diary, II, [133], Harvard Univ. Archives.

10. Tudor, *Life of Otis*, 9.

when in his junior and senior years the faculty granted him the privilege of eating "out of Commons at Night," shows that he became a serious and responsible student.[11] There can be no doubt, however, that James was highly emotional. The death of Russell shortly after Otis had celebrated graduation with him brought about despondency. Thereafter James's correspondence became formal and impersonal.

After graduation and Russell's death young Otis did little but read literature in preparation for the traditional second degree. If he had been allowed to follow his own wishes James probably would have devoted his life to the study of the classics. However, his father intended that the law should be his career. It was a sure road to influence and power. His mentor was Jeremiah Gridley, an old family friend and one of the most successful lawyers in Massachusetts. James's apprenticeship consisted in drawing up writs and wrestling with the old gothic "black letter" law books.[12] Aside from his studies, James took care of family business affairs when his father was absent from Boston. He kept his eyes open for cheap sugar and good claret.[13] And as his father was one of the leading backers of Governor Shirley's war policy in the House, he reported home all the latest political and military news. With youthful enthusiasm this young law clerk told of George II's acknowledgment of his "great obligation to this Province" for helping make possible the victory at Louisbourg. Shirley and Pepperrell each received from their grateful king the reward of a regiment, which James stated was worth £1,400 sterling.[14] James obviously enjoyed the bustle of Boston and hoped to settle in the capital. However, his father urged him to practice first in a small town.

In 1748, James Otis, Jr., put out his shingle in Plymouth. Here as a young attorney he had a chance to test himself, perfect a style,

11. 25 Sept. 1741, and 20 Sept. 1742, Faculty College Records, I, 159, 170, Harvard Univ. Archives.

12. James Otis, Jr., to Samuel A. Otis, 1760, in Tudor, *Life of Otis*, 10–11.

13. James Otis, Jr., to James Otis, Sr., July 1745, Otis Papers, I, 56, Mass. Hist. Soc., and 5 Dec. 1746, Otis Family MSS, I, 18, Butler Lib., Columbia.

14. James Otis, Jr., to James Otis, Sr., 2 Oct. 1745, Otis Papers, I, 65–66, Mass. Hist. Soc.

and above all, make mistakes where they would not count too heavily. And Plymouth was close enough to Barnstable so that the elder Otis could keep an eye on him. He sent James the proper executions, cautioned on charging fees, asked him to represent him in small matters, and did everything but give James the independence that he wanted.[15] As Plymouth was part of the elder Otis's circuit, sooner or later father and son would meet in court. Their first confrontation was over a debt action for 32s. in September 1748. James, Jr., won and had the added pleasure of seeing the verdict confirmed over his father's appeal to the Superior Court.[16] This served as a prelude to the famous case of Veazie *v.* Duxbury. The Rev. Samuel Veazie, who was Duxbury's pastor, sued the town for nonsupport. He hired the elder Otis to represent him, while the town elders countered by engaging James, Jr., to handle their defense. It was money well spent. Young Otis impeached Veazie's character by reading to the jury excerpts from the pastor's sermons which convinced the jury that this was not the "faithful, pious, and learned minister" for whom the town had contracted. His point was that as the pastor had not lived up to his end of the contract, so the town could not be legally bound to observe its part.[17] It was a solid victory. However, helping to oust a minister was probably not the best way of gaining country clients. The neighboring churches of Hanover, Halifax, Marshfield, and Plymouth resented Duxbury's action and finally condemned the town in solemn council for denying support to its old pastor and "Suffering the House of God to Lay wast[e]."[18] For this and other reasons James proved unable to attract the large load of common cases that alone made a country practice profitable. In May of 1749, young James handled one *de novo* action, while the leading local practitioners averaged fifteen,

15. James Otis, Sr., to James Otis, Jr., 10 June 1748, Otis Family MSS, I, 19, Butler Lib., Columbia.
16. Sept. 1748, No. 10, Minute Book, 1745–1749, and Inferior Court of Common Pleas Records, IX, 534, Plymouth. The judgment was confirmed in Aug. 1749, Superior Court of Judicature Records [XVII], 253, Suffolk County Court House.
17. Shipton, *et al.*, *Sibley's Harvard Graduates*, X, 87.
18. *Plymouth Church Records, 1620–1859* (New York, 1920), I, 299.

and his father garnered a third of the ninety-odd cases.[19] He must have realized that he was not fitted for this kind of work. No wonder young Otis preferred spending his time on the abstractions of his legal folios rather than trying to court local farmers. He utilized his last months in Plymouth preparing for his return to Boston. The intensity of his efforts worried his brother Joseph, who wrote the family that he "has taken so close to his Studies that he scarsely allows himself to Eat Decently or Sleep."[20]

Young Otis returned to Boston in 1750 as a gentleman with an obvious future. He was the first son of one of the hardest working supporters of the governor, he had both money and connections, while his former legal mentor thought highly of his talents and now sponsored his entry into St. John's masonic lodge.[21] James's clients were no longer crude farmers but polished merchants of the metropolis. He drew upon the connections of his own family as well as the Warrens of Plymouth, while the Bourns of Barnstable and Boston with their shipping and Halifax interests supplied additional clients.[22] Young James described himself as "naturally and constitutionally inclined to social pleasures."[23] He was affable, agreeable, and Harvard educated. While he stayed in Boston with the Allynes (his mother's family), he could come and go as he desired. He spent most of his time "dining out" and either making or renewing acquaintances with the leaders in trade, politics, and society.[24] James quickly counted as his clients such principal merchants and speculators as the Hancocks, Vassals, and Halls.[25] Nor was James's interest

19. May 1749 docket, Minute Book, 1745–1749, Inferior Court of Common Pleas, Plymouth.

20. Joseph Otis to James Otis, Sr., 8 Jan. 1749/50, Otis Family MSS, I, 21, Butler Lib., Columbia.

21. James Otis, Jr., to James Otis, Sr., 10 Sept. 1750, *ibid.*, I, 31; Shipton, *et al.*, *Sibley's Harvard Graduates*, XI, 248.

22. William Bourn to James Otis, Jr., Halifax, 1 Mar. 1754/5, Suffolk Court Files, 445: 04 (No. 72423), Suffolk County Court House.

23. *Boston Gazette*, 13 May 1765.

24. James Otis, Jr., to James Otis, Sr., Boston, 3 Aug. 1750 (copy), Gay-Otis Papers, Butler Lib., Columbia.

25. James Otis, Jr., to W. Vassall, 1 Sept. and 28 Sept. 1753, AM 1250 (No. 79, 80), Houghton Lib., Harvard; James Otis, Jr., "Account," 1750–1752, Suffolk Court

in trade solely based upon his legal practice, for he served as the family's Boston factor. He shopped for merchandise, arranged shipping, paid off the small notes of the Otis clan, and handled the legal writs connected with Barnstable.[26] In addition he represented the proprietors of the town of Gorham in Maine when they sought reconfirmation of their grant from the General Court.[27] Boston meant success, and in 1755 James took as his wife the beautiful Ruth Cunningham, a merchant's daughter and heiress to a fortune worth £ 10,000 O. T.[28] It had been an eventful five years.

It was but a matter of time before James Otis, Jr., entered the political world. As a young lawyer he served as liaison between his father and Governor Shirley. His appointment in 1756 as a justice of the peace for Suffolk showed his family's position. However, James was above all a Boston man with his own activities. He opposed the overtaxation of the trading towns by the back-country farmers and joined with the attorneys and merchants of the metropolis in petitioning against this injustice in December of 1755.[29] He was also instrumental in bringing about an accommodation between his father and Thomas Pownall, who had succeeded Shirley as governor. In this respect he continued in his role as go-between.[30] He served as the spokesman for his merchant clients in the new administration. Pownall found it advantageous to gather supporters from the country party of Otis, Sr., as well as from the city friends of James, Jr. The governor needed these allies to counterbalance the activities of his lieutenant-governor, Thomas Hutchinson, who was quietly gathering partisans in anticipation of obtaining the

Files, 442: 72 (No. 71910), Suffolk County Court House; Abram E. Brown, *John Hancock, His Book* (Boston, 1898), 34–35, 106.

26. James Otis, Jr., "Accounts" 1748–1758, fols. 1–6, Gay-Otis Papers, Butler Lib., Columbia.

27. 28 Dec. 1753, Mass. Archives, CXVI, 514–516.

28. Charles H. Tuttle, "Christopher Kilby of Boston," *New England Hist. and Gen. Register*, XXVI (1872), 44, n. 2.

29. The Petition of Sundry Gentlemen, Merchants and others, Inhabitants of the Town of Boston, 26 Dec. 1755, Mass. Archives, CXVII, 54.

30. James Otis, Jr., to James Otis, Sr., Boston, 3 Apr. 1758, in Tudor, *Life of Otis*, 18–19.

governorship himself.[31] Governor Pownall rewarded young Otis by making him deputy advocate-general of the Vice-Admiralty Court. This post yielded £200 a year and allowed James, Jr., to look after his friends.[32] The elder Otis, who had his own score to settle with Hutchinson and company as a result of the 1757 Council defeat, willingly joined up with the governor. Otis, Sr., again obtained the promise of the next vacant seat on the Superior Court. Before that occurred Pownall received promotion to the more valuable Carolina governorship. His last act approved Otis, Sr.'s election as speaker of the House, thereby placing his key supporter in a superior maneuvering position. The elder Otis took leave of Thomas Pownall at the "End of the Long Wharffe" with a deep feeling of regret.[33] Father and son now pondered what men and policies would guide their new governor, Francis Bernard. They both had vital interests to protect.

Bernard, the object of this anxiety, had served an uneventful term as governor of New Jersey. He had hoped that influential relatives would secure for him the lucrative governorship of either New York or Pennsylvania. However, the best Lord Barrington could do was to reshuffle him to Massachusetts.[34] Bernard had neither the practical experience of Shirley, who had fought his way to the top, nor the instinctive finesse of his immediate predecessor Thomas Pownall, who quickly mastered the perplexities of Massachusetts's shifting political structure. Moreover Governor Bernard's instructions from the home government required him to execute the long-ignored provisos of the 1733 Molasses Act which levied a prohibitive six pence a gallon on foreign rum.[35] For a man who wanted to

31. Thomas Hutchinson to Israel Williams, Boston, 8 Aug. 1759, Williams Papers, II, 151, Mass. Hist. Soc.; Malcolm Freiberg, "How to Become a Colonial Governor: Thomas Hutchinson of Massachusetts," *Review of Politics*, XXI (1959), 646–656.

32. Adams, ed., *Works of J. Adams*, X, 281; *Boston Gazette* 13 May 1765.

33. Albert Matthews, ed., "Notes on the Massachusetts Royal Commissioners, 1681–1775," Col. Soc. of Mass., *Pubs.*, XVII (1913–1914), 81.

34. Francis Bernard to Barrington, Perth Amboy, 23 May 1759, and Barrington to Francis Bernard, London, 14 Nov. 1759, Edward Channing, ed., *Barrington-Bernard Correspondence* . . . (Cambridge, Mass., 1912), 4–5, 7–8.

35. Pitt to Francis Bernard, 23 Aug. 1760, Mass. Archives, XXII, 163–165, and

provide for his family there was good reason for enforcing that act. As governor he would receive one third of all forfeitures. It seems as if from the very first Francis Bernard's interests and those of the province he was to serve would conflict.

Bernard was a governor who wanted to make his influence felt. He quickly stepped into the political arena by dealing with "T[y]ng and his adherents," who constituted the least important of the three parties in the House. Undoubtedly Bernard wanted to show his distance from the Otis men, who had recently backed Pownall, while at the same time remaining independent from Lieutenant-Governor Hutchinson's friends. However, Bernard's support of the Tyng clique, which was anathema to "Speaker [Otis] and so many of the principal members of the House," was a weak move in that it did not give him a majority to support his administration.[36] Sooner or later he would have to choose between the Otis and Hutchinson factions.

The death of Chief Justice Samuel Sewall on September 10, 1760, presented Bernard with the one patronage post that forced him to choose sides. It also involved the entire customs enforcement program, which his instructions and self-interest required him to put into effect. It was common knowledge that the old chief justice had taken a critical view of the general search warrants which the customs commissioners thought necessary for their crackdown on smuggling.[37] The new justice would have to pass upon the legality of those writs of assistance. The paramount concern of the elder Otis was the post itself, for custom required that a justice should be *ex officio* a member of the Council. He was probably neutral on the writs issue. However, James, Jr., as deputy advocate-general of the Vice-Admiralty Court did not favor a rigid enforcement policy which would hurt his mercantile clients. The elder Otis hoped to

see G[eorgius] R[ex], Orders and Instructions, 18 Mar. 1760, No. 13–16, Bernard Papers, XIII, 196–199, Houghton Lib., Harvard.

36. Thomas Hutchinson to Israel Williams, 25 Aug. 1760, Williams Papers, II, 155, Mass. Hist. Soc.

37. Hutchinson, *Hist. Mass.*, ed. Mayo, III, 68; *Boston Gazette*, 4 Jan. 1762; Adams to J. Morse, 29 Nov. 1815, Adams, ed., *Works of J. Adams*, X, 183.

reach an agreement with Thomas Hutchinson and Andrew Oliver for their support and sent his son to arrange it. Young James, who had heard rumors that the justiceship was to go to Hutchinson, asked him directly if he sought the position. Otis took what was a non-committal answer, that Hutchinson did not seek the office, to mean that he would not accept it.[38] But Bernard had ascertained that Hutchinson favored the legality of the writs.[39] And the lieutenant governor's friends, who promised him majority support in the House, convinced Bernard that there was no "ballancing between the two Candidates."[40] Hutchinson received the appointment on November 13 and took his seat on December 30. In the interval James, Jr., had resigned his admiralty position. He considered Hutchinson's conduct Janus-faced. Hutchinson's desire for the chief justiceship must have puzzled young Otis, for the lieutenant-governor had more than his share of honors. Did he now want this new post as balm for his ego after failing to obtain the governorship? Certainly Hutchinson did not have to worry about controlling the court with three of his relatives already justices. Did Hutchinson deliberately intend to block the Otises' rise to prominence by pre-empting the one post that the elder Otis had waited ten years for?[41] Young Otis, ever sensitive to family honor, might well have raised these questions in his heated exchange with the lieutenant-governor during which he "swore revenge."[42] Moreover, Hutchinson's appointment affronted other "old practitioners at the Bar," the foremost of whom was Colonel Brattle.[43] Bernard, by giving the chief justiceship to Thomas Hutchinson who was at one and the same time a member of the Council, judge of probate for Suffolk, lieutenant-governor and commander of Castle William, presented the opposi-

38. *Boston Gazette*, 4 Apr. 1763.

39. Thomas Bernard, *The Life of Francis Bernard* (London, 1790), 43–44.

40. Francis Bernard to Shelburne, Boston, 22 Dec. 1766, Bernard Papers, IV, 275, Houghton Lib., Harvard.

41. Waters and Schutz, "Patterns of Colonial Politics," *Wm. and Mary Qtly.*, 3d Ser., XXIV (1967), 561.

42. Thomas Hutchinson to Israel Williams, 21 Jan. 1761, Williams Papers, II, 155, Mass. Hist. Soc.

43. Palfrey to John Wilkes, Boston, 23–30 Oct. 1770, George M. Elsey, ed., "John Wilkes and William Palfrey," Col. Soc. of Mass., *Pubs.*, XXXIV (1937–1942), 419.

tion, whose ranks were now swelled with the disappointed, with the prime issue of plural office-holding.[44] It raised the cry of oligarchy which had been present in Massachusetts politics since Shirley's governorship.[45]

James Otis, Jr.'s career in Boston had been marked by particular concern for the welfare of the trading community. This was one of the factors Bernard considered in choosing Hutchinson over the elder Otis. James moreover had resigned from the Admiralty Court when he had been pressed for a really vigorous policy by the governor. Privately he told the merchants that the governor was the real beneficiary of the new trade policy and that "the L[ieutenant] G[overnor] was his friend."[46] Furthermore his knowledge of the vice-admiralty procedures convinced him that the present usage of that court was not only illegal but also a fraud against the commonwealth. The forfeiture law of George II called for a three-way division of these spoils, one third being for the use of the province, one third for the governor, and one third for the officials who made the seizure. In Massachusetts the court used the province's share to pay the assorted costs and charges of the informers, a procedure not warranted by law. On December 17, 1760, Otis presented the petition of his merchant friends to the General Court noting this irregularity and asking that the province sue the customs to recover its rightful third.[47] The House accepted the petition and directed the province's treasurer to bring suit for £475 against Charles Paxton, the collector of the customs. Governor Bernard was furious and refused his assent, claiming that only the attorney-general could sue.[48] The governor's position was both wrong in law and a pretext as Hutchinson admitted, but, he stated, Bernard's real reason was

44. Ellen E. Brennan, *Plural Office-Holding in Massachusetts, 1760–1780: Its Relationship to the "Separation" of Departments of Government* (Chapel Hill, 1945), 32–34.

45. Jonathan Mayhew, *A Discourse Occasioned by the Death of . . . Stephen Sewall . . .* (Boston, 1760), 37–38.

46. Thomas Hutchinson to Israel Williams, 21 Jan. 1761, Williams Papers, II, 155, Mass. Hist. Soc.

47. Mass. Archives, XLIV, 446.

48. *Mass. House of Reps. Jours., 1760–1761*, 242–247.

"to prevent Mr. Otis from carrying on the suit."[49] The House rejected Bernard's argument, and under prodding from the Council the governor on January 31, 1761, approved a resolve that made him look both selfish and ridiculous. Otis then twice sued Paxton in the common law Court of Common Pleas. Paxton's lawyer, the able Benjamin Prat, finally appealed to the Massachusetts Superior Court, claiming that as the Admiralty Court was a prerogative one, a disposition of its funds under its decree could not be recovered by an action in a common law court. The Superior Court, with Thomas Hutchinson sitting as chief justice, had to agree to the logic of the Paxton appeal and in February of 1762 instructed the jury to reverse the decisions of the inferior court.[50] If Otis had really been interested in recovering the £475 he should have brought an appeal before the prerogative High Court of Admiralty in England.

In effect, James Otis, Jr.'s handling of this entire matter displayed the brilliance of his pragmatic approach. First of all, the petition injected the whole issue of enforcement into the General Court and hence into the political realm.

Furthermore, it was certain that in the future the costs and charges of the informers would be deducted equally from the governor's and customs' thirds as the law required. That alone would reduce the incentive for strict trade enforcement by reducing the profits. Finally, Otis had publicly embarrassed Governor Bernard and had forced Lieutenant-Governor Thomas Hutchinson, acting in his new role as chief justice, to reverse a popular common law court decision and thus appear as a supporter of the prerogative.

Of course the major issue facing Thomas Hutchinson and the Superior Court was the legality of the writs of assistance. When this finally came up for a hearing in February 1761, Otis had resigned as the admiralty's advocate and appeared with his colleague Oxenbridge Thacher to speak in the name of the "inhabitants of

49. Hutchinson, *Hist. Mass.*, ed. Mayo, III, 64–66.
50. Josiah Quincy, Jr., comp., *Reports of Cases Argued and Adjudged in the Superior Court of Judicature of the Province of Massachusetts Bay between 1761 and 1772* (Boston, 1865), hereafter cited as Quincy, *Reports*, 541–547, 548–556.

Boston" against the writs. The task of presenting the customs petition fell to Jeremiah Gridley, Otis's teacher and friend. The customs desired that the Superior Court would issue these writs under its own seal and "in legal form and according to the usage of his Majesty's court of Exchequer." The determination of the court, Jeremiah Gridley stated, would concern two points: first, was it legal for the English Court of Exchequer to issue a general writ? and second, "whether the practice of the Court of Exchequer (admitting it to be legal) can warrant this court in the same practice." These writs, Gridley declared, had been authorized by Parliament in the time of Charles II, while in the reign of William III their application had been extended to the colonies. He realized that there was popular prejudice against these writs because they infringed upon the "common priviledges of Englishmen," but general search warrants were essential to the collection of revenue without which the state could not preserve itself from the "invasion of her foes, nor the tumults of her own subjects." Gridley concluded by stating that the "*Necessity* of having public Taxes effectually and speedily collected" was of "infinitely greater moment to the whole, than the liberty of any individual." There was no higher law than the survival of the state.[51]

Oxenbridge Thacher had prepared a careful legal rebuttal. First he questioned the exact form of the "writ prayed for," as it could not be found in the "*Natura Brevium*." This was a procedural point that the justices could not ignore, but Thacher's major contention was his denial that "this Court has the power of the Court of Exchequer." His reason for this was that the Massachusetts Superior Court lacked the chancery jurisdiction which the English court had. Thus in England the court that issued the writ had power to make the customs accountable for it while the Massachusetts Superior Court did not.[52] This he held was a juridical anomaly. Justice Hutchinson realized the force of at least the first argument and de-

51. "Substance of Mr. Gridleys Argument before the Superior Court in Favor of Writs of Assistance," Common Place Book, 5–8, Joseph Hawley Papers, II, New York Public Library, New York City, hereafter cited as Hawley Transcript.
52. John Adams, "Early Abstract," *ca.* 1761, Adams, ed., *Works of J. Adams*, II, 521.

termined to delay a decision until he could obtain information from England on exchequer procedure.[53]

So that none could doubt his motive James Otis, Jr., opened his own argument with a brief recitation of the events that now brought him to speak in favor of "British Liberty." He stated that the court had asked him previously to study the issue, and having done so, it would be absurd to charge him with a "desertion" of the admiralty advocacy. He would accept no fees for this case, he declared, but would speak only because of "principle." He did not need to remind his auditors that the writ prayed for was the "worst instrument of arbitrary power, the most destructive to English liberty, and the fundamental principles of the constitution." He declared that it was the very exercise of this kind of arbitrary power "which in former periods of English history, cost one king of England his head, and another his throne." All that the statutes cited by Mr. Gridley proved was that "*special writs directed to special offices, and to search certain houses etc. especially set forth in the writ*" are legal. Modern practice, however, would not allow a general writ that was universal and perpetual, for that would destroy all liberty. It would make masters subject to their servants. As for the so-called precedent, it "was in the zenith of arbitrary power" when Charles Stuart was king. A man's home should be his castle, and these search writs were a clear violation of constitutional rights. "An Act against the constitution is void." He told the court that it should "demolish this monster of oppression, and . . . tear into rags this remnant of Starchamber Tyranny." Even if Parliament had authorized a general search writ it still "would be void."[54] John Adams, the young lawyer scribbling away in his notebook, quickly summed up the essence of his master's position—the writs of assistance were "against the fundamental principles of law."[55]

If the presentation of the merchants' petition in December was a brilliant tactical maneuver on James Otis, Jr.'s part, his argument in

53. Thomas Hutchinson to Conway, 1 Oct. 1765, Mass. Archives, XXVI, 154–156; Hutchinson, *Hist. Mass.*, ed. Mayo, III, 68–69.
54. Hawley Transcript, 8–14, N. Y. Pub. Lib.
55. Adams, ed., *Works of J. Adams*, II, 521.

February against the writs of assistance embodied a constitutional principle of revolutionary consequence. He had answered Gridley by asserting that the unalterable law of nature took precedence over the survival of the state. As Otis must have expected, the Superior Court, having obtained an exact copy of the proper English writ, upheld the legality of writs that November.[56] From a narrow point of view he had neither recovered the £475 for the province nor convinced the court that these writs were illegal, but practically speaking, Otis had achieved his objectives. For one, the home government investigated the complaints against Bernard's trade enforcement policies. He was told that "the Fees and charges of proceedings in Admiralty Courts . . . are become so shamefully exorbitant, as to be matters of notice."[57] The harassing of the customs had its effect on morale. While statistical evidence is incomplete there are indications that by the spring of 1761 the early rigor of enforcement had yielded to a milder course. Such St. Eustatius merchants as William Fletcher were writing to friends who would well know how to use such information, "I have paid the Government in Martinique for a thousand hogsheads of Molasses."[58] And in May, so Samuel Allyne Otis informed his brother Joseph, Thomas Hancock had no difficulty running in his pipes of Madeira under the eyes of the Boston customs.[59] Politically, James, Jr., had forced the role of defending prerogative upon Thomas Hutchinson. That May the town of Boston showed its overwhelming approval of Otis's actions by electing him one of its four representatives. This Boston gentleman had earned his post as the defender of the town's essential mercantile interests.[60] Otis might have owed his start in

56. Quincy, Reports, 54–57; George G. Wolkins, "Bollan on Writs of Assistance," Mass. Hist. Soc., Procs., LIX (1925–1926), 430.

57. John Pownall to Francis Bernard, London, 22 July 1761, Bernard Papers, IX, 221, Houghton Lib., Harvard.

58. William Fletcher to Edmund Trowbridge, St. Eustatius, 9 Feb. 1761, Dana MSS, Mass. Hist. Soc.

59. Samuel A. Otis to [Joseph Otis], 14 May 1761, Otis Family MSS, II, 85, Butler Lib., Columbia.

60. [Edmund Trowbridge] to [William Bollan], [Boston], [May 1762], Dana MSS, Mass. Hist. Soc.

Boston politics to family influence, but the path he took, replete with maneuvering against Hutchinson and the hated writs of assistance, was his very own. If he was emotional he was also sensitive to the desires of his constituents. Family influence, education, important friends, intelligence were with James Otis, Jr., but they cannot explain his political genius. He was *sui generis*.

For the elder Otis the success of his son in Boston's social and political life came as heady wine. Yet even while he rejoiced in James's election to the House in 1761 it must have confirmed his feelings that James, Jr., really did not want to run the Barnstable bailiwick. By 1755, the year James took to wife a Boston heiress, the old colonel had become dependent upon the energy and talents of his second son Joseph for the management of the family's local business. This included marketing manufactured goods, as well as purchasing, trading, or putting up the fish, pork, oysters, onions, wheat, shingles, and homespun that he used to satisfy his Boston creditors. Otis was dependent upon others for merchandise and most of his shipping. In Barnstable this meant the Bourns who furnished Holland goods, rum, shipping, and the salt Otis used in processing fish and pork.[61] Only with his rise in provincial politics under Shirley and Pownall, when he expanded his business to include whaling and ship supplies, did he even start to challenge the Bourns' preeminence.[62]

To achieve his goal of an independent trading position in Barnstable, James Otis, Sr., needed additional sources of credit and supplies, and these he obtained through his children. He was the partial

61. For Holland goods see Isaac Freeman to Melatiah Bourn, [Barnstable], 24 Jan. 1749/50, Bourn Family Papers, I, 12, Houghton Lib., Harvard. The reference to James Otis, Sr., is in Sylvanus Bourn to Melatiah Bourn, 17 Apr. 1752, *ibid.*, V, 41. See also Edward Winslow's receipt for £620 (o.t.) from James Otis, Sr., on account of Melatiah Bourn, 28 Jan. 1748, Gay-Otis Papers, Butler Lib., Columbia. For exchange of Barnstable produce and homespun see Joseph Otis to ?, 6 Dec. 1762, *ibid.*

62. James Otis, Sr., to ?, 29 Nov. 1756, and Zacheus Macy to James Otis, Sr., Nantucket, 3 Aug. 1757, Otis Papers, I, 140, 154, Mass. Hist. Soc. See also J. Erving, Jr., to James Otis, Sr., Boston, 28 Oct. 1761, with request for 1755 and 1756 vouchers, and reply, James Otis, Sr., to J. Erving, Barnstable, 30 Oct. 1761, *ibid.*, II, 57–58. The total for these two years was £650.

beneficiary of three felicitous alliances. The marriage of his son Joseph to Maria Sturgis cemented already strong bonds with that shipowning family,[63] while Mercy's nuptials with James Warren of the distinguished Plymouth family made their existing commercial and political relationship even more intimate. Lastly, in 1764, with Samuel Allyne's alliance with the daughter of the provincial treasurer Harrison Gray, he gained access to a sure source of capital.[64]

The increasing success of the fifth generation of Otis males in the world of commerce was due to a combination of factors. First of all their father had provided a solid local foundation, which he had inherited from his father; and he had added to it the war contracts obtained from governors Shirley and Pownall. However, the radical trade expansion of the family came about through the cooperation of the sons themselves. Joseph proved a careful manager of the family store. He was also the advocate of an ambitious shipbuilding program that made trade expansion a necessity. The Sturgis in-laws supplied valuable Carolina business while the Warrens provided an introduction to the Philadelphia merchant Richard Smith, who was instrumental in increasing coastal shipping.[65] Finally in 1762 Samuel opened shop in Boston as the family agent of a partnership with his father and Joseph. He had a penchant for hard work, he skillfully bought stocks more profitable "than English goods," and he carefully evaded the provincial excise taxes.[66] Samuel's in-laws, the Gray family, provided choice Irish linens and knowledge of the overseas market. They also purchased whalebone, oil, and homespun.[67]

63. For the business part of this relationship see Elisha Glover, receipt, 26 Aug. 1754, Bourn Family Papers, V, 99, Houghton Lib., Harvard; Benjamin Ward to Sam Sturgis, N. C., 22 Sept. 1755, *ibid.*, V, 101; and Sam Sturgis to James Otis, Sr., (*ca.* 1757), account settling writ service, 1751 to 1756, *ibid.*, X, 40.

64. James Otis, Sr., to [Harrison Gray], Barnstable, 8 Sept. 1764, Harrison Gray Otis Papers, Box 1, Mass. Hist. Soc., in which he states his obligation for £500 sterling lent to Samuel A. Otis. As Samuel E. Morison indicated, Samuel A. Otis remained in the debt of Harrison Gray, in "The Property of Harrison Gray, Loyalist," Col. Soc. of Mass., *Pubs.*, XIV (1911–1913), 337.

65. James Otis, Sr., to Joseph Otis to [Richard Smith], Barnstable, 30 May 1761, Otis Papers, II, 47, Mass. Hist. Soc.

66. Samuel A. Otis to [Joseph Otis], Boston, 13 and 23 Sept. 1762, Gay-Otis Papers, Butler Lib., Columbia.

67. John Gray to James Otis, Sr., 11 Apr. 1764, Otis Family MSS, II, 109, *ibid.*; and Thomas Gray to Joseph Otis, 25 Apr. 1764, Otis Papers, II, 111, Mass. Hist. Soc.

Cousin Jonathan Otis of Newport secured his Jamaica-type fish for the West Indies trade from his Barnstable relatives.[68] In addition Caleb and Aaron Davis, two of the more prominent Boston merchants, traded rice, flour, and fish with Samuel A. Otis.[69]

At the same time that James Otis, Jr., entered political life his brothers were expanding the family business into new avenues of trade. From 1761 to 1765 there were voyages to the Carolinas and points south such as Georgia, Jamaica, and Guadeloupe. The southern colonies provided a market for beef, flour, rum, and finished wood products, which were exchanged for rice, naval goods, and specie. The West Indies consumed the cheaper grades of fish as well as large amounts of white oak, and in turn provided bills of exchange and large quantities of molasses. Of even greater value to the Otises was salt from Antigua.[70] Brother Joseph was an advocate of this southern trade even when keen Rhode Islanders kept the markets glutted. This was risky business, for low prices cyclically followed high ones, while the unexpected such as a smallpox epidemic in Charlestown all but ruined the *Dolphin* for a season. Fortunately a cousin, Amos Otis, was available to take charge.[71] Goods were also shipped to points north such as Nova Scotia, but with sharp competition both markets were depressed.[72] There was also one rather ordinary voyage to Liverpool.[73] However, Samuel

68. Jonathan Otis to James Otis, Sr., Newport, 18 Aug. 1761, Otis Papers, II, 52, Mass. Hist. Soc.

69. Receipts, 28 Apr. 1764, 6 July 1764, and 21 Nov. 1764, Caleb Davis Papers, V, Mass. Hist. Soc.

70. Josiah Freeman to James Otis, Sr., Middleborough, 15 Sept. 1762, Gay-Otis Papers, Butler Lib., Columbia; James Otis, Sr., to Joseph Otis, Boston, 30 Aug. 1764, Otis Family MSS, II, 120, *ibid.*; Samuel A. Otis to Joseph Otis, Boston, 17 June 1766, *ibid.*, II, 128.

71. Lot Thacher to James Otis, Sr., Charlestown, 15 Jan. 1761, Otis Papers, II, 45, Mass. Hist. Soc.; Lot Thacher to James Otis, Sr., 20 Dec. 1762, *ibid.*, II, 89; Samuel A. Otis to Joseph Otis, Boston, 8 Mar. 1763, Otis Family MSS, II, 100, Butler Lib., Columbia; see also Amos Otis's receipt for £6 from James and Joseph Otis, 12 May 1762, Barnstable County Papers, Mass. Hist. Soc.

72. James Otis, Sr., to Joseph Otis, Boston, 16 Apr. 1762, Otis Papers, II, 75, Mass. Hist. Soc.; James Otis, Sr., to Joseph Otis, Boston, 17 June 1767, Otis Family MSS, II, 134, Butler Lib., Columbia; Samuel A. Otis debt action against Jesse Dodge of Nova Scotia, Apr. 1767, Suffolk Court Files 509: 143 (No. 87672), Suffolk County Court House.

73. Insurance policy on the *Hope*, 17 Mar. 1764, Misc. Papers, Mass. Hist. Soc.

Allyne viewed these unprofitable ventures with alarm and proposed striking out into the Mediterranean as a remedy. Once the family established connections at Lisbon or Cadiz they would be able to "trade to advantage."[74]

In July of 1763 Samuel pushed for a Bilbao voyage. He offered to go himself as "super Cargo and think it a good Scheme much better than lounging here with my fingers in my mouth."[75] There was more to this than just the desire of a young man to see the world. Sam bitterly complained about the constant recriminations of his father and brother Joseph over his handling of the business. He told them that only the "Spirit of Divination" would enable him to do what they wanted and thus obey their "contradictory and far from explicit" instructions.[76] Before proposing the Bilbao trip he sent the family a demand for £500 to meet his obligations. As Samuel saw this relationship he was nothing but a factor "for the pretence of my being a partner is nothing in effect."[77] The old colonel had again frustrated the desire of one of his sons for independence.

These multiple commercial ventures, with their heavy employment of local talents and resources, were a continuing source of wealth and family influence in Barnstable, for in spite of mutual recriminations, profits grew and at times seemed almost unlimited. As Samuel told his brother Joseph: "If you reflect your goods are sold at what advance you please almost for homespun, etc. This Homespun purchases Lumber, employs people that owe you, whose Labor turns out cheap also. Your own vessell freights the Lumber, your own carts dragg it. In short all these matters are so within yourself, without advancing a farthing cash."[78] Proof of the success of this trade could be seen in the *Dolphin*, the *Success*, the *Tryall*, the *Coquette*, the *Mermaid*, and the well-named *Three Brothers*

74. Samuel A. Otis to Joseph Otis, July 1763, Gay-Otis Papers, Butler Lib., Columbia.

75. Samuel A. Otis to James Otis, Sr., Boston, 14 July 1763, Otis Family MSS, II, 103, *ibid*.

76. Samuel A. Otis to James Otis, Sr., Boston, 24 Nov. 1762, Gay-Otis Papers, *ibid*.

77. Samuel A. Otis to Joseph Otis, Boston, 10 June 1763, *ibid*.

78. Samuel A. Otis to Joseph Otis, 22 June 1767, *ibid*.

which sailed for the partners. Most of these were schooners or whalers. They averaged sixty to seventy-five tons and sold for £350 to £450. A good cargo would be worth roughly £800 with insurance figured at 4 per cent under normal conditions. However, in war areas during the year 1762 the premium was 8 per cent or better. The riggings and hardware, along with a large share of the freight, were secured in Boston by Samuel Allyne.[79] On occasion he let out the better schooners at £30 a month. While these shipping and trading ventures sustained a large volume of business, the real profits came from investing in whaling expeditions. The ship *Mermaid* paid costs in 1765, the first year of operation, and by September of the year following had returned a net profit of £400.[80] These combined enterprises produced profits of more than £1,100 every year from 1762 to 1765. Only in 1766, a year which opened with the Stamp Act in force, did the family operate in the red. Samuel Allyne offered two explanations for this: the first was that the partners under brother Joseph's proddings had overextended their nautical enterprises in proportion to what he termed "our Stock"; the second was that the whaling season had been unsuccessful, the result of the "frowns of Providence" rather "than any negligence" on the part of the Otises. Such loss proved but a temporary circumstance. Samuel reasoned that the family had *"Assiduity Skill and perseverance."* With such virtues (in effect the protestant ethic) it could not but prosper.[81]

Samuel Allyne Otis is the one member of his family who emerges from its complex commercial correspondence with a reputation still intact. As the letter writer for the firm he attempted to keep an openmindedness in dealing with clients. Unlike his father, Samuel refused to interpret every mistake or customer's error as intended fraud or a deliberate slight. He was in the "trading business" for money, and this meant a willingness to gamble on the market which

79. Samuel A. Otis to Joseph Otis, Boston, 23 Nov. 1762, same to same, Boston, 14 Nov. 1763, *ibid.*

80. Samuel A. Otis to Joseph Otis, Boston, 29 Sept. 1766, Otis Papers, II, 133, Mass. Hist. Soc.

81. Samuel A. Otis to [James Otis, Sr.], 22 Jan. 1767, *ibid.*, II, 137.

became a lifetime habit with him. Samuel's reports on the smuggling activities of John Hancock, the blunderings of Francis Bernard, and the antics of his brother James "Esq. Bluster," show a balanced, common-sense approach free of the partisanship found in so many of the patriots. Samuel also had a sense of humor. When someone made the threat to break the head of Representative Brown, he did not think the Court should waste its time on such a small matter, for it was well known that the "impenetrability of Browns Skull will forever be his security."[82] He had a lively interest in the opposite sex. For, while Samuel was curious to "see a young girls brain anatomized" in order to find out why women thought as they did, Boston had a broadening effect, and he later concluded simply that "they are the best bed fellows in the world, so god bless them."[83] He was his eldest brother's favorite and sought advice from him rather than his father. However, James, Jr., prudently kept out of the partners' bickerings.[84] Like James, Samuel also was subject to inherited melancholy. In 1764 with the sun shining on all his ventures he still felt "something which checks and seems to tell me Storms and tempests are consequent and necessarily connected with this sea of life."[85]

Joseph Otis, the boy who stayed home, resembled his hot-tempered father. He was jealous of his Harvard-educated brothers and allowed it to show in his constant suspicion of Samuel's business dealings. A little more patience would not have overburdened him.[86] On at least one occasion in 1762 Joseph delayed completing a shipping contract to take care of more profitable business, much to the annoyance of Samuel.[87] His market judgments were controlled by

82. Samuel A. Otis to Joseph Otis, Boston, 18 June 1763, Otis Family MSS, II, 102, Butler Lib., Columbia.

83. Samuel A. Otis to Joseph Otis, Boston, 13 Apr. 1762, Otis Papers, II, 74, Mass. Hist. Soc.

84. James Otis, Sr., to Joseph Otis, Boston, 30 May 1762, Otis Family MSS, II, 92, Butler Lib., Columbia; Samuel A. Otis to James Otis, Sr., Boston, 17 Mar. 1767, Otis Papers, II, 167, Mass. Hist. Soc.

85. James Otis, Sr., to Joseph Otis, 5 Dec. 1764, Otis Family MSS, II, 118, Butler Lib., Columbia.

86. James Otis, Sr., to Joseph Otis, 15 July 1766, *ibid.*, II, 130.

87. Samuel A. Otis to Joseph Otis, Boston, 27 Apr. 1762, Gay-Otis Papers, *ibid.*

price and not politics. If John Hancock, "a clever fellow," secured 150 barrels of whale oil, that was because he outbid the Grays who, in turn, outbid him on whalebone.[88] Joseph would continue the family influence in Barnstable.

All of the younger Otises attempted to keep clear of their father. As Samuel Allyne told Joseph after deciding to ship lumber without the father's knowledge, "I dont love to trouble him with the business."[89] The image of the old man projected by his sons is that of an awesome, overbearing, and jealous *pater familias* intent upon retaining control.[90] James, Jr., had cut out for himself a legal and political career in the capital which gave every promise of eclipsing the role of his father; Samuel Allyne showed a genuine feeling for the speculative nature of the marketplace, a skill in utilizing other people's capital, and a real talent for rationalizing business operations; and Joseph, for all his pettiness, knew Barnstable and how to use its resources to the utmost. The mutual bickerings, fears, and hostilities of these brothers testify to their insecurity before the dominating personality of their father. The elder Otis gave them the tools to achieve and the motivation to succeed, while at the same time bequeathing to them a feeling of personal inadequacy. He trained them to be useful to themselves, to work for the family, and to prosper in the world. These are strong, deeply etched personalities, held together as much by shared dislikes as by self-interest. They realized that public quarreling could only weaken their political import. Outside pressure as much as the need to defend their privileged positions would keep the Otises united during the next critical decade. They knew that in that "wild democracy" of Massachusetts politics there were "many who wish both here [in Boston] and else where to tread down every branch of our family."[91]

88. [Joseph Otis] to [James Otis, Sr.], and postscript, Samuel A. Otis to [James Otis, Sr.], [176–?], *ibid*.

89. Samuel A. Otis to Joseph Otis, 8 Jan. 1768, Otis Papers, II, 149, Mass. Hist. Soc.

90. Samuel A. Otis to Joseph Otis, 22 June 1767, Gay-Otis Papers, Butler Lib., Columbia.

91. Samuel A. Otis to Joseph Otis, 2 Mar. [1762?], *ibid*.

## ✕ VII.

# POWER, POLITICS, AND
# RIGHTS, 1761-1766

For more than two centuries the career of James Otis, Jr.,
has fascinated historians and political scientists. In fact James's role
in the early years of Governor Francis Bernard's administration is
still a matter of debate. Does one study the young Otis as the perfect combination of American hero and constitutional abstraction as
did his early biographer William Tudor in his 1823 *Life of James
Otis*? Or does one follow Bernard Bailyn's 1965 quest for a unifying
intellectual principle that would make sense out of the patriot's
actions from the "Writs of Assistance" issue to the *de facto* nullifi-
cation of the Stamp Act in 1766? Otis may be viewed as a brilliant
intellectual or as an emerging national hero. Contemporary judgments ranged from opportunism to madness. The customsman Samuel Waterhouse offered the former in his 1765 ditty, "So Jemmy
rail'd at *upper folks* while Jemmy's DAD was out, but Jemmy's
DAD now has *a place*, so Jemmy's turned about"; while Peter Oliver and even John Adams came to view Otis as the master of Bed-
lam.[1] Nor can James Otis's enemies be criticized for thinking that

1. *Boston Evening-Post*, 13 May 1765; entries for Apr. 1759, 5 June 1762, 5 Feb.
1763, Butterfield, *et al.*, eds., *Diary of Adams*, I, 84, 225–226, 235–236.

his 1764 tract on the *Rights of the British Colonies*, which denied that Britain could tax America, was contradicted the following year by his *Vindication of the British Colonies*, which argued for Parliament's "just and equitable right, power and authority" to impose both internal and external taxes.[2] That is the opinion of no less a scholar than Ellen Brennan who had an almost unrivaled grasp of the realities of Massachusetts politics.[3] Inconsistencies certainly marked most of James's actions. He rejected both slavery and the belief in Negro inferiority, arguing that as the "law of nature" made all men free it must be applied equally to "white or black."[4] Yet he never freed his own colored "boy." He said he loved George III; he wanted to see his "king, under God, the father of Mankind."[5] Yet Otis in the 1760's set in motion a train of events which he knew could lead to Massachusetts's independence! His sister, Mercy Otis Warren, aware of the self-tormenting uncertainty and complexity of her brother's inner psyche, cast him as the Brutus in her patriot play.[6] Mercy's portrayal of James constitutes the first psychological study of the patriot. Its very ambiguity raises the question whether Mercy perceived that the model for James's love-hate relationship with George III was her own father. After all, had not the elder Otis been both king and tyrant, father and antagonist to his own sons?

The starting point of almost all analyses of Otis's political thought is his statement that "an Act against the constitution is void." In the Writs of Assistance speech Otis claimed that he did no more than apply Lord Coke's dictum that "when an act of Parliament is against common right or reason, or repugnant, or impossible to be performed the common law [judges] will control it, and adjudge such act to be void." Bernard Bailyn holds that James Otis in citing

---

2. *Rights of the British Colonies*, 38, 42, and *A Vindication of the British Colonies . . .* (London, 1769), 4–5.
3. Ellen E. Brennan, "James Otis: Recreant and Patriot," *New England Quarterly*, XII (1939), 691–715.
4. *Rights of the British Colonies*, 29.
5. *Ibid.*, 40–41.
6. "The Adulateur" (1773), *Magazine of History*, Extra Number 63 [XVI] (1918), 229–259.

this seventeenth-century doctrine misread the text and at the same time supported a hopelessly outdated constitutional theory: Coke's dictum dealt with reading a statute and not interpreting the constitution; secondly, Otis did not realize that the Glorious Revolution had made Parliament the all-sovereign body. He could not recognize (as did Thomas Hutchinson) that the constitution was what Parliament made of it.[7] Rather Otis conceived of Parliament in seventeenth-century terms, as the supreme judicial as well as legislative body, all powerful, but bound by fundamental law not only because it recognized higher law as normative in interpreting statute law, but because it was part of the very nature of the constitution itself. The patriot followed the medieval idea that Parliament declares the law as it sees it (*jus dicere*) and does not make it (*jus dare*);[8] but in eighteenth-century England, Parliament made law and constitution independent of the Saxon past, Magna Carta, equity, natural law, or God. Then as now the past was either decorous or symbolic but neither binding nor controlling on the ministry. Professor Bailyn is of the opinion that James Otis's inability to comprehend this reality, combined with his surface understanding of Coke's position, was Otis's "tragedy."[9] But is this not a legalistic understanding of a complex issue? After all, Otis's use of Coke was a means to an end. His reading of that seventeenth-century jurist convinced him that the Bonham case could serve the defense of colonial rights. Otis recognized the reality of an American autonomy. He believed that we were already "a great people." He wanted to keep a connection with Britain but saw that the imperial violations of colonial rights would bring about an independence that he could not face. Independence from the parent state, he opined, "every good and honest man would wish delayed for ages, if possible, prevented for ever."[10] The act of separation constituted Otis's political and psychological stumbling block.

7. Bernard Bailyn, ed., *Pamphlets of the American Revolution, 1750–1776* (Cambridge, Mass., 1965), I, 100–102, 412.

8. Otis, *Rights of the British Colonies*, 47.

9. Bailyn, ed., *Pamphlets*, I, 413.

10. James Otis, Jr., to Mr. [Arthur] Jones, 26 Nov. 1768, Mass. Hist. Soc., *Procs.*, XLIII (1909–1910), 493.

In Otis's writings the major intent was to defend his concept of the colonial order. In a truly eclectic fashion the patriot quoted Locke, Harrington, Grotius, Rousseau, and other Enlightenment writers. He was aware of and utilized the English whig tradition; he accepted its belief in conspiracy as a way of understanding the past (which he might have picked up from the Harvard tutor Henry Flynt); and he saw his belief verified in the 1760's by the actions of the British ministries. He had read and would use the early Massachusetts charters as well as the puritans' chiliastic literature.[11] Finally, Otis found in the classics the antique vision of a colonial relationship free from the subordinate dependency which was then the essence of the European version of colonialism. The patriot summed up his ideal commonwealth in his title-page quote for the *Rights of the British Colonies Asserted and Proved* when he cited Virgil's *"et foederis aequas Dicamus leges, sociosque in regna vocemus"*—"let us promulgate an equal compact and let us invite them as partners to our state" (*Aeneid*, XI, 321–322). In looking at Otis's sources it is clear that he selected them because they either offered a check against parliamentary excess, provided a natural-law guarantee for property rights, or championed a noncolonial relationship. It is Virgil more than Coke, the New England tradition more than the Enlightenment, which shaped Otis's political reflections. Moreover, his political thought, which had started with a narrow defense of property interests in the Writs of Assistance case, had progressively developed by 1765 to include the "common Rights of Mankind." That evolution has its roots in Otis's role as a politician.

The popular image of Otis in our history owes as much to the hero worship of John Adams and William Tudor as it does to the dispatches of Francis Bernard. In 1766 Bernard wrote that the "Troubles in this Country take their rise from, and owe their Continuance to one Man." The governor's own conspiracy thesis held

11. See James Otis, Jr., to James Otis, Sr., Cambridge, 4 Apr. 1743, Otis Family MSS, I, 14, Butler Lib., Columbia; *Rights of the British Colonies*, 40; Henry Flynt's Diary, I, 44, 105–125, 146, 215–218, Harvard Univ. Archives; Bailyn, ed., *Pamphlets*, I, 24, 60–89.

Otis, Jr., to be the chief director of opposition in the Massachusetts House, the Council, the bar, and the Boston town meetings.[12] Adams and Tudor of course favored Otis and independence. Bernard did not, and as his awareness of his own impotence in the crisis increased so did the flow of epithets from his pen: Otis was cast as demagogue, as the Grand Incendiary, the firebrand, the madman. Would not all have been well in the American Eden if only the serpent had been silenced? While Governor Bernard's imagery is unforgettable its flaming colors ought not to hide the intellectual bankruptcy of its central unicausal analysis. As a young politician Otis was neither diabolical nor powerful, nor was he popular with the mob; when he entered the Assembly in 1761 he was the chosen representative of mercantile Boston. He had obtained his seat because of his defense of local trading interests against the "new" customs regulations. He had certainly not worked his way up the political byways. And unlike his colleagues Samuel Adams, John Hancock, and Royall Tyler, he did not try to gain popular support by having his chimney swept, his doors rehinged, or his barrels repaired before elections.[13] In an age which said it expected religious observance he never formally joined any church nor did he hold family prayer. In mimicry he once proposed a high treason bill for those misguided men who believed "in certain imaginary Beings called Devils."[14] Considering his ambiguous approach toward Congregationalism James may well have been a rationalist.[15] Whatever his own thoughts on religion, Otis was more than willing to exploit prejudice when it could be turned to political profit. However, he claimed that he did this to the "American Episcopalians" because of "their religious and political principles." For Otis "High Church" meant "Tory."[16] Yet in moments of vituperative fury he charged

12. Francis Bernard to Shelburne, Boston, 22 Dec. 1766, Bernard Papers, IV, 274–283, Houghton Lib., Harvard.

13. Tudor, *Life of Otis*, 91–92.

14. Dec. 1769, Butterfield, *et al.*, eds., *Diary of Adams*, I, 346.

15. James Otis, Sr., to James Otis, Jr., Barnstable, 1 Aug. 1772 (draft copy), Gay-Otis Papers, Butler Lib., Columbia.

16. James Otis, Jr., to Jasper Mauduit, 23 Apr., 28 Oct. 1762, *Jasper Mauduit, 1762–1765* (Mass. Hist. Soc., *Colls.*, LXXIV [1918]), 30, 77 (hereafter cited as *Jasper Mauduit*).

that his opponents equaled the basest of men, those "Jacobites and Jew-jobbers in Newport."[17] While Otis might not have had a private commitment to the Congregational way he defended the clergy. As Peter Oliver put it, Otis enlisted the "*black Regiment*" on his side while "*in nomine Domini incipit omne malum.*"[18] In short, there is little in Otis's early conduct in the House that indicates he opposed its norms. In no wise did he attempt to cater to the lower tradesmen or the so-called Boston mob. Even after the Stamp Act crisis his primary audience was the House of Representatives. His fellow legislators were not idiots, or a mob, or country bumpkins, but successful politicians. In the chamber he functioned as an opposition leader in the tradition of Elisha Cooke and James Allen. His conduct like theirs was wild and explosive, often unpredictable, spreading fear to enemy and friend alike, but his maneuvering won the left-handed praise of Thomas Hutchinson who called him a "clever fellow" who could adjust to the political situation.[19] Unlike Cooke he did not feign drunkenness to oppose the governor, and unlike Allen he was not expelled from the House; he was a charismatic speaker whose knowledge of the classics, the law, and language made him the object of admiration. And if Otis led this opposition to Bernard he did not call into existence those imperial measures which convinced the legislators that American liberty was at stake in the conflict with Britain.[20]

What distinguished the younger Otis from the majority of his political contemporaries was his unusual sensitivity to and an almost instinctive understanding of the popular temper. While his friend Oxenbridge Thacher wrote erudite tracts on finance and plural office-holding it was Otis who realized the political capital in these subjects.[21] Otis saw that a paper-money debate combined with an

17. *Brief Remarks on the Defence of the Halifax Libel* . . . (Boston, 1765), 7; see also Otis's anti-Semitic remarks in the *Boston Gazette*, 21 Dec. 1761.
18. Peter Oliver, *Origin and Progress of the American Rebellion*, eds. Douglass Adair and John A. Schutz (San Marino, 1961), 29.
19. Thomas Hutchinson to Col. John Cushing, 3 Jan. 1763, Mass. Archives, XXVI, 38.
20. Thomas Hutchinson to Richard Jackson, Boston, 21 Apr. 1766, *ibid.*, XXVI, 227.
21. See [Oxenbridge Thacher and Thomas Hutchinson], *Considerations on*

attack on Thomas Hutchinson's exalted status would both embarrass and undermine Governor Bernard's supporters in the House. He used the *Boston Gazette* to sell his views on colonial rights to its limited and elite subscribers throughout the province. While his idea of directing and pressuring deputies by means of the press was revolutionary in a tactical sense, he did this within the traditional power structures of his society. Although many Massachusetts towns had the legal option of sending two representatives to the House, the popular party did not attempt to increase its influence that way. While Otis was at the helm he sought to control the House rather than to change it. Yet if Otis was a popularizer and a disciple of realpolitik who made the legislature his central battleground, he was also a man who desperately needed approval for his course of action. It is in this respect alone that by 1765 he came to depend upon the Boston populace. The town meetings may well have supplied the psychological approbation that he felt his family had denied him. Long before the era of the common man Otis repaid the people of Boston by championing the "common Rights of Mankind."

Nothing could be further from the actual situation than to imagine that either Speaker Otis, who still represented Barnstable, or his son James, the newly elected representative from Boston, intended to go into opposition for the legislative year 1761–1762. The contrary was true. The popular party headed by Otis, Sr., in the House and William Brattle in the Council had every intention of capturing the government. To a politician as skilled in factions and maneuvering as the elder Otis the obvious thing to do was to reach an agreement with Francis Bernard. After all, by now the governor could be expected to have seen the folly of depending on Thomas Hutchinson. Was not the lieutenant-governor something of a liability to a man who had a legislative program to enact? The Otises for their part found themselves pressed by adherents who needed

*Lowering the Value of Gold Coins, within the Province of the Massachusetts-Bay* (Boston, 1762), 4–8, 13–17, and the "Considerations on the Election of Councellors Humbly Offered to the Electors," *Boston Gazette*, 26 Apr. 1762, which Ellen Brennan identified as being the work of Thacher in her *Plural Office-Holding*, 41.

favors and patronage.[22] For this arrangement to work the popular party demanded that Thomas Hutchinson and his friends be removed from their dominant position in the government. The natural corollary was that the governor's patronage and influence should be at the disposal of the Otis-Brattle alliance. Governor Bernard in turn would obtain those majorities necessary to enact his supply and defense measures, items that he was sure would impress the London authorities. Bernard, willing to compromise, was convinced "I shall accomplish my purpose of founding my administration on the broad bottom of a Collation."[23]

The fall session opened with the discovery that a large number of counterfeit notes were in circulation. Properly handled this could turn into a debate on the currency itself. Thomas Hutchinson, the father of the "fixed medium," proposed using this opportunity of calling in the bills to redress Massachusetts's unfavorable balance of trade. He was in favor of a devaluation of the currency in terms of silver, with the new ratios to be set in gold as a tender. If there was one issue which could be used to inflame public opinion this was it.[24] James Otis, Jr., while agreeing with the need for a fixed medium, argued that gold already was a legal tender (his father had helped to make it so during Shirley's administration). As he saw it, devaluation and the idea of frugality were high tory principles. James would solve the adverse trade balance by increasing exports, not by decreasing imports. In a reference aimed at the lieutenant-governor he remarked, "I know it is the maxim of some, that the common people in this town and country live too well; however . . . I do not think they live half well enough."[25] This sidetracked the issue.

22. Enoch Freeman to James Otis, Sr., Falmouth, 7 Apr. 1761, Otis Papers, II, 45, Mass. Hist. Soc., wanted the elder Otis to use his influence with Bernard to obtain the Registry of Deeds. And James Warren in writing to Otis, Sr., on 14 Jan. 1762 stated that their supporters now expected favors from young Otis's position of power, *ibid.*, II, 64.

23. Francis Bernard to Pownall, 28 Apr. [1761], Bernard Papers, I, 316, Houghton Lib.. Harvard.

24. Tudor, *Life of Otis*, 97–99; Hutchinson, *Hist. Mass.*, ed. Mayo, III, 71–72.

25. *Boston Gazette*, 21 Dec. 1761, continued 28 Dec. 1761.

James Otis now made his major attack against Hutchinson for being at one and the same time lieutenant-governor and chief justice. In the January 11, 1762, issue of the *Boston Gazette* he held that "checks and balances" were essential to proper government and that it was a basic principle "to keep the legislative, and executive powers, separate" as well as the judicial. This opening salvo was followed by more direct action. The House, with Otis, Sr., as "Speaker" and Otis, Jr., at the "heights of his power," made common cause with Hutchinson's enemies in the Council under the guidance of Colonel Brattle. They succeeded in reducing the salaries of the Superior Court justices from £750 to £700 in February of 1762.[26] The movement against the Hutchinson men was in high gear and by April 17, James, Jr., felt confident enough to bring out of committee a place bill which would have excluded the Superior Court justices from holding seats in the General Court. It was defeated by a handful of votes on a legal point, but Hutchinson, following the drift of events, was pessimistic over his political future. He had reason to be. In that same session William Bollan, a Hutchinson supporter, was dismissed as province agent.[27] Bollan was an Episcopalian and distrusted because of it. Young Otis particularly resented him for having secured the form of the exchequer writ that the Superior Court had accepted as legal in the Writs of Assistance hearing. James Otis now paid him for that service. With the agency vacant the lieutenant-governor's friends moved to elect him, while Bernard in a move for self-preservation pushed for his friend Richard Jackson. The popular party's stratagem had removed a *persona non grata* to Otis, Jr., and at the same time had split wide what was left of the Bernard-Hutchinson phalanx. James Otis, with obvious pleasure, wrote that "Mr. Bernard was and I believe now is against Mr. Hutchinson . . . from the motive of fear, lest he might thereby obtain the government."[28] The

26. 19 Feb. 1762, *Mass. House of Reps. Jours., 1761–1762*, 262.

27. Thomas Hutchinson to Bollan, Boston, 24 Apr. 1762, *Jasper Mauduit*, 32; 16 Apr. 1762, *Mass. House of Reps. Jours., 1761–1762*, 311, 319.

28. James Otis, Jr., to Jasper Mauduit, Boston, 28 Oct. 1762, *Jasper Mauduit*, 78.

popular party resolved the issue by setting up Jasper Mauduit as a compromise candidate for the agency with the understanding that Jackson would be his assistant. It was an easy victory.

More difficult to carry out was a scheme which was intended to destroy Hutchinson's influence. It was begun with an attack upon Israel Williams's plan for a college in Hampshire County. A defeat for this plan would discredit Hutchinson who backed the scheme. It also afforded an opportunity to defend Harvard and to further good relations with the Boston clergy whom he had been assiduously courting.[29] The western members together with Hutchinson's allies obtained a favorable vote for the new college in the House, but the Council rejected it. Governor Bernard intended to resolve the impasse by issuing a "charter himself by his own single authority." However, James Otis, Jr., quickly turned the debate into a constitutional issue by charging Bernard with a dangerous exercise of prerogative powers and managed to alarm both houses: if royal governors took to issuing charters, what would happen to the powers of the Massachusetts legislature! By cleverly manipulating the issue Otis had outmaneuvered both a House majority and the governor in order to deal Hutchinson and his western Massachusetts allies a stinging defeat.[30]

In 1762, James Otis, Jr., had his own pet bill calling for special Massachusetts writs of assistance, the objective being to replace the English exchequer form with a purely provincial instrument. The bill would have restrained the "Superior Court from issuing Writs of assistance except upon special information to a Custom house officer oath being made first, the informer mentioned and the person supposed to own the goods and the place where they are sus-

29. On 20 Jan. 1762 James Otis, Jr., joined with Jonathan Mayhew, Stephen Hall, Samuel Adams, James Bowdoin, Thomas Hancock, Harrison Gray, and Andrew Oliver, among others, in the formation of a society to promote Congregational missions to the Indians as opposed to the missions of the Anglican Church; see Mass. Archives, XIV, 289–290.

30. See Thacher to Pratt, (1762), Mass. Hist. Soc., *Procs.*, 1st Ser., XX (1882, 1883), 48; and Henry Lefavour, "The Proposed College in Hampshire County in 1762," *ibid.*, LXVI (1936–1941), 60–63.

pected to be concealed."[31] The bill was especially dear to James and the Boston merchants: it would have given them a legislative victory over the Hutchinson court and practical immunity from the customs. Politically, it kept alive Thomas Hutchinson's part in upholding a prerogative court procedure. The continuing popularity of the Writs of Assistance issue is seen in this bill's acceptance by both houses of the General Court. However, Francis Bernard vetoed it after obtaining a unanimous opinion of the Superior Court judges against it.[32] This solitary defeat only confirmed Otis's belief that the monopoly of public offices enjoyed by Thomas Hutchinson and company must be ended.

In general both Francis Bernard and the popular party of James Otis, Sr., and William Brattle were satisfied with the 1761–1762 legislative sessions. The governor had seen his supply bill pass with ease, and at the same time the assembly had granted him Desert Island, that enticing piece of real estate off the coast of Maine.[33] The younger Otis was convinced that Governor Bernard, who had fallen "into some of the worst hands" upon coming to Massachusetts, had come to realize his error and would now be guided by men whose "views are most nearly connected with the true interest of the province."[34] This was James's way of saying that Bernard was through with the Hutchinson clique and would now support the popular party. As for patronage, brother Joseph, who was being groomed to take over the Barnstable interests, found himself appointed sheriff as a result of six months' effort by his father. That May the elder Otis and his wife Mary made the trip to Boston. At long last the old man's day had come. It was fitting

31. Thomas Hutchinson to Bollan, Boston, 6 Mar. 1762, Mass. Archives, XXVI, 8–9; Joseph R. Frese, "James Otis and Writs of Assistance," *New England Qtly.*, XXX (1957), 499–501.

32. For the veto message see *Mass. House of Reps. Jours., 1761–1762,* 299, and Francis Bernard to Lords of Trade, Boston, 13 Apr. 1762, Bernard Papers, II, 58, Houghton Lib., Harvard. For the position of the justices see 6 Mar. 1762, Council Records, XV, 111, State House, Boston.

33. Francis Bernard to Egremont, Boston, 16 Apr. 1762, Bernard Papers, II, 180, Houghton Lib., Harvard; William Otis Sawtelle, "Sir Francis Bernard and His Grant of Mount Desert," Col. Soc. of Mass., *Pubs.,* XXIV (1920–1922), 207–209.

34. James Otis, Jr., to Jasper Mauduit, 23 Apr. 1762, *Jasper Mauduit,* 30.

that his wife should be there when he was elected to the Council with the governor's approbation.[35] It had been a most unusual year.

If James's first year in the General Court concluded with apparent victory for his family and party, the next year brought near ruin to both. In retrospect the reasons for this reversal seem fairly clear. In the first place James, Jr., misunderstood the nature of an accommodation with Francis Bernard. What the governor sought was "a balance to summa" Hutchinson, not a new master.[36] Bernard could be led, but he would not be pushed. True, Bernard had approved the reduction in the salaries of the justices. But all that this indicated was that he was playing politics for his own benefit. It is also possible that what qualms of conscience the governor had on this point were salved by the grant of Desert Island. The timing of that arrangement, which followed by eight days the salary cut for Hutchinson and cohorts, was too neat to be accidental. It indicates the hand of an old professional, probably the senior Otis who as speaker knew a trick or so himself.[37] Likewise the acceptance of Jasper Mauduit as agent protected Bernard's position. It demonstrated that Hutchinson needed the governor more than Bernard needed Hutchinson. At the same time Bernard had vetoed James's pet piece of legislation which would have substituted particular for general writs. What James Otis, Jr., took for victory was in reality something less. His father knew how to work with governors, realized that a display of deference was required, and understood how to make a deal, but the old man's influence, the one factor that might have modified his son's conduct, was now removed from the House by the father's elevation to the Council. It did not take long for the son's irascibility to show. Suddenly in May he resigned his seat, a step which he rescinded the following day. His brother Samuel informed the family that "such a pro-

35. See letter draft, 6 Jan. 1762, Otis Family MSS, II, 87, Butler Lib., Columbia; and Whitmore, *Massachusetts Civil List*, 106; James Otis, Sr., to Joseph Otis, Boston, 30 May 1762, Otis Family MSS, II, 92, Butler Lib., Columbia.

36. Thacher to Pratt, [1762], Mass. Hist. Soc., *Procs.*, 1st Ser., XX (1882, 1883), 46–47.

37. *Mass. House of Reps. Jours.*, 1761–1762, 262, 282.

ceedings can by no means be justified" and that "he acts for himself."[38] By that October the Otises understood the true state of
affairs: Bernard would not become a "convert."[39] The tactics of
collaboration had failed to lead to dominance. What might be
gained from a frontal attack on the Bernard administration?

Otis's answer to the situation in the fall of 1762 was *A Vindication of the Conduct of the House of Representatives*. This con-
tained his construction of past events and an outline of a reformed
Massachusetts government. The tract was intended to answer as
well as condemn the intersession activities of the governor and
Council. That summer, in response to pleas from Salem and Marblehead fishermen, Bernard had dispatched the province's armed
sloop to protect them from a rumored French invasion of New-
foundland. Francis Bernard, with the advice of the Council, increased the crew from six to twenty-six men. The extra costs were
met by the governor's warrants on the provincial treasury. When
Bernard sought approval for this action it was met with a violent
outcry from the younger Otis who claimed that a constitutional
issue was at stake. It was not the £72 but the fact that the military
establishment had been increased by the executive that was important. Were not those warrants "in effect taking from the house
their most darling priviledge, the right of originating all Taxes"?
That action was the equivalent of levying a tax. Otis held that necessity could never authorize such conduct.[40] He hoped that people would see this issue as he had defined it.

James Otis saw behind this constitutional issue a conflict of phi-
losophies. His opponents were following out the ideas of Robert
Filmer's *Patriarcha* and were supporters of the High Church belief
in divine rights. Otis rejected the medieval notion that society was
hierarchically ordained, for it was evident that "God made all men
naturally equal." He maintained that what differences did exist
among men were acquired through education or other means.

38. Samuel A. Otis to Joseph Otis, Boston, 31 May 1762, Otis Family MSS, II,
94, Butler Lib., Columbia.
39. James Otis, Jr., to Mauduit, 28 Oct. 1762, *Jasper Mauduit*, 76.
40. *A Vindication of the Conduct of the House of Representatives* ... (Boston,
1762), 6–7, 11–12, 15.

"Kings were (and plantation Governors should be) made for the good of the people, and not the people for them." Francis Bernard could not have missed the point. Otis rejected the blasphemy that made of a king "God's viceregent, cloathed with unlimited power, his will the supreme law, and not accountable . . . to any tribunal upon earth." That was the philosophy of tyranny. And he had noted earlier that if one could "levy taxes without parliament" one would be a tyrant. The domestic application was obvious: "A house of Representatives here at least, bears an equal proportion to a Governor, with that of a house of Commons to the King."[41] Otis, now convinced that the majority of the General Court would support this position, stated his conditions for cooperation with Francis Bernard: "If his Excellency will in all cases take the advice of the general assembly . . . his administration will be crowned with all the success he can desire." The governor had but to renounce the "advice of half a dozen" men opposed to the good of the commonwealth, a reference that Thomas Hutchinson could not have missed.[42] Whether Otis realized it or not, his schema would have seriously reduced the independence of the executive, while the earlier action he had sponsored in reducing the salaries of the superior court justices showed a rather limited concept of judicial independence. The General Assembly alone would have been supreme.

The test that would show whether the "Country Party" led by the Otises or the "Court Party" led by Thomas Hutchinson and his allies had control of the Assembly came in January of 1763. While the apparent issue at stake was the colonial agency, Bernard interpreted it as a power struggle that might jeopardize his own career. He told Richard Jackson that "it's given out by O[tis] and his party, that Mr. M[auduit] is with the help of the dissenting interests, to get me removed."[43] Obviously Bernard had had second thoughts about Jasper Mauduit, the past year's compromise

41. *Ibid.*, 17–21, 23–25.
42. *Ibid.*, 52.
43. Francis Bernard to Richard Jackson, Boston, 21 Feb. 1763, Bernard Papers, II, 263, Houghton Lib., Harvard.

candidate, and these were increased by James Otis's attempt to have Jasper's brother Israel appointed should Jasper resign because of ill health. The last thing Bernard wanted was to see the agency in hostile hands. And this time Thomas Hutchinson, who in the past had backed William Bollan, favored Richard Jackson, Mauduit's nominal assistant and the personal choice of Francis Bernard, if the status quo should be changed.[44] While Otis, Jr., managed a bare majority in a thin House for Israel, the Council rejected this action. This was followed by another House vote which was unfavorable to Israel's cause.[45] James tried to save face by explaining the rejection as due to the "additional expence" involved.[46] At best this was jesuitical casuistry masking defeat. Young Otis was despondent. He wrote to his friend Mauduit that Governor Francis Bernard's "administration is the weakest and most arbitrary that we have known since the Revolution." As he saw it the machinery of government was rotten, and the chief cause of that was Thomas Hutchinson's influence. If only the "Governor could be removed to some better place, and a wiser man sent in his room, that would act for himself, or if the Lieut. Governor could be confined to any one or two great posts, as Chief Justice or anything but Governor in Chief," the constitution might yet be restored. This sentiment was not lessened by Thomas Hutchinson's role in defeating Otis's move to back Israel Mauduit.[47] To his opponents the lieutenant-governor was the "Summa Potestatis." Hutchinson, knowing that he controlled the situation, coolly observed that Otis would find it advisable to adjust to the circumstances.[48]

James Otis, Jr., must have realized that February that his frontal

44. Thomas Hutchinson to Israel Williams, Boston, 17 Nov. 1763, Williams Papers, II, 158, Mass. Hist. Soc.

45. Francis Bernard to Richard Jackson, Boston, 23 Jan. 1763, Bernard Papers, II, 248–252, Houghton Lib., Harvard.

46. Bernard to Jackson, [Boston], 1 Feb. [1763], *ibid.*, II, 255–267; *Mass. House of Reps. Jours.*, 1762–1763, 138, 160, 189.

47. James Otis, Jr., to Mauduit, 14 Feb. 1763, *Jasper Mauduit*, 95.

48. Thomas Hutchinson to Col. Cushing, 3 Jan. 1763, Mass. Archives, XXVI, 38.

attack had failed. Unfortunately the host of tyrannies, endless tax-
ations, and arbitrary powers that the "Vindication" had conjured
up did not impress his colleagues as adding up to a faithful picture
of New England's situation. What Otis had shown was a potential
danger. At least one critic thought the intensity of the attack on
Bernard's administration was out of all proportion to the offense.[49]
Certainly Marblehead and Salem would not condemn an act that
defended their fishermen. Likewise, the attempt to manage the
House in regard to the agency was bound to annoy country members not interested in power politics. The move itself, as Otis, Sr.,
knew, was futile once Hutchinson and Bernard had agreed upon
a common policy. Moreover, young Otis had infuriated Bernard
and Hutchinson as much for the novelty of using the *Boston Gazette* to air public matters as for his *ad hominem* attacks upon their
reputations. Samuel Allyne recognized that his brother James had
made "many enemies" although he thought that James's friends
would stand by their "Esq. Bluster."[50] James's father, who was
much more a political realist, attempted to reach an understanding with Thomas Hutchinson before the advent of the next elections.[51] The disastrous defeat of the "Country Party" in the 1763
polling showed how wise he was. In fact, once Francis Bernard
had united his governor's patronage with Hutchinson's political
skills, their control of provincial politics was almost inevitable.
They immediately used their power to settle old scores. First, Edes
and Gill were turned out as printers because they had "printed
Mr. Otis's libells"; next the chaplain was purged as he "was supposed to be connected with Otis"; and finally a move was made
to take away the elder Otis's Council seat. Bernard was convinced
this could have been done except for the intervention of Harrison

49. Samuel Mather to Samuel Mather, Jr., Boston, 15 Mar. 1763, Samuel Mather
Letters, II, Mass. Hist. Soc.

50. Samuel A. Otis to Joseph Otis, Boston, 14 Feb., 18 Mar. 1763, Otis Family
MSS, II, 99, 100, Butler Lib., Columbia.

51. Thomas Hutchinson to Israel Williams, 15 Apr. 1763, Williams Papers, II,
157, Mass. Hist. Soc.

Gray, an old Otis friend and now a relative by marriage.[52] Politically this was the penultimate.

The world was indeed, as James Otis, Jr., opined, divided between the winners and the losers, *"between those who are discontented that they have no Power, and those who never think they can have enough."*[53] It was clear to Otis that he had failed in his endeavor to equate Bernard's spending £72 with tyranny. The administration had managed a capable campaign. And it shared in the victory of British arms that brought to a termination the French and Indian War in 1763. James rejoiced in that victory. It freed the border areas from the fear of Indian attacks and made "fellow-subjects" of the Canadians. These sentiments were part of his paean to the unfolding "universal monarchy" of the British nation. Woe to those who would divide it, for they should be mindful, Otis held, that "what God in his providence, has united let no man dare attempt to put asunder."[54] In the House, James steered a new course and moved in the first session to allow Governor Bernard his salary—although this action has been interpreted as a mockery. In what was becoming an annual event, James again resigned his seat only to reverse himself. There was something in Otis that impelled him to gain attention. Francis Bernard noted it all but did not rejoice. On the contrary, "Care must be taken to prevent" Otis from rallying his forces "which I doubt not he will be ready to do upon the first opportunity."[55]

Strange as it may seem, the problems that faced James Otis the younger and James Otis the elder for the next two years were anticipated in detail by Thomas Hutchinson in November of 1763. First of all, there was the disposition of the Barnstable bailiwick. The death of Sylvanus Bourn had left vacant the Probate Court as well as the chief justiceship of the Court of Common Pleas. These posts had been more or less in the Otis family since the early 1700's,

52. Francis Bernard to Shelburne, Castle William, 8 June 1763, Bernard Papers, III, 75–77, Houghton Lib., Harvard.

53. "The Preface," in *A Vindication of the Conduct of the House*, iv.

54. Francis Bowen, *Life of James Otis* (Boston, 1846), 92.

55. Francis Bernard to Jackson, Castle William, 8 June 1763, Bernard Papers, III, 75, Houghton Lib., Harvard.

and the old colonel wanted them. However, he would have a six-month wait. As Hutchinson summarized the situation, "The Governor keeps it off and both he and his son keep themselves silent."[56] This is the background of the alleged "deal" that made contemporaries somewhat less than sure about the Otises.[57] While the father might have made an arrangement with the administration, his son's independence was displayed in his vote against appointing Hutchinson as special agent in January of 1764.[58] This action was taken before Governor Bernard conferred the Probate and Common Pleas on James Otis, Sr., that February. At the time, the elder Otis was colonel of the county militia and a member of the Council, as nice a collection of plural offices as existed in Massachusetts. While James, Jr., flaunted his freedom by a vote against the special agency he is still open to the charge of inconsistency that was hurled at him by "Philo-Politiae" of Barnstable (in all probability Edward Bacon). Was not this the time for patriot Otis to serve his county as he had the province by pouring forth "all his zeal and eloquence to prevent any persons being commissioned for more than one department"?[59] Although James had a habit of missing the obvious, here was one barb that must have rankled the smooth smile of what had been the Bay Colony's leading opponent of plural office-holding.

The second piece of news that Hutchinson related was of larger interest. It concerned British plans to regulate the empire. He informed Israel Williams that a "revenue from the colonies will certainly be attempted the next Parliament sufficient at least to support the troops to be kept up here." In addition to that news, the "Molasses duty is to be enforced and a general stamp duty private letters say is also determined upon," although Hutchinson cautioned his friend, "This I would not have mentioned from me." The new

56. Thomas Hutchinson to Israel Williams, Boston, 17 Nov. 1763, Williams Papers, II, 158, and R. T. Paine "Diary," 22 Sept. 1763, Mass. Hist. Soc.

57. Francis Bernard to Shelburne, Boston, 22 Dec. 1766, Bernard Papers, IV, 278, Houghton Lib., Harvard.

58. Francis Bernard to Jackson, Cambridge, 2 Feb. 1764, *ibid.*, III, 123–127; Thomas Hutchinson to ?, Boston, 7 Feb. 1764, Mass. Archives, XXIV, 77–78.

59. *Boston Evening-Post*, 24 Oct. 1763.

policy would take all profit out of the agency while it required a
man of great judgment, and that clearly was not Jasper Mauduit.
Hutchinson was convinced that "Some of the friends of our new
Agent seem to be cool and growing sensible of his insufficiency."[60]
Thus the politics of the agency which had confounded Otis, Jr.,
for two years was sure to rise again. It would now be combined with
a revenue measure—the famed Sugar Act of 1764, while a stamp
act was in the works. There would be opportunity aplenty for
James Otis, Jr., both as politician and pamphleteer.

While it is generally recognized by historians today that the
Sugar Act rather than the Stamp Act marked the parting of the
waters, the initial implications of the 1764 act were recognized by
relatively few Americans.[61] The first Massachusetts reaction was
to fix the impending duty as low as possible. Thomas Cushing, a
leader of the popular party, held this attitude and as late as November of 1763 informed Mauduit that "if the Parliament should
think fitt to lower the Duty to an half penny or a penny per gallon . . . the Duty would be chearfully and universally paid."[62] It was
none other than Thomas Hutchinson who objected to this bargain-
ing approach, holding that it would establish a dangerous precedent.
He asked, "Will not this be introductory to taxes duties and ex-
cises upon other articles?" Would not such an act infringe upon
the "much esteemed privilege of English subjects—the being taxed
by their own representatives?"[63] The lieutenant-governor immediately laid bare the constitutional issue. Almost alone James Otis,
Jr., shared this position. With the convening of the December
Court James was appointed chairman of the committee to consider
the new acts. He quickly ended the drift by repudiating Cushing's
"private" instructions to Mauduit. He took a stand identical with

60. Thomas Hutchinson to Israel Williams, Boston, 17 Nov. 1763, Williams
Papers, II, 158, Mass. Hist. Soc.
61. Richard L. Merritt, "The Colonists Discover America: Attention Patterns
in the Colonial Press, 1735–1775," *Wm. and Mary Qtly.*, 3d Ser., XXI (1964),
270–287.
62. Thomas Cushing to Mauduit, Boston, 11 Nov. 1763, *Jasper Mauduit*, 139.
63. Thomas Hutchinson to Jackson, Boston, 3 Aug. 1763, Mass. Archives, XXVI,
65–66.

that of the lieutenant-governor. There was to be no temporizing with the intended act, "as it will be conceding to the Parliament having a Right to Tax our trade which we can't by any means think of admitting, as it wou'd be contrary to a fundamentall Principall of our Constitution vizt. That all Taxes ought to originate with the people."[64] Next the General Court decided to send Hutchinson as special agent to England to plead against the Sugar Act. Otis remained one of the few representatives to vote against the lieutenant-governor, perhaps because he thought the new instructions which he himself had helped to draft for Mauduit would suffice. However, province politics being what they were, the issue of the special agency bogged down over whether the lieutenant-governor should be excused from his posts in the province by grace of the General Court or should seek the king's permission for his absence. Bernard advocated the latter, not without mixed motives.[65] While the Assembly debated, Parliament on March 13, 1764, approved the Sugar Act. Jasper Mauduit had received no guidance save Cushing's letter of November which was without constitutional authority of any kind.

By June of 1764 young Otis had decided upon a plan of action. He began with an excoriation of Mauduit's handling of the 1764 Sugar Act which the agent had justified with the comment that it was wisest "to make a merit of our submission."[66] Mauduit was told that he had acted without instructions, that there could be no merit in submitting "to such an unconstitutional Measure," and that as the colonists were not represented in Parliament they could not be taxed by Parliament. As for Grenville's proposal to delay a stamp act for a year so that the colonials could come up with an equivalent, this was really saying "that if the Colonies will not tax themselves as they may be directed, the Parliament will Tax them." Mauduit was to work for a repeal of the Sugar Act and to oppose

64. Thomas Cushing to Mauduit, Boston, Jan. 1764, *Jasper Mauduit*, 145–146; Mass. Archives, XXII, 320.

65. Francis Bernard to Jackson, Cambridge, 2 Feb. 1764, Bernard Papers, III, 123–127, Houghton Lib., Harvard.

66. Jasper Mauduit to Speaker, 11 Feb. 1764, Mass. Hist. Soc., *Colls.*, 1st Ser., VI (1800), 194–195.

the impending Stamp Act on the basis of colonial rights. To make this perfectly clear, Otis sent him a copy of his latest political tract.[67]

James Otis, Jr.'s *Rights of the British Colonies . . .* was the logical development of the position he had taken against the writs of assistance in 1761. He turned once more to his earlier authorities—Coke, Locke, De Vattel, Grotius, Pufendorf, Harrington, and Hobbes—but now he rejected their various assertions that government was founded on grace, power, contract, or property. As Otis saw it government must have its origin in the *"unchangeable will of God,* the author of nature, whose laws never vary." Government must exist for the good of all. It was obvious that nature had intended that all men should be free. What was English history since the Norman conquest but the story of a people attempting to restore their ancient institutions? The essential meaning of the Glorious Revolution was the reestablishment of the "British constitution . . . with a professed design to lecture the liberties of all the subjects to all generations." Otis held that an American representation was required by equity, for Parliament, while absolute in its power, could not be arbitrary, bound as it was by a higher authority, God. "Should an act of parliament be against any of *his* natural laws, which are *immutably* true, their declaration would be contrary to eternal truth, equity and justice, and consequently void." Natural rights were beyond the jurisdiction of Parliament. Ever since the middle ages English law had affirmed that property could be taxed only with the consent of the taxpayer as represented in the Commons: *"Nostra statuta non ligant eos quia non mittant milites ad Parliamentum."* To tax Americans without representation was therefore illegal. There could be no distinction between internal and external taxes in this matter. Otis maintained that if "parliament have an equitable right to tax our trade . . . they have as good a one to tax our lands, and every thing else." But the fundamental law of God and immemorial English usage declared that they did not have this right. Otis's absolute parliament could not tax America.[68]

67. 13 June 1764, *Mass. House of Reps. Jours., 1764–1765,* 72–75, 77.
68. *Rights of the British Colonies,* 3–8, 31, 36–37, 42, 47–48, 61.

Having reaffirmed the theoretical grounds for resistance, James Otis now implemented his views by a really novel means. He had stated the Massachusetts position and now sought "the several Assemblies on this Continent to join with them in the same Measures." He realized that successful opposition to the Grenville program required a common colonial front. More than anything else this position alarmed Governor Bernard, who informed the Board of Trade that this was the "foundation for connecting the demagogues of the several governments in America to join together in opposition to all orders from Great Britain which don't square with their notions of the rights of the people."[69]

Having thrown down the gauntlet Otis promptly turned about and took actions which convinced his bewildered colleagues that he had sold out to Bernard. In January 1765 he voted for Richard Jackson as agent (with a three-year term), thus joining the Hutchinson men; while in February he provided the crucial vote that granted to Chief Justice Hutchinson £40 for what was termed the "faithful discharge" of his duties. This was in effect a partial restoration of the salary cut Otis had favored earlier. Francis Bernard, convinced that with a little encouragement James, Jr., would become an administration man, gave his assent to the election of young Otis as "Speaker pro tempore" to serve in the place of the ailing Samuel White for the rest of that session.[70] Worst of all, in his pamphlet, *Vindication of the British Colonies,* James seemed to admit that Parliament "has a just and equitable right, power and authority, to *impose taxes on the colonies, internal and external, on lands as well as on trade,*" thus repudiating his first position.[71] At this time he was again despondent, commenting to his father that "the time is come which we have long foreseen," for which he blamed "the people in England not half so much as I do our own."[72]

69. Francis Bernard to Board of Trade, 29 June 1764, Bernard Papers, III, 157–158, Houghton Lib., Harvard.

70. 23 Jan. 1765, 4 Feb. 1765, *Mass. House of Reps. Jours., 1764–1765,* 175, 210–211; Francis Bernard to Jackson, 25 Jan. 1765, Bernard Papers, III, 281, Houghton Lib., Harvard.

71. *Vindication of the British Colonies,* 4–5.

72. James Otis, Jr., to James Otis, Sr., (Dec. notation, 1764), Otis Family MSS, II, 117, Butler Lib., Columbia.

He had apparently backed Jackson for the agency because of the belief that Jackson would do something to protect Massachusetts's rights: was it not obvious to all but diehards in the popular party that Mauduit was incompetent? By joining with Hutchinson, James formed the equivalent of a "popular front" in the face of the impending Stamp Act. His repudiation of the *Rights of the Colonies* by the *Vindication*, which he reiterated further in his *Brief Remarks*, may well have been based upon a fear of the "consequences of denying the right of Parliament to tax the colonies and of justifying revolution against arbitrary power," as Ellen Brennan has suggested.[73] On the other hand this change of face may also be explained as arising from the depths of Otis's own psyche. It seemed to be part of his mental makeup to take an extreme stand, to wait for the praise, and then to nullify it by a moderate remark. Is this not the tone of his reflection that he wished the British "Island was sunk in the Sea, so that the King and his Family were Saved"?[74]

The popular party was not pleased with young Otis's many turns. Governor Bernard expressed the opinion that the *Vindication* alone "is like to cost him his seat in the Assembly altho' he had every vote at the last Election."[75] What may have saved him from defeat was the song "Jemmibullero," which went, "And Jemmy is a madman, and Jemmy is an ass / And Jemmy has a leaden head, and forehead spread with brass." This scurrilous ditty printed in the May 13 issue of the *Boston Evening-Post* was the brainchild of Samuel Waterhouse of the customs. John Adams thought it convinced many that anyone so unpopular with the administration deserved to be reelected. Success at the polls threw Otis increasingly into a world of town meetings and protests: he had become a politician dependent upon the approval of the populace.[76]

73. Brennan, "James Otis," *New England Qtly.*, XII (1939), 701.
74. Francis Bernard to Shelburne, Boston, 22 Dec. 1766, Bernard Papers, IV, 279, Houghton Lib., Harvard. For the original copy see Bernard to Shelburne, Colonial Office Group, 5/756, 9, P.R.O.
75. Francis Bernard to Pownall, 6 May 1765, Bernard Papers, III, 289, Houghton Lib., Harvard.
76. Adams to Tudor, 11 Mar. 1818, Adams, ed., *Works of J. Adams*, X, 296.

The Stamp Act had created an explosive atmosphere in the American colonies, where opposition to it was virtually unanimous. Men of such different views as the conservative (and future loyalist) Martin Gay of Hingham and the radical John Hancock of Boston, as well as Thomas Hutchinson and the James Otises, were united in protest.[77] Seldom has there been such a consensus of opinion on a major issue in American politics. The most unexpected development of the protest movement was the Stamp Act Congress scheduled to convene in New York in October. William Gordon in his *History of Independence* is the authority for the statement that the Congress was hatched at the Warren household during a conference of the Warrens and Otises.[78] Otis, Jr., as a member of the House committee to consider the Grenville program was in a key position to implement a plan of concerted opposition which had the unanimous endorsement of the Massachusetts House. It proceeded to elect the young Otis as one of its three delegates to the New York Congress, and all indications are that James acted with unexpected moderation.[79] Bernard reported James Otis's telling General Thomas Gage that "the province of Massachusetts would never be in order, until the Council was appointed from home." However, considering that the appointments board was then in the hands of the Hutchinson-Oliver faction it need hardly be pointed out that this remark is open to a double meaning.[80]

James Otis, Jr.'s most recent political work, the *Considerations on Behalf of the Colonists*, was also moderate. In that tract he claimed that *"no Englishman, nor indeed any other freeman, is or can be rightfully taxed, except by his own actual consent . . . or by . . . those who are chosen by himself."* He stressed that Parliament had

77. For the first see Martin Gay to Jotham Gay, Boston, 26 Aug. 1765, Gay-Otis Papers, Butler Lib., Columbia; and John Hancock to Barnard, 5 Apr., 11 Sept. 1765, Hancock Letter Books, V, Baker Lib., Harvard.

78. William Gordon, *The History of the Rise, Progress, and Establishment of the Independence of the United States of America* (New York, 1794), I, 119.

79. Jon. Watts to Gen. Monckton, N.Y., 12 Oct. 1765, *Aspinwall Papers*, II (Mass. Hist. Soc., *Colls.*, 4th Ser., X [1871]), 580.

80. Francis Bernard to Pownall, 5 Nov. 1765, Bernard Papers, V, 22, Houghton Lib., Harvard.

unlimited authority, declaring that the "power and authority of parliament is not to be questioned." Otis also pointed out that the idea of American representation was "generally much disliked in the colonies." Now if representation remained the sine qua non for the right to tax, Otis had really granted nothing to Parliament. He still dreamed of a "beneficial union of these colonies to the realm ... so that all the parts of the empire may be compacted and consolidated, and the constitution flourish with new vigor" and of a veritable golden age of "national strength, power and importance" which would "shine with far greater splendor than ever yet hath been seen by the sons of man."[81]

Both James Otis's *Considerations* and his conservative, moderate, and sensible conduct at the Stamp Act Congress served to convince the delegates of other colonies that Massachusetts was not in the hands of levelers. This had become imperative, for on August 14 the first of a series of demonstrations had occurred in Boston that spelled direct resistance. These Stamp Act riots aimed at destroying the machinery that would have enforced the new tax. The victims were Andrew Oliver, the would-be collector and brother-in-law of the lieutenant-governor, and then Hutchinson himself, who had his house and papers ransacked by a "mob" rioting in "tumult."[82] These demonstrations against the Stamp Act, along with those of the twenty-sixth which sacked vice-admiralty and customs records, clearly showed a conscious design on the part of the mob. Otis could not have disapproved of the results, although he realized that these actions compromised a movement that had as its motto "Liberty and Property." The Boston patriots insisted that the destruction of Thomas Hutchinson's house had been done by a lawless rabble and not by true Americans. James Otis expressed his utter amazement at the "violent proceedings" that swept over the eastern

---

81. *Considerations on Behalf of the Colonists in a Letter to a Noble Lord* (London, 1765), 5, 36, 40, 41 (first printed as a serial in the *Boston Gazette*, 22 July 1765 ff).

82. Samuel A. Otis to Joseph Otis, Boston, 16 Aug. 1765, Otis Family MSS, II, 121, Butler Lib., Columbia. See also Francis Bernard to Halifax, 15 and 16 Aug. 1765, Stowe MSS, 264: 161–168, British Museum.

seaboard from New York to Charleston. He told a Connecticut correspondent, William Samuel Johnson, that he and his friends solemnly detested the attacks on "private property" and feared the consequences. He thought that Parliament would "charge The Colonies with presenting Petitions in one hand and a daggar in the other."[83] His sentiments were identical with those of the wealthy merchant Martin Gay, who prayed for "Peace and good order."[84] James Otis feared the dangerous potential of mob activity, but it was his colleague Samuel Adams who regained control—if indeed he had ever lost it—of the Boston rioters. This was made evident on November 1. That day the hated act took effect, greeted by tolling bells and a subdued citizenry. The real test came on Guy Fawkes or Pope's Day, the fifth of November. This time the north and south mobs joined together in union under the auspices of the popular party.[85] To make certain that there would be no property damage, Negroes were excluded from the ranks of these lower-class tradesmen and worker demonstrators. They danced to Otis's tune, chanting, "Who will Seize Merchants Goods, what Judge will condemn them, what court will dare to grant Writs of Assistance now."[86]

The popular party skillfully organized the resentment that had been generated by the "Black Act." Its activities had the single intent of nullifying the Stamp Act. Newspapers were printed without stamps, commerce was continued, while legal means were employed to force the courts to reopen. The placard before the province house expressed the sentiments of a mercantile community: "Open your Courts and let Justice prevail / Open your Offices and let not Trade fail." On December 20, 1765, Jeremiah Gridley, James Otis, Jr., and John Adams appeared before the governor in

83. James Otis, Jr., to William Samuel Johnson, Boston, 12 Nov. 1765, William Samuel Johnson Correspondence, Connecticut Historical Society, Hartford.

84. Martin Gay to W. Longe, Boston, 9 Sept. 1765, Gay-Otis Papers, Butler Lib., Columbia.

85. George P. Anderson, "Ebenezer Mackintosh: Stamp Act Rioter and Patriot," and "A Note on Ebenezer Mackintosh," Col. Soc. of Mass., *Pubs.*, XXVI (1924–1926), 15–64, 348–361.

86. Francis Bernard to Pownall, Boston, 26 Nov. 1765, Stowe MSS, 264: 20–21, British Museum.

Council to urge the opening of the courts. Adams declared the
Stamp Act to be "utterly void" in law and to have no force within
the province because it was unconstitutional. Otis drew from the
entire philosophy of the whigs and the English revolution of 1688,
for he declared that the absence of the courts was tantamount to
an "abdication" of government, which if continued would place
men back in a state of nature. This was identical in substance with
the charge that had been brought against James II. Gridley's plea
was based solely on inconvenience. Francis Bernard held that the
arguments "were very good ones" and should be used "before the
Judges of the Executive Courts." In short he shifted the problem to
the Superior Court by suggesting that it was the proper body to
consider fine points of the law. Actually both the Probate and Inferior Court in Suffolk had decided to function without stamps, but
the Superior Court remained closed until March term. The House
indicated its sentiment on January 24, 1766, by resolving eighty-one
to five that all courts within the province should be opened. By
March it was common rumor that the Stamp Act would be repealed,
and Hutchinson was conveniently absent from the court. This time
the justices shifted their stand by noting that they would proceed *if*
the lawyers initiated a pleading. Not even James Otis was willing,
however, to take the option of beginning what could be an illegal
action. The Superior Court in effect postponed opening until news
of the repeal.[87]

The popular party, rightfully or not, exploited its opposition to
the "Black Act" by a campaign directed against the so-called supporters of the ministry. In simple language this meant that the court
party, which was in reality a provincial group, would pay the price
of that imperial blunder known as the Stamp Act. The May elections of 1766 brought forward a triumphant popular party. Not
surprisingly, the first act of the House was to elect James Otis, Jr.,

87. Francis Bernard to Conway, 19 Dec. 1765, Bernard Papers, IV, 184, Hough-
ton Lib., Harvard; Quincy, *Reports*, 202–206; 19 Dec. 1765, Butterfield, *et al.*, eds.,
*Diary of Adams*, I, 265–267; Edmund S. and Helen M. Morgan, *The Stamp Act
Crisis: Prologue to Revolution* (Chapel Hill, 1953), 140–143.

its speaker. The popular party, its majority swelled by malcontents and enemies of the Hutchinson-Oliver combination, proceeded to purge the Council of its court party members, including Thomas Hutchinson, the lieutenant-governor, Andrew Oliver, province secretary, Edmund Trowbridge, the attorney-general, and Peter Oliver, a justice of the Superior Court (but not Treasurer Harrison Gray now twice related to the Otises by marriage).[88] In effect, the popular party used its victory in exactly the same manner as had Hutchinson and Bernard in 1763 when they had cast out the Otis family supporters. The one exception then had been James Otis, Sr., whose seat had been saved by the intervention of Harrison Gray. Now in 1766, the popular party removed its opponents, who also wore the stigma of the Stamp Act, with the sole exception of Harrison Gray. While Francis Bernard deeply resented the purge, a more prudent governor would have accepted it and have sought a working agreement with the popular party.

May of 1766 was as propitious a time as Francis Bernard would ever have to form a broad-bottomed government. News of the Stamp Act repeal should have removed the major item of contention. Certainly the Otises had shown their willingness to work with any administration that would share its patronage and give recognition to their talents. Francis Bernard, however, destroyed any possibility of accommodation by acts that the astute Thomas Hutchinson thought ill advised. He refused to confirm James Otis, Jr., as speaker, giving as a reason his notorious "treatment of all Persons acting under the King's Authority both British and provincial," and then followed his veto (an almost unheard of event in itself) by negating the four newly elected councilors and, for good measure, both colonels Otis and Sparhawk of the popular party.[89] The governor intended this as a preliminary move to be followed by a compromise: "He should be glad to see Colls. Otis and Sparhawk

88. Richard Dana to Edm. Dana, Boston, 20 May 1766, Dana MSS, Mass. Hist. Soc.

89. Francis Bernard to Pownall, 30 May 1766, Bernard Papers, V, 115, Houghton Lib., Harvard.

at the Board provided his 4 friends might return." However, the House, which knew "a trick worth two of his," refused.[90] It did not intend to barter away the fruits of victory. Bernard now hectored the Assembly. He impugned the motives of the popular party in voting out of office the best of men, "whose only crime is their fidelity to the Crown," in a tactless speech which superimposed a constitutional issue upon party politics. It was answered for the House by the young Otis. Quoting Bernard verbatim, Otis replied that the House was at a loss "to conceive how a full, free, and fair election can be called 'an attack upon the government in form,' 'a professed intention to deprive it of its best and most able servants,' 'an ill-judged and ill-timed oppugnation of the king's authority.' " These were serious charges which if true meant that the General Court was guilty of high treason. What these free elections had done was to release the judges of the Superior Court "from the cares and perplexities of politics" and to return them to study and perfection within the law.[91] Constitutionally, the House in turn claimed Bernard to be guilty of executive interference. It refused to elect new members to the Council after Bernard's heavy-handed vetoes, thus adhering to its own 1741 precedent which it had used against Governor Belcher's attempted *coup de main*.[92] This deadlock resulted in a decline in the Council's position within the government.

In more than five years of constant agitation James Otis, Jr., had helped to form the first stable Massachusetts party structure since the administration of William Shirley. Even more significant was the nature of the campaign the popular party waged in the May 1766 elections, in which it declared open war against thirty-two representatives of the "Court Party." Nineteen of them went down to defeat wearing the Stamp Act albatross. This was the first province-

90. Samuel A. Otis to [Joseph Otis], Boston, 17 June 1766, Otis Family MSS, II, 128, Butler Lib., Columbia.

91. Alden Bradford, ed., *Speeches of the Governors from 1765 to 1775; And the Answers of the House of Representatives . . . with Their Resolutions* (Boston, 1818), 74–75. Thomas Hutchinson in his *Hist. Mass.*, ed. Mayo, III, 107–108, is the authority for attributing authorship to James Otis, Jr.

92. Hutchinson, *Hist. Mass.*, ed. Mayo, II, 303–304, III, 110.

wide electoral campaign in Massachusetts history. James Otis, John Adams, and Samuel Adams, moreover, had brilliantly utilized the *Boston Gazette* and the *Boston Evening-Post* to identify the Bernard-Hutchinson-Oliver clique as supporters of the prerogative.[93] Otis achieved this by championing American nationalism against imperial regulations and taxes. The success of this campaign startled Hutchinson. "Had our confusions, in this province, proceeded from any interior cause we have good men enough in the country towns to have united in restoring peace and order and would have put an end to the influence of the plebian party in the town of Boston over the rest of the province," but as a result of Otis's influence the rural representatives "unite with those whom they would otherwise abhor under a notion of opposing by a common interest a power which we have no voice in creating, and which they say has a distinct and separate interest from us."[94]

While James Otis, Jr.'s arguments in favor of opening up the courts during this crisis period were also revolutionary, he held back from any overt act. In fact, he considered himself as a defender of the empire and told his sister Mercy that he dared not leave Boston lest the radicals push things to a crisis.[95] He had inspired a party of opposition, helped of course by Bernard's blunders. Otis's guide had been the protection of mercantile interests in 1761, but by 1765 he had come to defend those "certain essential Rights of the *British* Constitution of Government which are founded in the Law of God and Nature, and are the common Rights of Mankind."[96] He was uncertain where his path would lead him, he feared what his party would do, but he rejoiced in his victory over arbitrary government. It was more than a boast when James Otis, Jr., signed his letters "*Anno Libertatis Primo.*"[97]

93. See *Boston Evening-Post*, 3 Feb., 28 Apr. 1766; *Boston Gazette*, 31 Mar. 1766.

94. Thomas Hutchinson to Richard Jackson, Boston, 21 Apr. 1766, Mass. Archives, XXVI, 227.

95. James Otis, Jr., to Mercy Warren, 11 Apr. 1766, *Warren-Adams Letters*, I (Mass. Hist. Soc., *Colls.*, LXXII [1917]), 1–3.

96. 29 Oct. 1765, *Mass. House of Reps. Jours.*, *1765–1766*, 153.

97. James Otis, Jr., to R. T. Paine, 14 Aug. 1766, R. T. Paine Papers, Mass. Hist. Soc.

## ✹ VIII.

# THE TWILIGHT OF
# PROVINCIAL POLITICS

In 1766 the "Patriot Party" owed its victory to its successful mobilization of the province-wide opposition to the Stamp Act.
It had campaigned on the issue of colonial rights. It had followed the
Otises' charge that the court party was a tool of Governor Bernard
and the English ministry in their evil attempt to infringe charter
liberties, the rights of Englishmen, and the law of nature. The
columns of the *Boston News-Letter* and the *Boston Gazette* carried
this propaganda throughout Massachusetts.[1] The May 1766 elections, in which nineteen of the court party went down to defeat,
testified to the popular party's political acumen. The patriots, following the eighteenth-century precedents of colonial politics, used
their victory to purge the Council of the opposition. After all, was
this not what Bernard and Hutchinson had done when they had won
in 1763? Francis Bernard had decided not to play this game, however. He showed this when he excoriated the General Court on its
duties, vetoed Otis, Jr., as speaker, barred the elder Otis from his
old Council seat, and negated the four new Council men from the

1. Arthur M. Schlesinger, *Prelude to Independence*; *The Newspaper War on
Britain, 1764–1776* (New York, 1958), 67–84.

country party. In effect, the governor changed the rules in the middle of the game. He undoubtedly considered the patriot party's victory a temporary phenomenon and counted on the next election to restore his control of the Assembly. In the meantime the Otises were denied the honors and profits of office, which was precisely what was needed to unite that family.

Both the country and the court parties prepared early for the showdown. The elder Otis, who felt "pretty Easy in my own Chimney Corner" that cold winter, outlined the strategy for the coming May election of 1767. It had no ideological flavor, calling as it did upon the country party representatives to maintain the status quo. Son James was told, "Keep Exactly to the Last years Plan and Chose the Same Councellors that was the Last year Chosen unless there was a fair Chance to Drop a few of the Torrey Part Behind." The elder Otis had started this letter with the observation that "sometimes the Whiggs a Little overdo as to the Strick Truth of things."[2] This reflection upon the polemics in the *Gazette* mirrored the different worlds of father and son. To be in power, to work with the administration, to make a bargain, to get on with business—these were old Otis's values and those of his Barnstable constituents. When he saw that it was to his interest, he had used his influence in the General Court to back the opposition to the Sugar and Stamp Acts, but in the Council he had sided more frequently with the administration than with the radicals. It came as a shock to him when Governor Bernard took on the role of a "searcher of hearts" and again barred him from the Council, declaring that the "Fathers Principles and the Sons were Both a Like but the father was not so open."[3] The elder Otis, a careful, realistic, provincial politician who had weathered every storm for more than two decades, found himself forced into a position he did not welcome and identified with an ideology he could not support.

James Otis, Jr.'s political orientation had been initially as con-

2. James Otis, Sr., to James Otis, Jr., Barnstable, 24 Jan. 1767, Otis Papers, II, 137, Mass. Hist. Soc.
3. James Otis, Sr., to Joseph Otis, Boston, 12 June 1767, *ibid.*, II, 142.

servative as his father's. He had started his career in Boston affairs
with his spirited defence of her merchants against the writs of assistance. His whole-hearted efforts quickly gained the approbation
of the capital's mercantile community. Its traders, shipowners, shop-
keepers, small distillers, and artisans elected him as their representative in 1761, and he had continued to champion their special interests in the face of the hostile Hutchinson-dominated Superior
Court, a more efficient customs, and renewed admiralty activity.
Otis certainly understood the popular temper. This was shown at
the time of the 1765 Stamp Act riots when the demonstrators cried,
"Who will Seize Merchants Goods, what Judge will condemn
them, what court will dare to grant Writs of Assistance now." Yet
while the crowd mouthed Otis's thoughts he secretly abhorred
their attacks on "private property" and the violence of their proceedings. He doubted that Parliament would give way to mob intimidation.[4] In short, Otis was consistently for a legal, peaceful
resistance. He knew that some of his associates wanted to bring on
a crisis as early as April of 1766 and had resolved to block them. In
fact, he had informed his sister Mercy that he dared not leave Boston in their hands.[5] Moreover, James felt that his position in Boston,
unlike his father's in conservative Barnstable, required a dynamic
and popular approach if he was to retain and direct public opinion.
Undoubtedly James had charisma. Equally important was his es-
pousal of an ever more egalitarian political doctrine. He posited
that the "representation of the whole people should be as equal as
possible." That alone was balm to overtaxed and underrepresented
Boston, but James went even further in insisting that every man by
nature had "his life and liberty" and that even if he lacked property
he should have a vote.[6] This radical position was directly opposed
to the beliefs of James Otis, Sr., who in the Barnstable town meeting

4. James Otis, Jr., to William Samuel Johnson, Boston, 12 Nov. 1765, W. S.
Johnson Correspondence, Conn. Hist. Soc.
5. James Otis, Jr., to Mercy Warren, 11 Apr. 1766, *Warren-Adams Letters*, I,
1–3.
6. *Considerations on Behalf of the Colonists*, 5–6. See also the *Boston Gazette*,
22 July 1765.

had insisted upon the necessity of property qualifications for taking part in the political process.[7] In the past the vote had been tied in one way or another to property. Undoubtedly Massachusetts had many voters simply because most of her people had property, but that was a fortuitous circumstance. James Otis's argument was revolutionary in so far as it insisted that participation in politics flowed from human rather than from property rights. Otis had made Locke obsolete.

If Otis dreamed of a new order within Massachusetts he also called for external changes which would have made the province autonomous. He had now come to the point of denying the *right* of Parliament to legislate for the colonies. When this new stand was challenged by a representative who said he "knew the time when the House would have readily assisted the Governor in executing the Laws of Trade," Otis responded passionately that "the times were altered; they now knew what their Rights were, *then* they did not."[8] This position was a logical development of James's 1765 realization that England's power to veto colonial laws worked a hardship on the people of Massachusetts. It also reflected his awareness that the "principal Merchants, thro' the Continent" were dissatisfied with the mother country's mercantile policy. The trading interests still looked to James Otis, Jr., for guidance and direction.[9] Only a man of his genius could bring together such diverse elements as mobs and private property, mercantile interests and universal manhood suffrage, union and autonomy.

Francis Bernard did not understand the Otises, but he did realize what was at stake in the May 1767 elections. He took over the patronage distribution and by his lack of judgment alienated the more principled members of the court party. Judge John Cushing, one of Hutchinson's friends, remarked that the governor was "gitting into office Scandalous and unfit persons and Throwing about Com-

7. Barnstable Town Records, II, 129.

8. Francis Bernard to the Earl of Shelburne, Boston, 24 Dec. 1766, C. O. 5/756, 19–29, P.R.O.

9. John Cruger, *et al.*, to James Otis, Jr., N. Y., 24 Nov. 1766, Ezekiel Price Papers, No. 30, Mass. Hist. Soc.

missions and promising almost Everybody" places if they would back his candidates in the coming elections.[10] Bernard knew that the popular party with young Otis as its penman had started up the old maneuver of writing to England against him.[11] By January of 1767 he had lost confidence in himself and spent his time outlining a conspiracy thesis. In the past, he noted, the faction had forced Governor Samuel Shute out of office, the "best natured and inoffensive man living," it had broken the heart of Governor William Burnet, a man exemplary in all his qualifications, and it had displaced Governor Jonathan Belcher, whose chief fault was his attachment to England. His two immediate predecessors had been spared this ordeal, William Shirley, because his recall followed a change in the ministry at home, and Thomas Pownall, whose stay in the Bay Colony was too short for the faction to combine against him. Bernard, on the verge of panic, concluded by informing Lord Shelburne that the popular party was now determined to remove him. The director of this machination was James Otis, Jr.[12]

The May 1767 elections confirmed the governor's worst fears. He again failed to round up enough votes to elect Hutchinson and Oliver. He apparently approached several of the popular party head men and proposed a compromise arrangement. He told Shelburne that he agreed to settle for the joint elections of Hutchinson, Oliver, Sparhawk, and the elder Otis to the Council. But the Otises would make a deal only if he excluded Thomas Hutchinson.[13] However, James Otis, Sr., who returned to Boston that year as Barnstable's representative, was told by his friends on the Council that Bernard opposed a place for him because of his dangerous principles. The elder Otis's "old friends" refused to sell out on the colonel.[14] If one follows the Otis document on the proposed com-

---

10. John Cushing to Thomas Hutchinson, 15 Dec. 1766, Mass. Archives, XXV, 116–117.

11. James Otis, Jr., to Sec. Conway, Boston, 9 June 1766, C. O. 5/755, 523, P.R.O.

12. Francis Bernard to Shelburne, Boston, 24 Jan. 1767, New England Papers, II, 23–24, Sparks MSS, Houghton Lib., Harvard.

13. Francis Bernard to Shelburne, Boston, 30 May 1767, Bernard Papers, VI, 211–212, *ibid*.

14. James Otis, Sr., to Joseph Otis, Boston, 12 June 1767, Otis Papers, II, 142, Mass. Hist. Soc.

promise, it was Francis Bernard's stated animus—which he had expressed earlier in his conspiracy thesis diatribe—that ruined the chance for a settlement. The following year when Lieutenant-Governor Thomas Hutchinson again failed in his bid for a Council seat, Governor Bernard countered by negativing Otis, Sr., and five other whig leaders. On that occasion Hutchinson had come very close to election. As he related it, he would have made it except for the ingratitude of Artemas Ward, a "very sulky fellow who I thought I could bring over by giving him a L[ieutenant's] Commission in the Provincial forces."[15] Failure again greeted the court party in May of 1769. In fury Bernard now negated eleven proposed members of the board. In effect the governor's use of his veto had reduced the Council from its normal twenty-eight members to but sixteen in 1769. This diminution weakened the voice of the board in joint ballots with the House, and Bernard was forced to admit finally in 1769 that he had failed to retain its loyalty.[16] Thomas Hutchinson opposed Bernard's rigid adherence to barring the opposition and termed it "absolutely impracticable."[17] By 1769 the Council, which was intended as a check on the House, had been transformed from an important pro-administration instrument to apparently a rump subservient to the popular party.[18]

What is one to make of the Bernard administration's loss of control in the Council in the years 1766 to 1769? Is one to accept the governor's opinion that the election of the Otises' supporters was political subversion? What is the real meaning of the governor's recommendation to the ministry that the crown should guarantee an independent Council? Actually, as Francis Bernard realized, the key to the control of the Council rested in the House, for under the charter government the new councilors were chosen by joint ballot

15. Thomas Hutchinson to Pownall, June 1768, Mass. Archives, XXV, 262.

16. Francis Bernard to Pownall, Boston, 23 Apr. 1769, Bernard Papers, VII, 285, Houghton Lib., Harvard.

17. Thomas Hutchinson to Francis Bernard, Boston, 15 Sept. 1770, Mass. Archives, XXVII, 1.

18. Francis G. Walett, "The Massachusetts Council, 1766–1774: The Transformation of a Conservative Institution," *Wm. and Mary Qtly.*, 3d Ser., VI (1949), 605–609.

of the twenty-eight "old" members of the board and the newly
elected one hundred-odd representatives. Assuming that the administration controlled the "old" Council, its party would have to
muster but a third of the representatives present to yield the needed
majorities by joint ballot.[19] To gain this end Francis Bernard had at
his disposal the governorship's customary patronage. Considering
that the method of electing the Council gave the incumbents the
decided advantage of being able to vote for themselves and that
the patronage was a potent weapon in obtaining additional support,
the inability of the Bernard administration to win in the Council
elections from 1766 to 1769 stands out as an unprecedented turn
in the politics of provincial Massachusetts. What Bernard believed
to be subversion of the Council was in reality the constitutional
functioning of the traditional electoral processes. From 1766 on
the popular party controlled at least two-thirds of the representatives. In effect, when the governor called for an independent board
he meant that it should be free from the dictates of the Bay Colony's
voters. Nothing indicates more clearly Governor Bernard's political
failures than his 1769 position that the "Reformation of the Council
must now be made in the Body and Not in the Members. It must be
done at Westminster and cant be done here."[20] Bernard's desired
reform called for the subversion of the traditionally elected Council
and its replacement by crown-appointed placemen.

Why had Governor Bernard failed? What produced the governmental impasse that drove Bernard to seek British intervention as
the only means of restoring his political authority in the colony?
The element of personality is central to this problem. In most respects Bernard proved himself an inept politician. His actions were
precipitate and tactless; even Hutchinson viewed his handling of the
Otises and the Council as obtuse.[21] His own mistakes were always,
in Bernard's eyes, the faults of others. His weakness during the

19. Hutchinson, *Hist. Mass.*, ed. Mayo, II, 6–7, for election procedures.
20. Francis Bernard to Pownall (Private), 15 Apr. 1769, Bernard Papers, VII,
292, Houghton Lib., Harvard.
21. Hutchinson, *Hist. Mass.*, ed. Mayo, III, 107–110.

Stamp Act crisis was evident, while his vacillating conduct during
the 1768 difficulties merited from Lord Hillsborough the rejoinder,
"It is You, to whom the Crown has delegated its Authority, and
You alone are responsible for the due Exercise of it."[22] The British
general, Thomas Gage, held that the governor would not take responsibility for the measures he called for.[23] This was summed up
by Colonel John Dalrymple, who wrote that the governor "means
to avail himself of others, to do that which he himself ought to have
done long since."[24] Bernard also had a less than effective lieutenant-
governor, who was resented by many of the representatives because of his dominance of the political scene.[25] The Otises exploited
the issue of plural office-holding on the part of the Hutchinsons
and Olivers; they did not invent it. In fact after the 1767 defeat
Bernard in a private letter declared that he had failed because of
his alliance with Hutchinson and his "endeavouring to support him
and his offices."[26] Clearly, Hutchinson was never totally in the
governor's confidence. After all, Thomas Hutchinson aspired to
the governor's chair himself. The court party, divided internally,
its leaders both jealous and suspicious of each other, lacked the
needed insight and energy to preserve itself from the assaults of the
popular party and identification with the hated imperial measures
of the British ministries.

If anything killed the appeal of the court party within Massachusetts it was the string of imperial edicts hung upon it by Parliament. From 1764 to 1775 the unstable and irresponsible ministries that formed the government of Great Britain floundered from
one expedient to another in a futile quest for colonial revenue and
imperium.[27] The Sugar Act certainly did not win popularity in a

22. Hillsborough to Francis Bernard, 11 June 1768, Bernard Papers, XI, 192,
Houghton Lib., Harvard.

23. Gage to Francis Bernard, 11 July 1768, Gage Manuscripts, W. L. Clements
Library, Ann Arbor, Mich.

24. Dalrymple to Gage, 10 July 1768, *ibid*.

25. Francis Bernard to Shelburne, Boston, 24 Jan. 1767, New England Papers,
II, 23–24, Sparks MSS, Houghton Lib., Harvard.

26. Francis Bernard to Richard Jackson, 29 July 1767, Bernard Papers, VI, 31,
*ibid*.

27. As John Brooke observed, "It was in the years from 1766 to 1770 that the

trading community. The Stamp Act was even more repugnant to the Bay Colony's electorate. While its repeal in 1766 should have restored some harmony, that year was embittered by the "Malcom affair" which revived the debate about writs of assistance. Surely it was an act of folly when in September of 1766 the customs officers attempted to enter the cellar of Captain Daniel Malcom in search of French brandy. Of course Malcom refused to admit them, and when they sought a writ of assistance, Malcom countered by hiring Otis as his attorney. Once again James Otis did battle against the Hutchinson-controlled Superior Court. Otis insisted that it was illegal for the court to issue such a writ (an opinion sustained that October by Attorney-General William De Grey of Great Britain).[28] And Parliament's threat to suspend the New York Assembly in 1767 for its refusal to comply with the Quartering Act called forth sympathetic support in defence of colonial rights. James Otis, Jr., brought the moral home to the readers of the *Boston Gazette*, declaring that if "our legislative authority can be suspended whenever we refuse obedience to laws we never consented to, we may as well send home our representatives, and acknowledge ourselves slaves."[29] Lastly, the Townshend Duties in 1767 resurrected the issue of colonial taxation.

Each of these measures fortified the Otises, Warrens, and Adamses in their policy of resistance. They placed the blame for these measures on the court party and its English friends. The popular party summed up its philosophy when it replied to the Townshend Duties with its "Circular Letter" declaring that the act—which was intended to raise a colonial revenue—was a violation of

alienation of the colonies from Great Britain increased with alarming rapidity; and it was the irresponsibility of Charles Townsend, the narrow, shortsighted views of Hillsborough, the refusal of Chatham to direct the Administration he had formed, the struggles of the Rockinghams to force themselves back into power, and the timidity of Grafton and Camden, the friends of America, which brought about a situation almost beyond the powers of statesmanship to handle," *The Chatham Administration, 1766–1768* (London, 1956), 26–27.

28. George G. Wolkins, "Daniel Malcom and Writs of Assistance," *Mass. Hist. Soc., Procs.*, LVIII (1924–1925), 13–16, and William De Grey, Opinion of the Attorney General, 17 Oct. 1766, *ibid.*, 71–73.

29. "A. F.," *Boston Gazette*, 31 Aug. 1767.

the natural and constitutional rights of the Americans. When Lord Hillsborough ordered Governor Bernard to secure the rescission of the Circular Letter, the governor realized that this command might well ruin the court party, yet he obeyed it.[30] Only 17 out of 109 representatives were willing to follow that order. These votes came from the governor's hard core of supporters; they equaled but 15 per cent of the House. Is it any wonder that by the following June, Bernard doubted he could find ten supporters for his policies in the Assembly?[31] The popular party owed a large part of its success to the impolitic conduct of Francis Bernard and the program of a British government intent upon a revolutionary change in colonial relations. This is by no means a novel interpretation. In 1774 Francis Bernard himself realized that he would still be drawing a salary "if the Parliament had not taxed the colonies" or if he had not "in the height of my Zeal for my Mother Country, and the Service of the King tho't it my Duty to support the authority of Parliament."[32]

James Otis, Jr.'s belief in peaceful, legal resistance received its major test as he organized the people of Boston against the Town-shend Duties of 1767. To many this act, which in its preamble affirmed the right of American taxation to defray "the Charge of the Administration of Justice, and the Support of Civil Government, in such Provinces where it shall be found necessary," violated everything the colonials believed in and negated the Stamp Act repeal. To enforce the new duties an American Board of Customs was created, located at Boston, and headed by none other than Francis Bernard's old friend Charles Paxton. In Boston the first recorded opposition to the Revenue Act came from a town meeting chaired by Otis which proposed a nonimportation movement to take effect that October. This movement's motto was classically conservative: "No Mobs and Tumults, let the Person and Properties of our

30. Francis Bernard to Lord Barrington, Boston, 18 June 1768, Channing, ed., *Barrington-Bernard Correspondence*, 160–161.
31. Francis Bernard to Pownall, Boston, 1 June 1769, Bernard Papers, VII, 295–296, Houghton Lib., Harvard.
32. Francis Bernard, Aylesbury, 4 Jan. 1774, Channing, ed., *Barrington-Bernard Correspondence*, 218.

most inveterate Enemies be safe—Save your Money and you save your Country."[33] On November 20, the day the Townshend Duties went into effect, James again held the town's rostrum and declared the tax unconstitutional. His emphasis was, "*Let our burthens be ever so heavy, or our taxes ever so great,*" there was nothing at present which would justify "*private tumults and disorders.*" He reminded his listeners that their forefathers had prayed to God and petitioned Charles I for fifteen years "*before they would betake themselves to any forceable measures.*" They should be mindful that "*during the course of the revolution which placed king William on the throne, there was no tumults or disorder.*"[34] This speech was illustrative of Otis's style. Its logic insisted upon order while its rhetoric hearkened back to the revolutionary tradition of the seventeenth century. Momentarily, the patriot shared in the sentiments of the conservative John Dickinson, the famous author of *Letters from a Farmer in Pennsylvania*, who wrote him, "We have constitutional methods of seeking Redress; and they are the best Methods."[35]

The Massachusetts Assembly, conscious of its past, protested to its agent against the new tax measures. Closely following Locke, the members reasserted that property was essential for the support of civil government. Was not the "great end of government" the security of "right and property"? What property, it asked, could the "colonists be conceived to have, if their money may be taken away by others, without their consent?" In the past an arbitrary monarch and his minion Governor Andros had violated the sacred rights of the people. Now it was the Parliament. James, the author of this document, concluded by returning to the riddle he would not solve: "We are taxed, and can appeal for relief, from their final decision, to no power on earth; for there is no power on earth

33. *Boston Gazette*, 9 Nov. 1767.
34. This quotation is from the body of the speech as reported in the *Boston Evening-Post*, 23 Nov. 1767. In the *Boston Gazette*, 30 Nov. 1767, Otis denied that the introductory comments favorable to the customs were his, but he did not repudiate the main text.
35. John Dickinson to James Otis, Jr., Philadelphia, 5 Dec. 1767, *Warren-Adams Letters*, I, 4.

above them."[36] But if James Otis, Jr., could not cut that knot there were others who would.

The Circular Letter of February 1768 epitomized the dualism of James Otis, Jr.'s position. It denied the right of Parliament to tax the colonies, held that the intent of utilizing the revenues to pay governors and judges was a usurpation, affirmed loyalty to the crown, and concluded with a denial that America was seeking independence.[37] Otis was the great exponent of colonial rights, while he loved the power, the majesty, and the order of the British empire.[38] He thought it essential that he should be on the scene just as he had been during the Stamp Act crisis. He did not trust Samuel Adams and took pains to establish his own authorship of these 1768 propositions, at the same time that he deprecated Adams's influence: "I have written them all, and handed them to Sam to *quieuvicue* [polish] them" was a boast that masked uncertainty.[39]

The Commissioners of the Customs in Boston interpreted Otis's Circular Letter as denying the very authority on which the Townshend Revenue Acts rested. What they wanted to back up their position, as did Francis Bernard, were troops. They interpreted this document as sedition and declared that it made it "totally impracticable to inforce the execution of the Revenue Laws, untill the hand of Government is properly strengthened."[40] On March 18, the anniversary day of the Stamp Act repeal, the Boston patriots showed their feelings about Commissioner Paxton by hanging his effigy from the Liberty Tree. Lieutenant-Governor Hutchinson, who had developed a skill in judging popular demonstrations, considered this one as "only such a Mob as we have long been used to the 5 of Nov. and other Holidays." Nevertheless the commissioners again demanded armed protection from the home government and

36. House to DeBerdt, 12 Jan. 1768, in Bradford, ed., *Speeches of Governors*, 126.
37. *Ibid.*, 134–136.
38. James Otis, Jr., to the Earl of Buchan, Boston, 18 July 1768, Otis Papers, II, 159, Mass. Hist. Soc.
39. Bowen, *Life of Otis*, 154.
40. Commissioners to Lords of the Treasury, Boston, 12 Feb. 1768, as reprinted in George G. Wolkins, "The Seizure of John Hancock's Sloop *Liberty*," Mass. Hist. Soc., *Procs.*, LV (1921–1922), 263–267.

this time the ministry would give it.[41] In the meantime the radical fringe of the popular party under the direction of Sam Adams summoned a "Massachusetts Convention" to meet in Boston that September. In part this was a protest against Governor Bernard's proroguing the General Court for its refusal to rescind the Circular Letter.

James Otis, Jr., was as much opposed to offensive measures in the convention as to the coming of troops. He was not elected one of its officers and did not attend until the fourth day.[42] Yet the drift of affairs in Boston was upsetting. James had long feared a standing army and considered it an instrument of intimidation if not of outright coercion. He could see no justification for stationing troops in the town, a position shared by their commander, General Alexander Mackay, who was of the opinion, "There is not the smallest Intention of any Revolt."[43] Both father and son thought of themselves as loyal subjects. The father had been rankled to note that the English press wrote of him as "one of the most active" in his "opposition to Government."[44] The son considered himself above reproach in this matter. It came as a rude shock that General Thomas Gage while visiting Boston in October should refuse a dinner invitation extended to him by young Otis.[45] As painful as James might find it, he was forced to reflect upon the turn of events. In writing to a British friend that November, he summarized his views on the

41. Commissioners to Lords of Treasury, 28 Mar. 1768, *ibid.*, 268–271. This letter was received by the Lords on 4 June 1768 along with the "duplicate" letter of 12 Feb. 1768 cited above. It was on the basis of the so-called demonstration of 18 Mar. that troops were finally ordered to Boston and not because of the June 10 *Liberty* riot. See Hillsborough to Gage, 10 June 1768, Clarence E. Carter, ed., *The Correspondence of General Thomas Gage* (New Haven, 1931–1933), II, 68–69, and Hillsborough to the Admiralty Lords, 11 June 1768, C.O. 5/757, 165, P.R.O. See Thomas Hutchinson to Richard Jackson, 23 Mar. 1768, Mass. Archives, XXV, 295–296, for the lieutenant-governor's evaluation of the disturbance.

42. John C. Miller, "The Massachusetts Convention: 1768," *New England Qtly.*, VII (1934), 445–474.

43. Alexander Mackay to Thomas Gage, Boston, 5 July 1769, Gage MSS, Clements Lib.

44. Extract, July 1767, "Gentleman's Magazine," as copied in the hand of James Otis, Sr., Otis Family MSS, II, 133, Butler Lib., Columbia.

45. Andrew Oliver to John Spooner, Boston, 28 Oct. 1768, Oliver Letter Books, I, 41–45, Mass. Hist. Soc.

American experience. The first point was that his ancestors were good and free men whose patrimony he wanted to preserve. If England would not allow autonomy, then the Americans would become "a great people." With the marching of redcoats in the streets young Otis warned that the "present measures can have no Tendency but to hasten on with great rapidity events which every good and honest man would wish delayed for ages, if possible, prevented for ever."[46] The implication, too painful to be uttered, was independence.

James Otis, Jr.'s actions during this critical period were essentially moderate. He had not favored Samuel Adams's convoking the "Massachusetts Convention," with its obvious references to the Convention of 1689 which had given England a new government, nor could he see the justification in the customs' call for troops, which paralleled the Stuart tyrants' dependence upon foreign aid. The results of the 1769 election demonstrated that Otis's middle position as formulated in the Circular Letter was a better reading of the sentiments of his fellow citizens than those of his opponents. Eighty-one of the "Glorious Ninety-two" representatives who voted against rescinding the Circular Letter were reelected, while twelve of the infamous "seventeen" rescinders went down to defeat. Looking over the wreckage of the court party, Governor Bernard despairingly commented, "Otis, Adams, etc. are now in full possession of the government."[47]

A factor which contributed to the defeat of the court party in the 1769 elections was the admiralty trial of Michael Corbet, a Marblehead sailor who had resisted the attempt of Lieutenant Henry Gibson Panton of H.M.S. *Rose* to impress by killing that officer. Corbet's representatives, John Adams and James Otis, Jr., argued for a jury trial but were denied it by a legal decision of the chief justice. Undoubtedly Thomas Hutchinson was correct in

46. James Otis, Jr., to Jones, 26 Nov. 1768, Mass. Hist. Soc., *Procs.*, XLIII (1909–1910), 493.

47. Francis Bernard to Pownall, 1 June 1769, Bernard Papers, VII, 295–296, Houghton Lib., Harvard.

holding for admiralty jurisdiction. Yet any trial before a prerogative court was sure to touch an exposed nerve in the Bay Colony. James Otis, although defeated in his plea over jurisdiction, went on to show he had lost none of his legal acumen by raising the crucial question upon which acquittal hung. Otis's crossexamination disclosed that Lieutenant Panton had said nothing to Corbet "about his being a custom house officer or his having a right to search for goods."[48] Once it was established that neither Panton nor his superiors had "any warrant or special authority" to impress, the crown's case collapsed.[49]

The news that Francis Bernard would return to England must have pleased Otis as much as his legal victory. Bernard, who had been made a baronet, gave as the ostensible reason for his trip home the need to inform George III about conditions in Massachusetts, but local gossip interpreted this move as a graceful way of removing Bernard, obviously a *persona non grata*, from the local scene. This was coupled with the news that the 1767 Revenue Act would be repealed, save for the tax on tea.[50] That August, Boston exulted over Governor Bernard's departure: "The bells were rung, guns were fired from Mr. Hancock's wharf, liberty tree was covered with flags, and in the evening a great bonfire was made upon Fort Hill."[51]

Success seemed only to increase James Otis, Jr.'s many doubts. In part they sprang from an unwillingness to recognize the likely results of a situation, a personal refusal to be identified with a uniform course of action. Above all he considered himself loyal to his king. Never in his speeches had James attacked the person of the monarch, the unassailable father figure. Now, however, Otis was forced to champion the nonimportation movement against British

48. John Adams, "Testimony Taken in Case of Michael Corbet," *Mass. Hist. Soc., Procs.*, XLIV (1910–1911), 438.

49. Hutchinson, *Hist. Mass.*, ed. Mayo, III, 167.

50. Samuel A. Otis to [Joseph Otis], [Boston], [1769], Otis Family MSS, IV, 323, Butler Lib., Columbia; Col. John Pomeroy to Thomas Gage, 15 May 1769, Gage MSS, Clements Lib.

51. Hutchinson, *Hist. Mass.*, ed. Mayo, III, 182.

goods as the most effective means of forcing the ministry to repeal the Townshend Duties, although he realized that a successful boycott would deprive the parent state of its lifeblood. In Massachusetts the nonimportation movement received near universal compliance, and Otis smiled enigmatically at its success.[52] It must have been discouraging to a man of Otis's principles to find out that some of his Barnstable supporters used this movement as the pretext for destroying certain Scottish merchants.[53] Earlier that fall James became enraged when he learned that Commissioner John Robinson of the customs had written home that Otis was an enemy to the "rights of the crown and disaffected to his Majesty." A violent fight occurred on the night of September 5 when these two antagonists encountered each other in the British Coffee House. Otis received the worst of it including a cut on the head.[54] It is impossible to evaluate the physical or psychological effects that this humiliating defeat at the hands of one of the king's officers had on an already precarious constitution. Even before the fight John Adams had recorded signs indicating the breakdown of his hero.[55] The tensions within James Otis, Jr.'s personality, the ambiguity of his political position, and the growing popularity of other politicians such as William Molineux, Rev. Dr. Samuel Cooper, and Sam Adams combined to destroy him.[56]

That November, James Otis oscillated toward the court party. This may have been due to his mental instability. However, his whig contemporaries winced at what appeared to them as yet another example of the Otises' political opportunism. But James gave up what was left of his law practice and confided to his doctor that he feared death. He had meant well in his past actions but now

52. Thomas Hutchinson to Francis Bernard, Boston, 8 Aug. 1769, Mass. Archives, XXVI, 361.
53. Benjamin Crocker to [James Otis, Jr.?], Falmouth, 4 Nov. 1769, Otis Papers, II, 172, Mass. Hist. Soc.
54. Shipton, *et al.*, *Sibley's Harvard Graduates*, XI, 277.
55. John Adams, 3 Sept., and Nov. 1769, and cf. 16 Jan. and 26 Feb. 1770, Butterfield, *et al.*, eds., *Diary of Adams*, I, 343, 345, 348–350.
56. Thomas Hutchinson to Francis Bernard, Boston, 17 Oct. 1769, Mass. Archives, XXVI, 389.

realized they were wrong and that his country approached ruin. In anguish he concluded this confession with, "*Cursed be the day I was born.*"[57] He took more and more to drink. His conversation ran with "Trash, Obsceneness, Profaneness and Distraction."[58] In January 1770 Otis wrote to Lord Hillsborough urging him to read the Bible and affirmed that he was "his majesty's liege, true and faithful subject."[59] That March he broke the windows of the Town House and fired off his guns on the Sabbath. His family prudently removed his weapons.[60] It came as no surprise that he was not renominated for his Boston seat that year, yet his return to private life did not seem to depress him. Otis told Thomas Hutchinson that he rested "in the peace of God and the King, that he considered me as the Representative of the King, and the King, as the Representative of God."[61] By the following May, Otis's absence from the political scene had restored his health sufficiently for him to be again elected to the House. However, his "Conversion to Toryism" seemed to be complete. In the 1771 General Court he fought against Sam Adams's interpretation of the charter, declaring for the right of the governor to convene the Court wherever he willed.[62] While this turnabout might seem to be an abrupt departure from Otis's role as opposition leader it cannot be explained simply in either abstract political or psychological terms. After all, Otis, Jr., was now as much against Sam Adams as he was for Thomas Hutchinson, and it was no secret in Boston that he strongly opposed Sam Adams's tactics, his desire for conflict, and his political tastes.[63] Otis was also jealous of Adams's increasing popularity, and in turn both John and Sam

57. Thomas Hutchinson to Francis Bernard, Boston, Nov. 1769, *ibid.*, XXVI, 409.

58. 16 Jan. 1770, Butterfield, *et al.*, eds., *Diary of Adams*, I, 348.

59. James Otis, Jr., to Lord Hillsborough, 13 Jan. 1770, in Tudor, *Life of Otis*, 476.

60. Joseph Otis to [James Otis, Sr.], Barnstable, 19 Mar. 1770, Otis Family MSS, II, 142, Butler Lib., Columbia.

61. Thomas Hutchinson, "Annotated Almanac," 11 Aug. 1770, British Museum, as quoted in Shipton, *et al.*, *Sibley's Harvard Graduates*, XI, 281–282.

62. 2 and 6 June 1771, Butterfield, *et al.*, eds., *Diary of Adams*, II, 20, 26; Thomas Hutchinson to ?, Boston, 5 June 1771, Mass. Archives, XXVII, 180–181.

63. Francis Bernard to Hillsborough, 9 July 1768, Bernard Papers, VI, 295, Houghton Lib., Harvard.

Adams resented James's vanity, his wealth, and his family's quest for office and influence. As John Adams put the case, James had used politics to get his "Father chosen Speaker and Councillor," his "Brother in Law chosen into the House and Chosen Speaker of it," and a "Brother in Laws Brother in Law into the House and Council." Adams concluded by looking at his own virtue, noting that never "did I ever turn about in the House, betray my Friends and rant on the side of Prerogative, for an whole Year, to get a father into a Probate Office, and a first Justice of a Court of Common Pleas, and a Brother into a Clerks Office."[64] Moreover, Hutchinson was a consummate politician; unlike Bernard, he treated the House "with great Complaisance."[65] Hutchinson was willing to flatter Otis and expected much from his support.[66] It was not Otis's politics but his nerves that failed. His brother Samuel Allyne tried to take care of him but by December the family had decided upon his confinement.[67] But had not James Otis, Jr.'s political leadership in the whig cause come to an end even before then?

The advent of Thomas Hutchinson, who received his governor's commission in March of 1771, had presented the Otises with an ideal opportunity for an arrangement. What with Francis Bernard gone and the Townshend Duties repealed save for the tax on tea, the whigs had lost their source of unity. As Samuel Allyne Otis saw their weakness, "There is but little honor amongst them" and "even less dependence to be had one upon another." With unconscious irony Sam went on to report the extremely significant point that "Father has been to pay his compliments to his Excellency for which [I] am not sorry."[68] May elections saw the return of James, Jr., to the House and James, Sr., to the Council. Governor Hutch-

64. John Adams, 2 June 1771 and 27 Oct. 1772, Butterfield, *et al.*, eds., *Diary of Adams*, II, 20, 66.

65. Joseph Hawley to Mary Hawley, Cambridge, 3 Apr. 1770, Hawley Papers, N. Y. Pub. Lib.

66. Thomas Hutchinson to ?, Boston, 5 June 1771, Mass. Archives, XXVII, 178–179.

67. Samuel A. Otis to Joseph Otis, 16 Nov. 1771, Otis Papers, III, 34, Mass. Hist. Soc.

68. Samuel A. Otis to Joseph Otis, 16 Apr. 1771, *ibid.*, III, 21.

inson, reversing Bernard's policy, gave his approval to the elder
Otis's election and was prepared to walk an extra mile. Brother
Joseph obtained the rank of major in the Barnstable militia while
his father received the profitable guardianship of the Plymouth Indians.[69] And James Otis, Jr., in his more lucid moments attempted
to salvage his legal practice by serving on the side of the admiralty.[70] In short, as long as England refrained from any overt attempt
to change the status quo the Otises were willing to cooperate with
the administration. For the Otises this was the natural thing to do.
Samuel Allyne had gone no further than to sign the nonimportation agreement in 1768.[71] Joseph Otis followed his father's lead in
maintaining the family's interests in Barnstable, and the elder Otis
looked with obvious distaste on the Boston radicals. It is doubtful
that he ever considered the possibility of independence during this
crucial period. He certainly lost no time in 1771, when it seemed
as if the whig party was at its nadir, in paying court to Governor
Thomas Hutchinson. In the midst of the Revolutionary crisis the
old man remained a petty provincial horsetrader. Only James Otis,
Jr., saw above the trifling considerations of his time. It was his
theoretical opposition to imperial taxation combined with his family's influence that raised the Otises to the brief prominence they
commanded in the 1760's. But James Otis envisioned the anarchy
of separation that independence might produce and refused to proceed, leaving to the Adamses both leadership and prominence.

The mental breakdown of James Otis, Jr., presents a more difficult problem in evaluation than do his or his family's political
changes. His father summed up most of the manifestations in a let-

69. For the election of Col. Otis to the guardianship of the Black Ground In-
dians of Plymouth and Sandwich, see 2 June 1772, Minutes, Mass. Archives,
XXXIII, 561. The confirmation by Hutchinson is in Suffolk Court Files, 1280: 84
(No. 173509), Suffolk County Court House.

70. James Otis, Jr., to Ruth Otis, 22 Mar. 1773, Otis Papers, III, 46, Mass. Hist.
Soc., for the attempt to regain a practice. For the admiralty case see Samuel
Adams to Arthur Lee, Boston, 22 Apr. 1773, Alonzo Cushing, ed., The Writings
of Samuel Adams, III (New York, 1907), 37.

71. See 1 Mar. 1768 nonimportation agreement in S. P. Savage Papers, Mass.
Hist. Soc.

ter he wrote to James in August of 1772. He was hurt that James did not write and was especially annoyed at the abuse which James had hurled at him and the family. James's distractions, his depressions, and now his giving up his legal practice were observed facts. James, Sr., warned, "If you Continue to go on this way your family will be Ruined and you will Destroy yourself Both Soul and Body." He was forced to ask himself if his son deliberately sought to bring an aged parent to the grave. The old man declared that he had done everything to educate his "first born." He had spared nothing in anticipation of the "fine prospect" his son would have to be "useful to himself and family and the world." All these hopes were now "blasted." Junior's unruly passions, his constant blasphemies, his giving in to the "Temptations of the Evil on[e]," his lack of belief—all were bringing him to the edge of the pit. The only salvation was for James to "Sett up the Worship of God in your family" and pray. These were the thoughts of an "afflicted father."[72] The elder Otis thus blamed his son's yielding to the devil for his mental instability. The whigs in turn were only too delighted to charge it to the tories because of Robinson's attempted "Assassination" of the patriot.[73] Lastly, the tories saw in James's madness a prophetic answering of his alleged cry that he would set the province in flames though he perished in the attempt.[74] Today we know that the Otises were given to melancholia and that the family history was marked by mental instability. The crisis of loyalty was too much for James Otis, Jr.'s disposition. Tension also broke the mind of James's cousin Ignatius.[75] James Otis, Jr., could not serve equally George III, Massachusetts liberty, and his family.

72. James Otis, Sr., to James Otis, Jr., Barnstable, 1 Aug. 1772 (draft copy), Gay-Otis Papers, Butler Lib., Columbia.

73. Shipton, *et al.*, *Sibley's Harvard Graduates*, XI, 279–280.

74. Oliver, *Origin and Progress*, eds. Adair and Schutz, 163.

75. For Ignatius Otis see Horatio N. Otis, "Genealogical and Historical Memoir of the Otis Family," *New England Hist. and Gen. Register*, II (1848), 292. The Plymouth Probate Records, Plymouth, Mass., list at least five members of the Otis family in the 19th century who were so unbalanced that their property had to be placed in custody: Abijah, spendthrift—1818; Ensign, spendthrift—1822; Job, insane—1825; Amy, insane—1846; and another Amy, insane—1869.

For a brief twilight period it seemed as if Thomas Hutchinson would restore the old political order within the province.[76] He succeeded only so long as England did not press the imperial issue, but the British ministry had decided to pay Hutchinson's salary as a servant of the king. In July of 1772 the Court protested against this "dangerous innovation." That October alarm spread throughout the province when it was known that the justices of the Superior Court were to be paid by the royal warrant on the customs.[77] Sam Adams vigorously protested against these changes in the constitution, as did James Otis, Jr.[78] However, it took a combination of parliamentary largesse and the stupidity of the East India Company to bring this situation to a boil in Boston Harbor. In 1773, Parliament, in an attempt to save the company from bankruptcy, reduced the tea tax to a point where legal tea would undersell the smuggled Bohea. The East India Company, so as to maximize its profits, consigned its tea to a select group of friends, thereby excluding the majority of the colonial merchants. In Boston the consignees included, as could be anticipated, two sons and a nephew of Governor Thomas Hutchinson, who owned stock in the company. This move alienated the one sector of Massachusetts society which realized the value of the imperial connection, and excluded merchants joined hands with radicals to oppose the monopoly.[79] That November, Boston united in unanimous opposition to this measure of a foreign Parliament. The General Assembly now considered itself independent from the British legislature, declaring that when the people of America had settled the province "it was not and never had been the sense of the Kingdom that they were to remain subject to the supreme Authority of Parliament."[80]The arrival of

76. James Warren to Joseph Otis, Plymouth, 18 Apr. 1771, Otis Papers, III, 22, Mass. Hist. Soc.; Andrew Oliver to Henry Bromfield, 20 Apr. 1771, Oliver Letter Books, II, 9–10, Mass. Hist. Soc.; see also Catherine Barton Mayo, ed., *Additions to Thomas Hutchinson's "History of Massachusetts Bay"* (American Antiquarian Society, *Proceedings*, LIX [1949]), 38.

77. Hutchinson, *Hist. Mass.*, ed. Mayo, III, 259–262.

78. John Adams, 27 Oct. 1773, Butterfield, *et al.*, eds., *Diary of Adams*, II, 64–65.

79. Arthur M. Schlesinger, *The Colonial Merchants and the American Revolution: 1763–1776* (New York, 1957), 280.

80. The Massachusetts Assembly reply to Thomas Hutchinson, 1773, Additional MSS, 38342: 32–33, British Museum.

the East India tea, symbolizing subjection, resulted in the Boston Tea Party. The "Promised Land" now purged itself of the luxuries of tribute. The news of this resistance to the tea and parliamentary authority brought forth from Britain the cry, *"Delenda est Bostoniensis."* The arrival of the new governor in May of 1774 signified the end of the old charter government. General Thomas Gage had been vested by the crown with a plenitude of power over his province, which made all local officials subject to his dismissal. The popular town meetings were to be gagged, and an appointed Council was to reign. In Massachusetts this was the "Intolerable Act" which precluded any compromise.[81]

81. Lawrence H. Gipson, *The Coming of the Revolution, 1763–1775* (New York, 1954), 224.

## ✖ IX.

# INDEPENDENCE

The Barnstable town scribe wrote of 1774 as a "time of Difficulty, Darkness and Distress." For the Otises this crisis year ushered in a period of confusion. Prophetically, almost a decade earlier James Otis, Jr., had been one of the first to recognize the grounds for separation from England, but he had fled from his own reasoning. Recognizing that Massachusetts faced civil conflagration, he was passive while the elder Otis, in poor health for the past two years, had simply refused to consider the possibility of an armed conflict with Britain. In fact, he had invested the better part of his liquid capital in Massachusetts provincial bonds which could not help depreciating rapidly if the imperial link were severed.[1] Otis, Sr.'s dominant place in his local court system and his Council seat, summing up a lifetime's activity, would not be cast off at the first ill wind. General Thomas Gage, the new British governor, recognized Otis's special position in Barnstable and allowed him to retain his old Council seat in 1774, although Gage felt compelled to negate

1. Barnstable Town Records, III, 60; Harrison Gray, Treasurer, "Province of the Massachusetts," 2 Apr. 1771, for £1,000 in silver ($3,300) on two notes, in Boston Athenaeum. These notes were still outstanding in 1777, see *Mass. Acts and Resolves*, XIX, 519.

thirteen whig radicals.[2] The alteration of the charter called for an appointed Council, removing one of the props which held the elder Otis's loyalty to the crown. Son Joseph, now fully in charge of the Barnstable business operations, had taken time out from profit-making in 1773 to place in front of his store a large sign bearing the single word "Liberty."[3] He would follow whatever path the family took. Samuel Allyne Otis, aware of the financial and trading opportunities afforded by the British connection, thought the Boston politicians that summer were "driving matters to extremity" and would find it very difficult to restrain the people.[4] Above all, the family counseled moderation.

For more than forty years James Otis, Sr., had dominated the local scene in Barnstable County. He had come to know the lawyers, doctors, ministers, whalers, and prosperous farmers of the Cape personally and continued to meet most of them in their capacities as justices of the peace, militia officers, and representatives. His power, while it legally rested upon the various royal commissions that at one time or another designated him colonel, judge of probate, chief justice of Common Pleas, and councilor, was in a more fundamental sense derived from the acquiescence of his fellow citizens. Barnstable was the elder Otis's bailiwick, and he was its leading man. He intended to avoid any hasty action which might jeopardize his legal position or the town's safety.

The elder Otis was unnerved that September 27 when an armed mass of his neighbors gathered to prevent his convening the Inferior Court. He declared that his was a "legal and constitutional court," that the proof was plain to see, for the court "had suffered no mutations," and that "the juries have been drawn from the boxes as the law directs." He asked why its proceedings should be interrupted. The old patriarch, perhaps sensing that the people were not

2. Gage to Dartmouth, Boston, 31 May 1774, Albert Matthews, ed., "Documents Relating to the Last Meetings of the Massachusetts Royal Council, 1774–1776," Col. Soc. of Mass., *Pubs.*, XXXII (1933–1937), 467.

3. Peter Oliver to ?, Mashpee [Barnstable], 23 May 1773, Otis Family MSS, II, 149, Butler Lib., Columbia.

4. Samuel A. Otis to [Joseph Otis], [summer, 1774], *ibid.*, IV, 325.

interested in his legalistic argument, concluded with the prudential, "Why do you make a leap before you get to the hedge?" The
people's reply was that any appeal from the local court must be
heard by the prerogative justices of the Superior Court, who now
held office at the king's pleasure and would favor the unconstitutional Intolerable Acts. They echoed James Otis, Jr.'s arguments
against the writs of assistance and prerogative measures in general.
In effect, this gathering affirmed the sanctity of the old charter government. Otis then ordered them "in his majesty's name," as was his
duty, "to disperse and give the court the opportunity to perform
the business of the county." The people not only refused to move,
but also insisted upon exacting a promise that Otis, Sr., as a member
of the legal Council, would defend the old charter.[5] Although some
commentators have interpreted such actions as mob rule, these
September protesters knew exactly what they wanted: a clearcut
rejection of the jurisdiction of the prerogative justices in particular
and of the new royal government in general.

James Otis, Sr., understood the sentiments of his neighbors and
sympathized with their claim that the new Massachusetts Government Act, with its mandamus Council, represented a violation of
the legal rights of the province. Joseph Warren epitomized this
popular opinion when he wrote that the people "do not swerve
from their allegiance by opposing any measures taken by any man
or set of men to deprive them of their liberties. They conceive that
they are the King's enemies who would destroy the Constitution;
for the King is annihilated when the Constitution is destroyed."[6]
The elder Otis was and continued to be a "constitutional member
of his majesty's council . . . by the royal charter" and saw no inconsistency in forming the Massachusetts Provincial Congress.[7] In

5. Trayser, ed., *Barnstable*, 122–123; Francis T. Bowles, "The Loyalty of Barnstable in the Revolution," Col. Soc. of Mass., *Pubs.*, XXV (1922–1924), 336–337.
6. Joseph Warren to Arthur Lee, Boston, 20 Feb. 1775, Samuel E. Morison, ed.,
*Sources and Documents Illustrating the American Revolution . . .* (New York,
1929), 140.
7. *The Journals of Each Provincial Congress of Massachusetts in 1774 and
1775 . . .* (Boston, 1838), 37–40.

January 1775, Otis pushed the Barnstable town meeting to stop paying its taxes to the royal government of Thomas Gage, although he could not persuade his fellow citizens to agree to purchase small arms or to subscribe to a nonimportation agreement against Britain.[8] The old colonel did however secure donations for the relief of the Boston port from his Indian clients.[9] The family prudence ended only with the clash of arms and the bloodshed of April 19, 1775. Joseph Otis was now called upon to play his first major role, opening it with the command to the militia, "Forward—Lexington eighty miles away." The troops, including James Otis, Jr., who acted his last part in a revolution he had done so much to start, marched to Marshfield before receiving word to turn back.[10] James Otis, Sr., recognized by local towns as the Cape's leader, gave his declining energies to the establishment of a wartime government for Massachusetts.[11] The election of Joseph Otis as Barnstable's new representative ratified the family's control of its county.[12]

Old Otis's service within the provincial government in effect equaled the enrollment of Barnstable in favor of the war. He understood that Barnstable town did not favor change, and he realized also that his primary mission on the local scene was to encourage the lukewarm to join the patriot cause, while neutralizing hostile tory elements. He showed his desire to defend law and order in May of 1776 when he protested the tarring and feathering of the widow Abigail Freeman by young rebels who had attacked her because of her shrewish tory comments. Many of Otis's patriot friends disapproved of his defense of the old tory widow although it probably

8. Barnstable Town Records, III, 61–62.

9. John Soley to James Otis, Sr., Boston, 25 Jan. 1775, Mass. Hist. Soc., *Colls.*, 4th Ser., III (1858), 215.

10. Trayser, ed., *Barnstable*, 448; "List of Men . . . ," 22 Apr. 1775, Otis Papers, III, 49, Mass. Hist. Soc.; Hinckley Papers, Misc. 32, New England Historic Genealogical Society, Boston.

11. Gideon Bates to James Otis, Sr., and Amos Knowles, Watertown, Eastham, 7 Aug. 1775, Otis Family MSS, III, 170, Butler Lib., Columbia; James Otis, Sr., Council Order, Watertown, 13 Oct. 1775, Sparks MSS, 49.2(71), Houghton Lib., Harvard; Commission of Captain Leighton, Watertown, 29 Apr. 1776, "December Meeting, 1883," Mass. Hist. Soc., *Procs.*, 1st Ser., XX (1882, 1883), 401.

12. Barnstable Town Records, III, 64.

helped him to maintain his leadership in a divided community.[13] Otis knew that Barnstable had a large loyalist faction and an even larger number of voters who would not leap until they reached the hedge. At the town meeting called to instruct for American independence, thirty voters were for it, thirty-five against it, while sixty-five electors chose not to cast a ballot, a negative vote which showed the fence-sitters to be clearly in the majority. A little more than a quarter of the electorate gave Barnstable the dubious distinction of being the only town in Massachusetts known to have voted against immediate independence in 1776.[14] The leader of this opposition group was Edward Bacon, Otis's old opponent and kinsman. He led the small merchants and farmers and played upon their fears of retaliatory action from the English fleet, stressing their dependence upon the sea and Britain's control of it. James Otis, Sr., tolerated these pacifist and loyalist elements as long as they posed no real threat to his control. The Otises' independence party included the major landowners, traders, and merchants, the law enforcement officers, the local clergy, and those who commanded the militia. The elder Otis by a combination of political skill and police power kept his town favorable to the patriot cause until shortly before his death in 1778.

Joseph Otis, by utilizing his family's widespread commercial contacts, enlisted a host of extralegal resources that he combined with the Barnstable independence party to effect almost total mobilization for the war effort. Samuel Allyne Otis in the course of his work for the war department called upon Joseph for needed requisitions while reciprocally supplying hard-to-get commodities such as salt.[15] A cousin, Jonathan Otis of Newport, naturally turned to the Otis stores in February of 1775 when he needed uniforms for

13. Trayser, ed., *Barnstable*, 124.
14. Joseph Otis to Mr. Edes, Barnstable, 18 July 1776, in Bowles, "Loyalty of Barnstable," Col. Soc. of Mass., *Pubs.*, XXV (1922–1924), 291.
15. Receipts, 7 Apr. and 5 May 1777, Otis Family MSS, 205, Butler Lib., Columbia; Samuel A. Otis to Joseph Otis, Boston, 8 June 1778, in Samuel E. Morison, *The Life and Letters of Harrison Gray Otis, Federalist, 1765–1848* (Boston, 1913), I, 22.

eighty soldiers.[16] In addition, friends throughout the Cape sought guidance and supplied valuable information. Even before Joseph's appointment as muster master for Barnstable in December of 1776, his Wellfleet correspondent Elisha Cobb considered him the proper authority to deal with the disaffected. The immediate case involved two runaways, an apprentice and a Negro man who had supplied "fresh Provisions and refreshments" to an English ship lying offshore. The Negro was sent back to his master and the patriots took care to keep the incident out of the "Publick Papers." The talk of liberty had permeated the consciousness of at least one Negro, part of a minority that formed the bottom 2 per cent of the county's population of thirteen thousand people. Cobb saw a pressing need to watch the discontented so that "they may not be able to feed our Enemies or to take revenge by coming here with an armed Force."[17] In fact, throughout the Revolutionary War the independence party by its control of most of the communication channels suppressed news unfavorable to the cause. Joseph Otis held the reins as his county's leading merchant, its muster master and brigadier general of militia, and representative to the General Court. In 1776 Joseph added the collectorship of the newly created Barnstable customs district to his portfolio. He finally completed his list of offices the following year when he became clerk of the Inferior Court. The fusion of commercial, commissary, military, fiscal, and political functions in one person was a source of immediate strength to the patriot cause. It insured control of Barnstable and meant that its silver and gold, matériel, and men were at the disposal of the "United States of America."[18]

16. Jonathan Otis to Joseph Otis, Newport, 8 Feb. 1775, Gay-Otis Papers, Butler Lib., Columbia.

17. Elisha Cobb to Joseph Otis, Wellfleet, 7 Sept. 1775, Otis Family MSS, III, 173, *ibid.*; for population figures see Evarts B. Greene and Virginia D. Harrington, *American Population before the Federal Census of 1790* (New York, 1932), 21, 29–30, and "1777 Census" for Barnstable Town, Hinckley Papers, New Eng. Hist. Gen. Soc.

18. For muster master see *Mass. Acts and Resolves*, XIX, 736 (28 Dec. 1776); the customs, Trayser, ed., *Barnstable*, 336; and clerkship, Barnstable 1777, in Records of the Superior Court of Judicature [XVI], Suffolk County Court House; *Mass. Acts and Resolves*, XIX, 265–266.

From December 1776, when the British fleet captured Newport, Rhode Island, thereby gaining control of its deep, defensible harbor and command of Long Island Sound, until October of 1779 when Sir Henry Clinton evacuated the port in order to concentrate his military forces in the South, the defense of Rhode Island consumed most of Barnstable's wartime energies.[19] For the first year of the British occupation the towns of Harwich, Yarmouth, Eastham, and Chatham enthusiastically met their quotas for the defense of American soil, even though a fifth of the militia was away whaling and fishing.[20] There was little difficulty in supplying the troops out of commercial stores and home resources, while the acceptance of the relatively stable paper money did not put any noticeable strains on the local economy. However, when the British navy consolidated its control of Narragansett Bay in the spring of 1778, thereby stopping all shipping from Chatham to Bedford, the patriots' position changed radically.[21] The blockade cut off the importation of vital matériel, which could no longer be obtained from heavily depleted local resources. Moreover, Joseph Otis, convinced that Barnstable had given more than its just proportion of men for the land and sea forces, sympathized with his neighbors in their reluctance to serve away from home in the face of the British fleet offshore.[22] The town of Falmouth, which was more "Exposed than any Part of the Cape" to British attack, absolutely refused to comply with its spring quota, declaring that the "Town is imposed upon." Its officers said "they shall Do Nothing About the Mater" even if "they Must Abide by the consequences."[23] Joseph Otis did what he could, but

19. James Warren to Joseph Otis, Plymouth, 8 Dec. 1776, Misc. Bound MSS, XV, Mass. Hist. Soc.; Jeremiah Powell to Joseph Otis, Boston, 23 Dec. 1777, Otis Family MSS, III, 209, Butler Lib., Columbia; John Avery to Joseph Otis, Boston, 3 Apr. 1779, and Sam Adams to Joseph Otis, Boston, 9 July 1779, Misc. MSS, Box 8, Mass. Hist. Soc.

20. Gamaliel Cahoon to [Joseph Otis], Harwich, 14 Dec. 1776, Otis Family MSS, III, 199, Butler Lib., Columbia; Enoch Hallet to [Joseph Otis], Yarmouth, 16 Dec. 1776, ibid., 200; Edward Knowles to Joseph Otis, Eastham, 16 Dec. 1776, ibid., 201; Joseph Doane to James Rider to [Joseph Otis], Chatham, 26 Dec. 1776, and see also Doane's letter of 9 Aug. 1776, ibid., 203, 182.

21. Joseph Otis to Dept. of War, Barnstable, 4 May 1778, ibid., III, 221.

22. Joseph Otis to the Council, Barnstable, 29 May 1778, ibid., III, 228.

23. Joseph Dimmick to Joseph Otis, Falmouth, 11 June 1778, ibid., III, 235.

when he raised troops he lacked the means to supply them. The Boston authorities, who knew how tight his supplies were by the end of 1778, could only suggest that if he had "not bread for the Prisoners [of War] let them live without, as many better men have done before them."[24] Total war had come to Barnstable.

At the end of 1778 Joseph Otis saw the war machine he had so artfully constructed and so painfully sustained verging toward collapse. He feared the "Seditious Party" within Barnstable and resolved to sacrifice his "Life or Interest" to serve his country.[25] Had he not recruited the soldiers, supplied them out of his store while he could, and finally equipped them by requisitions of shoes, stockings, and blankets taken from the very bodies and beds of the townsmen![26] Otis considered the prosecution of the war the greatest event in his life. However, many of his fellow citizens could not help thinking that his activities were responsible for bringing them to ruin. Some now prayed that the "kings troops might prevail that we might live in quietness and peace as we used to under the kings laws." Those with eyes could see that the "people here was tearing one another to peaces." Only the authority of the monarch could terminate Barnstable's internecine strife. A party of opposition had reformed within the town, encouraged no doubt by British control of Narragansett Bay. At first composed of small merchants, farmers, and political failures, all of whom lacked power, it was now joined by the lower class. These radicals parroted loyalty to George III at the same time that they contemplated the elimination of Barnstable's old elite. As one of these levelers put it: "If Colonel otis Brigadier Otis and Davis was took up and carried off they could do well Enough in Barnstable."[27] Edward Bacon, ceaseless in his enmity, rallied the discontented and the war-weary around his banner. When the price of molasses hit $30 a cask he told one farmer to be "thankfull we was not obliged to Carry our money about in Corn

24. Jeremiah Powell to Joseph Otis, Boston, 6 Nov. 1778, *ibid.*, III, 245.
25. Joseph Otis to the Council, Barnstable, 1 Dec. 1778, *ibid.*, III, 246.
26. *Mass. Acts and Resolves*, XIX, 769, 807.
27. Deposition of Edward Davis, 28 May 1779, Bowles, "Loyalty of Barnstable," Col. Soc. of Mass., *Pubs.*, XXV (1922–1924), 325.

Baskets"; another reported that Bacon said it made no difference whether the continental currency was "Counterfeit or not," thereby implying its worthlessness.[28] Joseph Otis was constitutionally unable to see the validity of such complaining in a time of crisis. He did not comprehend that a war leader must carry the burdens of defeat if he were also to claim the glory of victory.

In part it was the general resentment against the hardness of war, the continual shortages of necessities, and high taxes combined with inflation that persuaded the Barnstable electorate to choose Edward Bacon as its representative in May 1778. However, Bacon's reelection when he vacated his first term in March of 1779, and his success in gaining a second term in May of 1779 also revealed Joseph Otis's failure as a politician.[29] Joseph Otis was insensitive in his dealings with his fellow citizens. He accused other merchants of not accepting the almost worthless paper money while his own insolvency forced him to make contracts in terms of milled silver dollars.[30] Furthermore he sought the state's intervention to exclude Edward Bacon from the legislature. Although Otis stated that his motivation in this matter was of highest principle as Bacon was both "an Abetter of Bernard and Hutchinsons wicked Measures, . . . and a professed Enemy to the Independency of America," the town remembered the Otis family's conflict with Bacon stretching back more than twenty years. The town meeting declared that Joseph Otis's wish to unseat Bacon was due to "an old family quarrel and was the effect of envy rather than matters of truth."[31] Whatever Barnstable might believe, Otis convinced the Assembly that Representative Bacon *"hath been inimical to the revolution of the government and independency of this State, and of the other United States of America."* On June 3, 1779, the House by a vote of ninety-

28. Deposition of Prince Bearse, 6 Jan. 1779, and Rowland Hallett, 6 Jan. 1779, *ibid.,* 305–306.

29. *Ibid.,* 271–274.

30. Samuel A. Otis to Joseph Otis, Boston, 15 July 1779, and Joseph Otis to [Will Crocker], Barnstable, 8 Aug. 1780, Gay-Otis Papers, Butler Lib., Columbia.

31. Petition of Joseph Otis and Others, 22 May 1778, Bowles, "Loyalty of Barnstable," Col. Soc. of Mass., *Pubs.,* XXV (1922–1924), 294; Barnstable Town Records, transcript, *ibid.,* 300 (16 Dec. 1778).

five to five excluded Edward Bacon from his seat.[32] The state government, with Narragansett Bay still under British control, realized that Brigadier Joseph Otis must be sustained in his actions. However, Barnstable, smarting under Otis's dictatorial ways, charged him with destroying "the invaluable right of free election and representation."[33] Joseph Otis had deeply offended the sentiments of a community that had always prized its representative government.

If Joseph Otis had reflected upon his predicament in 1783 he might have realized that the needs of the war itself, rather than any intended principle of revolution or government, had turned Barnstable topsy-turvy. In 1778, acting on his belief that his town would not elect a representative who was "soft" on independence, he petitioned the central government to exclude Edward Bacon "from the publick Councils for ever." Otis claimed that Bacon was in reality a minority candidate who had a majority ballot from a small town meeting; he certainly did not represent a majority of the Barnstable electorate.[34] However, Bacon's two subsequent elections gave the lie to this claim. Yet Joseph Otis felt compelled to have Bacon ejected from the Assembly and in so doing utterly failed to convince the voters of the justice of his position. Barnstable reacted by charging him with violating the right of free election and named Bacon its delegate to the 1780 Massachusetts Constitutional Convention.[35] Nor did Joseph Otis gain popularity when as the collector of customs he searched for smuggled and contraband goods in the county.[36] He was also involved in raising the £89,000 tax assessment in 1780 (worth about $1,600 in Spanish silver).[37] Moreover, Joseph Otis was connected in the popular mind with other repressive measures that violated the fundamental norms of his community. Men who pleaded that conscience forbade them to

32. *Ibid.*, 277.
33. Barnstable Town Records, III, 110 (6 July 1779).
34. Bowles, "Loyalty of Barnstable," Col. Soc. of Mass., *Pubs.*, XXV (1922–1924), 293–294.
35. *Ibid.*, 282.
36. Joseph Otis to Capt. ?, 22 Oct. 1779, Otis Family MSS, IV, 270, Butler Lib., Columbia.
37. Assessors of Barnstable to Joseph Otis, 15 Nov. 1780, Gay-Otis Papers, *ibid.*

fight against the king were threatened with the "taking away [of] their Entrest because they would not go into the servis."[38] And the enforcement of the 1779 "Act for and Confiscating the Estates of Certain Persons Commonly Called Absentees," which proclaimed that any man who refused to serve the state justly forfeited "all his property, right and liberties, holden under and derived from the constitution of government," did violence to the belief in the natural law right to property.[39] This 1779 law, the most radical statute of the entire Revolutionary era, repudiated the intellectual foundations of James Otis, Jr.'s argument against British tyranny. By the end of the war Joseph Otis had been forced to support a series of measures that paralleled the stated causes of the Revolution against Great Britain: outside intervention in elections, curtailment of smuggling, onerous taxes, coercion of conscience, and a prerogative-like confiscation of property. Joseph Otis's services to the Revolutionary cause and the Boston authorities had eroded his political position in Barnstable. In the future he would be dependent upon the state government for his posts of profit.

The key to understanding Barnstable's conduct during the Revolutionary era is to be found in the town's concept of itself as a little country, a *patria chica* in the Latin American sense of the term. It had its own mores in its own understanding of an absolute natural law which bound it as surely as did the sea, the eternal low hills, and its salt marshes. Barnstable neither expected nor wanted the break with Britain, and from the very beginning of the armed struggle in 1776 town voters had resented the outside influences that the Revolution brought into play. They considered themselves competent to judge their own and protested the early extralegal activities of the Revolutionary party which had spirited away its opponents

---

38. Bowles, "Loyalty of Barnstable," Col. Soc. of Mass., *Pubs.*, XXV (1922–1924), 325.

39. *Mass. Acts and Resolves*, V, 968, following Richard D. Brown, "The Confiscation and Disposition of Loyalists' Estates in Suffolk County, Massachusetts," *Wm. and Mary Qtly.*, 3d Ser., XXI (1964), 539. For Barnstable see the proceedings of the Court of Common Pleas against Seth and Thomas Perry, Apr. 1782, Otis Family MSS, IV, 276, Butler Lib., Columbia.

for trial outside of Barnstable.[40] As the war progressed they found themselves less and less the masters of their own fate. And the symbol of this outside mastery was Joseph Otis who took his orders from Boston. He signed the passes for ships leaving the harbor, conscripted their men and grain, collected their taxes, and also supplied the trickle of scarce goods, such as tea at $12 a pound, that entered the community.[41] Moreover, the consensus of the town held him guilty of a "wrong and Perjurious Representation" against its legal but helpless representative, Edward Bacon. As expected, the town's voters opposed the Articles of Confederation because they considered them a surrender of power to the central government. They did not believe that any outside agency should have the right to make peace and war or to issue money.[42] Yet Barnstable did carry a heavy burden and even when hard pressed it still made special provision for its troops at Providence and Peekskill as well as for their families at home.[43] Barnstable gave its men and wealth to the war effort, but it conceived of its duties in a parochial rather than in a state or national way.

The Reverend Oakes Shaw, the pastor of Barnstable's West Parish, sensed the intrusion of the Revolution and its concomitant ideologies into the world he had known. While one could read into his surviving 1779 sermon a political identification—after all, II Samuel, dealing as the pastor put it with Absalom's "unnatural rebellion" against David, his father and king, was not exactly a revolutionary text, that would miss the point of a sermon which argued for the overruling hand of God and His "righteous displeasure and . . . Chastisement" against all sinners.[44] And in his 1782 fast day sermon Shaw stated that the "great revolution" must be viewed as a moral failure, since it had not brought about a general reformation. Rather the land had come under a "flood of vice and Iniquity." Un-

40. Barnstable Town Records, III, 68 (5 Mar. 1776).

41. Joseph Otis to Mrs. Oakes Shaw, Lemuel Shaw Papers, Mass. Hist. Soc.; Barnstable Town Records, III, 65, 254.

42. Barnstable Town Records, III, 84 (23 Feb. 1778).

43. *Ibid.*, 95, 104.

44. Oakes Shaw's 16 May 1779 sermon, Lemuel Shaw Papers, Mass. Hist. Soc.

less the faithful reformed they would be visited with more misery and chastisement. The pastor declared that now was the proper time "to lay aside the distinction of Whig and Torey and all to be united" for the commonwealth; society must restore its old morality; "family Government and family prayer [must] be maintained and observed"; only then could sinful man expect the "Smiles of heaven."[45] Undoubtedly Oakes Shaw correctly realized that the Revolution had undermined Barnstable's moral and political cohesiveness, and while his idiom sounds archaic to our ears his thoughts more aptly expressed the values of his people than did Joseph Otis's advocacy of the national state.

When Barnstable's electorate voted for a heavily amended state constitution in 1780 it showed its desire for a legal frame of government that hopefully would end the indecision, anarchy, and arbitrariness of the various Revolutionary tribunals. This certainly did not mean a wholehearted support of the new state or of Revolutionary principles. In fact, the establishment of a legal government proffered the perfect opportunity to protest more military bounties and additional high taxes.[46] By December of 1782 the town had reached the end of its patience and, by its own reading, its resources. It now took the unprecedented step of ordering its assessors to make only the town rate, declaring that it would consider itself liable for "all Damage that the said assessors shall Receive in Consequence of not making said [state] Taxes."[47] Joseph Otis and the Revolutionary party, who already stood accused of reviling "others to keep themselves and their Connections in office," should have realized that this was an inappropriate time to wave the bloody shirt.[48] Nor could Joseph Otis have had any doubts about his general popularity when he received a total of four votes from Barnstable in the April 1783 senatorial elections.[49] However, the Revolutionary party felt impelled to fight any implementation of

45. Oakes Shaw's 25 Apr. 1782 Fast Day Sermon, *ibid.*
46. Barnstable Town Records, III, 134.
47. *Ibid.*, 148.
48. *Ibid.*, 119 (29 Mar. 1780).
49. *Ibid.*, 179.

the fifth and sixth articles of the 1783 Treaty of Paris which would have enabled loyalists to recover certain debts and properties. It warned that "every Effort of the Enemies of your Country will be exerted, by their friends, who are among us, and who lie in wait and are watching to deceive" and betray the cause.[50] The patriot party counted Captain Sam Hinckley on its side and probably hoped to defeat Shearjashub Bourn, the other incumbent in the 1784 elections. However, Bourn retained his seat and was joined by a moderate, Nymphas Marston.[51] In short, Barnstable intended to follow pastor Oakes Shaw's admonition and forget the "distinction of Whig and Torey." And while the town now voted for a governor as well as for local representatives and senators, at no time during this period did the gubernatorial vote surpass the totals for the representatives and senators. The most active contests involved local and regional candidates, for the community still believed that political life should follow parochial norms.[52] Moreover, when in 1786 it instructed its representatives "not to vote in General Court for Emiting Paper money and making the same a Lawfull Tender and likewise not to vote to make lands Personal Estate etc. a Lawfull Tender," it affirmed its ancient adherence to fundamentalist fiscal concepts.[53] Strictly speaking, Barnstable's actions during this era were not counterrevolutionary but rather restorationist in intent. It had followed the Otises in protesting British innovations of the past and now it just as consistently rejected the *novus ordo saeculorum*. Samuel Allyne Otis, viewing the turmoil within the state, saw this consistent pattern when he wrote that to suppose that the people of Massachusetts, after opposing the "infringement of their liberty and property from abroad, will suffer them to be overturned by licentious abandoned people at home, is to suppose like causes produce directly contrary effect."[54]

50. Mutilated manuscript [1784], Lemuel Shaw Papers, Mass. Hist. Soc.
51. Barnstable Town Records, III, 185.
52. *Ibid.*, 137–267 (1781 to 1789).
53. *Ibid.*, 197.
54. Samuel A. Otis to Theodore Sedgwick, Boston, 30 July 1782, Theodore Sedgwick Papers, Mass. Hist. Soc.

The real irony in the Otises' loss of leadership and deference was that, by and large, the three brothers sympathized with Barnstable's traditional polity. While James Otis, Jr.'s breakdown precluded his taking a part in the conflict, he did not approve of the new men who emerged as leaders of the commonwealth. He vented his feelings of disgust in his observation that when the "pot boils the scum arises." His death in May of 1783, which came as he had hoped it would by a bolt of lightning, removed from the scene Barnstable's greatest defender of fundamental law.[55] Joseph Otis, now fiscally and politically impoverished by the independence movement, had tried to preserve the status quo as he understood it. Events had been beyond the control of both brothers. And finally there was Samuel Otis, whose class-based conservatism mirrored Barnstable's own values. However, he had chosen to act upon another stage.

Samuel Allyne Otis's earliest revolutionary sentiments, recorded in 1776, called for the establishment of an "American Bank" of England. He was even willing to turn in his silver shoe buckles to augment its supply of "hard money."[56] This became the *idée fixe* of his career. In the first years of the war he found the Congress weak and ineffectual. It would not support its own agents and did not understand finances; however, he was convinced that if a "greater part of the Honorable Body were Merchants, or at least . . . had Studied the Theory of Commerce," proper remedies would be found for the nation's problems.[57] Yet while critical of quotidian events he became one of the most effective "Collectors of Clothing for the Continental Army," for which he supplied eighteen thousand uniforms.[58] He also organized an exchange system which traded hides for shoes, gave advice to the army on how to issue and even guard

55. John Eliot to Jeremy Belknap, Boston, 12 Jan. 1777, *Belknap Papers*, III (Mass. Hist. Soc., *Colls.*, 6th Ser., IV [1891]), 104; *Boston Gazette*, 26 May 1783.

56. Samuel A. Otis to Robert Treat Paine, 28 Oct. 1776, R. T. Paine Papers, Mass. Hist. Soc.

57. Samuel A. Otis to Elbridge Gerry, Boston, 8 Apr. 1780, Gerry-Knight Papers, *ibid.*

58. See Morison, *Life of H. G. Otis*, I, 20–23; Samuel A. Otis to Sam Savage, 11 July 1777 (?), S. P. Savage Papers, Mass. Hist. Soc.; Samuel A. Otis to Elbridge Gerry, Boston, 22 Feb. 1778, Gerry-Knight Papers, *ibid.*

its military stores, and supplied the French fleet at a profit.[59] Nor had Sam neglected his political career. He served as a Boston representative, a faithful committee member, and following family tradition, became speaker of the House. But wartime politics distressed him as did the seven years of fighting and the derangement of commerce.[60] Like his brother James he could not stomach the new class of men who pressured for bills "cancelling debts and sacred contracts, or paying them off in pine boards."[61] By July of 1782 he told his confidant and fellow contractor Theodore Sedgwick that he was "almost sick of breathing the contaminated air of the House." However, Sam concluded with a prudent reminder to "Burn my communications."[62] He was realist enough to comprehend that "all revolutions are founded in blood."[63] Otis was frightened by the change, the uncertainty of politics, the passing of old values.

It was clear to Samuel Allyne Otis that his own business ventures as well as the family properties had been adversely affected by the long war, the inflation of the late 1770's, and then the recession. The Otises' large speculative holdings of rural lands, which had seemed so promising in the 1760's, were now nothing but tax quagmires.[64] Truthfully Sam wrote in 1782 that the "want of money plagues all the world."[65] However, his shortage of capital did not stop him from making large imports from his British factors with the coming of peace, and it was his own extension of credit to shaky outport merchants such as his brother that later brought about his ruin.[66]

59. Samuel A. Otis to Gen. William Heath, 27 Feb. 1778, 7 May 1779, Wm. Heath Papers, VIII, 138, 161, Mass. Hist. Soc.; Samuel A. Otis to Theodore Sedgwick, Boston, 30 July 1782, Sedgwick Papers, *ibid.*

60. Samuel A. Otis to Theodore Sedgwick, Boston, 8 July 1782, Sedgwick Papers, *ibid.*

61. *Ibid.*

62. Samuel A. Otis to Theodore Sedgwick, Boston, 10 July 1782, *ibid.*

63. Samuel A. Otis to Theodore Sedgwick, Boston, 30 July 1782, *ibid.*

64. See "Col. Otis Minutes" for land in Murryfield, 1762–1767, in Box 1 of the Harrison Gray Otis Papers, Mass. Hist. Soc.

65. Samuel A. Otis to Theodore Sedgwick, Boston, 12 Nov. 1782, Theodore Sedgwick Papers, *ibid.*

66. Samuel A. Otis to Joseph Otis, Boston, 22 Apr. 1784, Gay-Otis Papers, Butler Lib., Columbia.

Moreover, he had reviewed the family ledgers and had informed Joseph that only the most vigorous action would save what was left of the family patrimony. Samuel tried to convince his brother that the surest way to raise capital was to sell the Barnstable properties. He told Joseph, who had enmeshed his business accounts with receipts owed the commonwealth as well as with cash due him, quickly to "commence suits around you, and take the peoples land and pay your own debts, for charity begins at home." He refused point blank to form a partnership with Joseph, who already owed him in excess of £6,000.[67] Joseph on his part would neither sell the farm nor sue his neighbors no matter how much his brother needed money. However, Samuel felt obliged to lobby for Joseph's retention of the court clerkship and counseled him to retain also the "excise off[ice] as every little helps."[68] These two posts, along with the collectorship of the Barnstable customs, meant survival for the man who had done more than anyone in Barnstable to insure the success of the American Revolution. In this matter Samuel Allyne had been forced to act quickly while he still had influence. By the spring of 1785 he knew he would probably not be able to meet his own fiscal obligations; that August he prudently deeded his Boston household to his children.[69] The first of the family to go under was cousin John Otis V who saw himself become a town charge after his property had been sold at public auction.[70] Joseph Otis hardly needed his brother's advice to take the necessary steps to prevent the family property being "torn from you by angry Creditors." He proceeded to make a series of secret transfers which included the Barnstable store, family heirlooms, the warehouse and wharf, the farm and all equipment, furniture and goods in both stores, as well as "all transferable debts by book or bonds."[71] He

67. Samuel A. Otis to Joseph Otis, Boston, 4 Aug. 1783, Otis Family MSS, IV, 278, *ibid.*

68. Samuel A. Otis to Joseph Nye, Boston, 2 May 1785, and Samuel A. Otis to Joseph Otis, Boston, 18 May 1785, *ibid.*, IV, 294, 297.

69. Suffolk Deeds, 147.260, 151.6, 16 Feb., 27 Aug. 1785, Suffolk County Court House.

70. Barnstable Town Records, III, 187–191.

71. Joseph Otis to Samuel A. Otis, Barnstable, 24 Apr., 29 Apr. 1785, and Samuel A. Otis to Joseph Otis, Boston, 14 May 1785, Otis Family MSS, IV, 291, 293, 296, Butler Lib., Columbia.

was insolvent, but his heirs would be property owners. For Samuel Otis the September deluge found him bankrupt for lack of £30,000 lawful money.[72] The patrician might speak of "sacred contracts" in 1782, but in 1785 Samuel Allyne Otis opted for the older law of survival.

The next five years were probably the most difficult times in Samuel Otis's life. In a very literal sense he was a captain without a ship in search of both cargo and port. He could not fall back on minor posts and petty community services as did his brother Joseph.[73] He knew that his bankruptcy had ruined his mercantile reputation in Boston, while he had seen his sense of honor disintegrate in the deluge. He had retained his prejudices, if not his principles, and they now found reinforcement in the narrow circle of federally minded men.[74] He had no sympathy with John Hancock's governorship, although he realized that Hancock's enormous popularity could not be overcome at the polls. Yet his position required circumspection, as he depended in one form or another on Hancock's approbation for a political spot.[75] After all, he was no longer a marketable political commodity within the state's politics. If for no other reason than the pay allowance, he had welcomed his election to the Confederation Congress in 1787. However, his own letters make it abundantly clear that the Congress was an impotent side show of has-beens and nonentities. The national government's weakness equaled its lack of dignity. What could be sadder than the country's treasury "without supplies, Their troops stationed to secure the frontiers, and the Civil list of Congress destitute of provision"?[76] He found consolation among like-minded friends and in acting out his symbolic role in the one organ which pre-

72. George Partridge to Samuel Holten, Duxbury, 20 Sept. 1785, in Edmund C. Burnett, ed., *Letters of Members of the Continental Congress* (Washington, D.C., 1921–1938), VIII, 220.

73. Joseph Otis, *et al.*, subscribers, Barnstable, 18 July 1787, Lemuel Shaw Papers, Mass. Hist. Soc.

74. Samuel A. Otis to Theodore Sedgwick, N. Y., 25 Dec. 1787, Sedgwick Papers, Mass. Hist. Soc.

75. Samuel A. Otis to Theodore Sedgwick, N. Y., 13 Oct. 1788, *ibid.*

76. Samuel A. Otis to [James Warren], N. Y., 6 Feb. 1788, Burnett, ed., *Letters of Continental Congress*, VIII, 696.

served the "semblance of a foederal Government."[77] But his hope was in the plans for a "new energetic Government." In the meantime he boarded for $2.50 a week.[78]

It was the bark Constitution that ultimately cargoed Samuel Allyne Otis's future. By the spring of 1788 he was confident she would accommodate the nation's different interests and reach port. News from the South was as favorable as that from Massachusetts, a matter for rejoicing which held no fear: "N England united, will forever counterpoise any cabals and manoeuvres of the South."[79] Otis saw the central problem of the new nation as a fiscal rather than a sectional one. His prejudices were obvious in his expressed hope that the federal government would refund the war debt as the chief means of restoring business confidence. Only federal refunding would "reanimate a dead mass of useless paper, and instantly make it an efficient Capital, for the farmer, the merchant, and every man in the Community." Otis was not concerned with the moral right or wrong of refunding. He insisted that the real issue was the beneficial effect it would have upon the national life.[80]

Samuel A. Otis wanted to play a part in the new government, and it was therefore a bitter disappointment when the Massachusetts General Court failed to elect him to the federal Congress. Having no "commercial prospects," he had hoped to capitalize on his knowledge of public affairs. His solution to unemployment was a successful hunt for an administrative post, which was rewarded in April of 1789 with his election as secretary of the United States Senate.[81] Sam was now more optimistic than ever about the government and its securities.[82] From his inside seat in the Senate he saw that Madison

77. Samuel A. Otis to Benjamin Lincoln, N. Y., 8 May 1788, *ibid.*, 730.
78. George Thatcher to Nathan Dane, N. Y., 2 Oct. 1788, *ibid.*, 802.
79. Samuel A. Otis to George Thatcher, N. Y., 18 [May] 1788, *ibid.*, 735–736.
80. Samuel A. Otis to James Warren, N. Y., 26 Apr. 1788, Mass. Hist. Soc., *Procs.*, XLV (1911–1912), 333–336.
81. Samuel A. Otis to Jeremiah Wadsworth, N. Y., 12 Jan. 1789, Burnett, ed., *Letters of Continental Congress*, VIII, 814–815; "In Senate," 8 Apr. 1789, Harrison Gray Otis Papers, Box 1, Mass. Hist. Soc.
82. Samuel A. Otis to Mr. Templemon, N. Y., 27 Dec. 1789, C. E. French Papers, Mass. Hist. Soc.

and his friends would not defeat the impending assumption measures for the state debts. This information provided him with a golden opportunity to speculate and to refloat his family's fortune. In complete confidence he wrote to William Smith, declaring, "I have a disposition to make the most of things for the benefit of my family, but it would not be well for one to be seen much in business, as my [Senate] office might be injured thereby; I am however of opinion that something might be made by underwriting if I could by lodging a sum with a confidential friend, induce him to take prudent sums from." There were few epitaphs so important to him as "he has left handsome property to his family."[83] He was able to do just that by cashing in on new opportunities. The Revolution would feed its children; the sixth generation of Otises would not want. Nor is it surprising that Samuel Allyne Otis became an early advocate of a strong central government. Its real advantage was that it gave him a second chance. Backing its bonds was as much a psychic as an economic measure for him. By championing the new federal Union he restored his faith in himself, in the protestant belief that success was a sign of salvation, and in the rule of the elite.

83. Samuel A. Otis to William Smith, N. Y., 27 Feb. 1790, Smith-Carter Papers, Mass. Hist. Soc.

# ❧ X.
## REFLECTIONS

Our study of the Otises began with the England of King Charles I and the puritans. It concludes 160 years later with Commonwealth Massachusetts's ratification of the federal Constitution. We know little about Richard Otis, the ancestor of this line. Simply stated, he was a weaver from Glastonbury who spent his last days in a beneficed alms house either as a pensioner or a minor official. Richard Otis's place in his society was on the fringe of respectability. For his son John immigration to America meant both change and material improvement. He ended his days in his own house with an income of £10 a year. His son, the second John Otis, stored up £1,500 of treasure before quitting this life. His son, John Otis III, concluded his life as an honored member of the king's Council in Massachusetts and chief justice of the Inferior Court of Common Pleas in Barnstable County. His success testified to his society's mobility. But it represents a variant of the "rags to riches" theme of popular literature insofar as the rise took three generations. Might not this pattern be typical of social mobility in early Massachusetts?

The rise of the Otis family to influence and power in Barnstable is in reality the unfolding of unusual talent in a revolutionary situation. When John Otis III served as the first representative of his town under the Massachusetts charter government of 1692 he was the servant of a new order. The old regime, as represented by Governor Thomas Hinckley of Plymouth, had never recovered the verve it lost because of the Indian wars and subjection to the Dominion of New England. A push from the social discontents brought down a leadership that lacked faith in itself. The impetus came from the young members of an exploding population who were part of an economy that had ceased to expand. If John Otis III's foundations of political power rested upon such ruins, the new structure was fashioned out of increased trade, political opportunity, and active participation in a market economy. In his lifetime John Otis III tripled his assets, thus continuing what had become a family tradition. This grandson of an immigrant farmer left his sons an estate worth £5,000.

In the agrarian society of colonial Massachusetts the success of the Otises rested on a multitude of factors. The first was biological. Many sons were a blessing, and the Otises averaged two male members for every female. For three generations this family's birth and survival rates were remarkably high. One is tempted to see a connection between sustained biological fertility and income. There can be no doubt that there was a connection between property-holding and political office. Those who held positions of responsibility came from the most propertied class in Barnstable. But after all, who else but the first families had either the time or the inclination to serve at Boston!

Yet this was not a matter of simple inheritance. The first Colonel James Otis was the last, not the first son of John Otis III. A political career rested upon deference, talent, achievement, and performance. And each year the retention of one's political post was subject to the approval of a large electorate. There is every indication that the Otises and the other leaders represented the aims and beliefs of their freemen neighbors. However, both social and political mobility in the Barnstable structure declined as its first families formed a closed circle. Increasing stratification marked this society as the Revolutionary period approached.

The career of James Otis the elder was forged out of new materials. Law, commerce, and political influence were combined to give James Otis, Senior, status in his county and in Boston as well. The elder Otis was an extraordinarily gifted politician whose climb to success has been all but eclipsed by the brilliance of his son James Otis, Junior. Yet if the son was a constitutional theorizer and political innovator, the father was a first-rate tactician and practical politician. The victories of the popular party during the crucial decade of the Bernard administration testify to the fruitfulness of a collaboration of talents. Rather than looking at the patriot as the "great man," it is more fruitful to judge the young Otis's proper import within the context of the family-political apparatus.

The crisis brought on by the Sugar Act of 1764 lasted with but the briefest respite until Massachusetts declared its independence in 1776. It was the argument of the Otises that the real revolutionaries were the British, and after all, the Massachusetts Government Act of 1774 did promise to change the structure of government that had been in effect since the end of the seventeenth century. The Otises did not see themselves as social or political innovators. In Barnstable they were the upholders of the status quo, and in 1776 it was their intent to fight for home rule, not revolution. The struggle engaged in was for "Independence."

However much the Otises might have desired to retain a known and stable society as well as their leadership within it, they could not control the war process itself. In a very real sense it was war that produced the greatest social, economic, and political innovations their society had witnessed since the establishment of the charter government at the end of the seventeenth century.

Barnstable's wartime leader, Joseph Otis, lacked tact in his dealings with his countrymen, but it was not within his power either to control the inflationary spiral or to heal the ideological divisions that had split his community in two. He attempted to mediate the state's demands upon Barnstable when they clearly exceeded the town's ability to comply. Yet while he might moderate certain requisitions he could not restore his community's traditional autonomy. In fact, the town held him responsible for war exactions and the erosion of its customary way of life. When peace came the town refused to invest Joseph Otis with office. The war itself, with its state and national demands, clearly had destroyed the parochial basis of Joseph Otis's career in Barnstable.

In serving the Revolutionary cause Samuel Allyne Otis contributed his ability to organize, to rationalize, to get results, and therefore to profit. He was a merchant with an absolute conviction that the business of his country was business, that his class alone possessed those virtues that could make the commonwealth flourish, that his role as a leader was justified by his family's past performance and his own pragmatic success. His bankruptcy in the 1780's severely strained the image he had of himself, limited his participation in Massachusetts politics, and forced him to look further afield. It was his line, however, who maintained the elite status of their Otis forefathers.

His namesake, Samuel Allyne Otis (II) (1768–1814), settled at Cape Francis, Haiti, but was driven from his plantation by the successful Negro rebellion which ended white colonial rule on that island. He resettled at Newburyport, Massachusetts, and joined the Federalist pandits, sharing fully in their hatred of the egalitarian philosophy of the Jeffersonians. His son, the Reverend George Otis (1797–1828) graduated from Harvard, became professor of Latin, and ultimately, rector of Christ Church, Cambridge. However, the most prominent of the sixth generation was Samuel A. Otis's first son, Harrison Gray Otis (1765–1848). He alone continued the tradition of public service. Harrison Gray succeeded Fisher Ames in 1797 as congressman from the Suffolk district. Like his father and grandfather before him he held the speakership of the Massachusetts House and also served as president of the state Senate. He helped moderate the secession sentiments of the Hartford Convention in 1814. His fruitful public life included election as senator to the Sixteenth Congress in 1817, an unsuccessful bid as the Federalist candidate for the governorship in 1823, and election as

Boston's third mayor in 1829. He invested heavily in Maine and Georgia and in western lands. His wealth allowed his sons and grandsons to live in genteel elegance.

Harrison Gray Otis II (1797–1827) of the seventh generation attended Harvard, married Elizabeth Boardman of the India and China trade family, and died young. His widow presided over one of Boston's most fashionable salons and was a prime advocate in the drive to adopt Washington's birthday as a state holiday in 1845. His brother, James William Otis (1800–1869), became president of the North America Fire Insurance Company of New York. James William Otis's son, William Church Otis (1831–1889), contemplated life from the exclusive haunts of the Somerset Club. And his son, Harrison Gray (1856–1915), was also a clubman, who, however, married an Elizabeth McNamara and died in Dublin. Finally, Harrison Gray Otis I's ninth child, William Foster Otis (1801–1858), lived easily in Versailles. His daughter Emily Marshall married Samuel Eliot of another old Yankee line. Her grandson, Samuel Eliot Morison of the tenth generation, may justly lay claim to his family's tradition of service, attachment to Harvard, and prominence in his own right as one of the twentieth century's most distinguished historians.

To have records tracing the activities of an American family for ten generations is a priceless boon for the social historian. The lines we have looked at in this study had their famous men and their failures. For the most part the descendants of the elder James Otis were content to follow careers whose patterns had been established by the colonial generations. The progress of these lines was not linear, and there were always more clerks than senators. Yet if the line of the elder Otis and his three sons declined in terms of political eminence during the nineteenth century, there were many prominent Otises who also were descendants from the first John Otis. Their fame—as inventors and scientists, elevator manufacturers and newspaper publishers, generals and Jesuit priests—constitutes an unwritten chapter in the continuing history of a mobile people.

## ❧ NOTE ON SOURCES

The ordinary bibliography usually hides as much as it reveals. In the case of the "Otis Family" that would be especially true. Most of what has been written about the Otises deals directly with the "Patriot" James Otis, Junior. Strange as it may seem, the only full length work on the patriot of any historical value is William Tudor's *Life of James Otis*, which was published in 1823. Tudor used his sources intelligently. He did have a tendency to suppress personal material. He also flavored his account with a dash of whiggery. Tudor's *Life of James Otis* is the story of a hero. It belongs to the "great man" tradition in history. In 1846 Francis Bowen presented another *Life of James Otis*. This formed volume thirteen of Jared Sparks's "Library of American Biography." The key to this book was patriotism and that theme was replayed by John C. Ridpath's *James Otis the Pre-Revolutionist* (Chicago, 1898). Both Bowen and Ridpath were strong on virtue, edification, and morality. However, most of their information came from Tudor's 1823 account.

Modern research starts with Ellen Brennan's "James Otis, Recreant and Patriot," *New England Quarterly*, XII (1939), 691–725. This is a superb analysis of the young Otis's political writings. In addition her *Plural Office-Holding in Massachusetts, 1760–1780* (Chapel Hill, 1945) is invaluable for the politics of that era. In 1954 Alice Vering wrote a dissertation at the University of Nebraska on James Otis. It is a study of the patriot as seen in the dispatches of Governor Francis Bernard. The now available manuscripts at Columbia University would have changed its direction and intent. However, Clifford K. Shipton has supplied a classic biographical account of James Otis in volume eleven of *Sibley's Harvard Graduates* (1960). It would be inexact to say that it is biased against the patriot, but it does reflect a heavy dependency upon the views of Thomas Hutchinson, Andrew Oliver, and Francis Bernard, who were of the tory party. A more eulogistic treatment of Otis's ideals—as distinct from his political conduct—may be found in the first volume of Bernard Bailyn's *Pamphlets of the American Revolution* (Cambridge, Mass., 1965).

No scholarly account exists on the "Otis Family" as such. Horatio N. Otis gathered some information in his "Genealogical and Historical Memoir of the Otis Family," *New England Historical and Genealogical Register*, II (1848), 281–296. He suppressed details in the 1611 will of his ancestor Richard Otis which indicated that Richard spent his last days in an almshouse. This pietistic attitude is also seen in William A. Otis's *A Genealogical and Historical Memoir of the Otis Family in America* (Chicago, 1924). The Somerset Record Office at Taunton and the Exeter Diocesan Record Office yielded additional background materials.

George D. Langdon, Jr.'s *Pilgrim Colony, A History of New Plymouth, 1620–1691* (New Haven, 1966) is a prudential study of the "Old Colony." Unfortunately the late date of its availability precluded an intensive use of its findings in my own study. Little exists in print of value on Hingham, Scituate, or Plymouth and Barnstable counties under the charter government. Some important information is in Harvey H. Pratt's *The Early Planters of Scituate* (Scituate, 1929), and Donald G. Trayser's *Barnstable, Three Centuries of a Cape Cod Town* (Barnstable, 1939).

In attempting to understand the workings of the towns of Hingham, Scituate, and Barnstable I have had heavy recourse to non-narrative sources. Tax rolls, church lists, land distribution plans, which were based upon total property ownership, and quantitative studies of law dockets, wills, and inventories have supplied most of the data on the social structure of these societies. The historian gains little from knowing that John Otis III left an estate worth £5,000. That datum has meaning only when a comparative analysis shows that Otis was the richest man in his town and one of the three men in his county of that estate. The files of the Barnstable Registry of Probate, Barnstable, the Plymouth Registry of Probate, Plymouth, the Suffolk Registry of Probate, Boston, and the Old Colony Records, Plymouth Registry of Deeds, Plymouth, supplied the better part of this kind of evidence. In addition the Records of the Inferior Court of Common Pleas for Plymouth, at Plymouth, the Minute Books of Common Pleas for Barnstable, and the Records of the Superior Court of Judicature, as well as the Suffolk Court Files, Suffolk County Court House, Boston, were heavily utilized.

The town records of Hingham, Scituate, and Barnstable, as well as the Massachusetts Archives, proved invaluable.

This thesis, originally entitled The Otis Family in Provincial and Revolutionary Massachusetts (Ph.D. diss., Columbia University, 1965), is in part a reply to the challenge raised by Edmund S. Morgan's "The American Revolution: Revisions in Need of Revising," *William and Mary Quarterly*, XIV (1957), 14. The possibilities inherent in studying family and political relationships to explain a social structure received fruitful formulation in Friedrich Münzer's *Römische Adelsparteien und Adelsfamilien* (Stuttgart, 1920). This was brought to a brilliant synthesis by Ronald Syme in his *The Roman Revolution* (Oxford, 1939). In between these two works Sir Lewis Namier utilized this methodology in his famous *The Structure of Politics at the Accession of George III* (London, 1929). In a somewhat different fashion James B. Hedges explored *The Browns of Providence Plantations, Colonial Years* (Cambridge, Mass., 1952), Byron Fairchild examined *Messrs. William Pepperrell: Merchants at Piscataqua* (Ithaca, 1954), Aubrey C. Land wrote about *The Dulanys of Maryland* (Baltimore, 1955), and Richard S. Dunn gave us his fine analysis of *Puritans and Yankees: The Winthrop Dynasty of New England, 1630–1717* (Princeton, 1962). These works, with the various questions they posed, helped me in approaching the Otises. However, the formulations within this essay are based on my understanding of the "Otis Family" and its papers.

My study of the Otises is a familial sketch within given localities. It belongs to a recent class of historical literature which is concerned with the "way government worked on the local level." It is an addition to such regional studies as Lee N. Newcomer's *The Embattled Farmers* (New York, 1953), and Robert J. Taylor's parallel investigation of *Western Massachusetts in the Revolution* (Providence, 1954). Although the first chapters of this study were written before the appearance of Sumner C. Powell's meticulous *Puritan Village* (Middletown, 1963) and Benjamin W. Labaree's *Patriots and Partisans, The Merchants of Newburyport, 1764–1815* (Cambridge, Mass., 1962), it is evident that we share a common methodology. This is also true for a third recent book in local history, Darrett B. Rutman's *Winthrop's Boston* (Chapel Hill, 1965).

There are four important manuscript collections dealing with the Otises upon which this study is built: (1) The Otis Papers in the Massachusetts Historical Society; (2) Miscellaneous Papers and other documents in the care of the Supreme Judicial Court (the famous Suffolk Court Files) at Boston; (3) the Gay-Otis Papers, and (4) the Otis Family Manuscripts, now in Special Collections, Butler Library, Columbia University. Of these documents only (1) and (2) have been previously available to scholars. The first, the three volumes of Otis

Papers, were selected from a larger corpus. They are of a public nature as the Society in 1836 returned the "private" documents to William Otis. The Miscellaneous Papers in 1896 were transferred to what is now the Suffolk Court Files (see Massachusetts Historical Society, *Proceedings*, 1st Ser., II [1835–1855], 45; *ibid.*, 2d Ser., XI [1896, 1897], 221–225). Only Clifford K. Shipton has made extensive use of the first two series of these documents. In addition there exists a bound volume in the Suffolk Court Files entitled Otis Legal Memoranda, which was borrowed from the Massachusetts Historical Society in 1918 (of which the Society has no record). Collections (3) and (4) constitute the "private documents" returned to William Otis and material inherited by the Gay family. This paper has made heavy use of these four series, two of which are used in depth for the first time.

A second equally important group of materials consists of the Francis Bernard Papers, Houghton Library, Harvard, the Hutchinson Correspondence in the Massachusetts Archives, as well as letters in the Israel Williams Papers in the Massachusetts Historical Society. These papers have been common domain for a century. Needless to say they represent views which I have attempted to reconsider in the light of the Otis Papers taken as a whole. The Hancock Letter Books at Baker Library, Harvard, and the Massachusetts Historical Society, were important sources for the relationship between trade and politics. The Bourn Papers at Houghton, Harvard, were of aid in studying Barnstable's trade and commerce.

Several minor collections repaid searching. The Richard Dana Manuscripts, the Nathan Dane Papers, the Samuel Mather Letters, II, the Oliver Letter Books, the R. T. Paine Papers, and the Ezekiel Price Papers, of the Massachusetts Historical Society, were used to profit. Likewise, the Miscellaneous Bound Manuscripts, the Miscellaneous Manuscripts, the Miscellaneous Papers, the Belknap Papers, the Caleb Davis Papers, the John Davis Papers, and the J. M. Robbins Papers of the Society were consulted. One or more key interpretative documents came from the C. E. French Papers, the Gerry-Knight Papers, the Wm. Heath Papers, the S. P. Savage Papers, the Theodore Sedgwick Papers, and the Lemuel Shaw Papers of the Massachusetts Historical Society. Harvard University Archives supplied Faculty Records, I, II, as well as Tutor Flynt's Diary. The Joseph Hawley Papers at the New York Public Library, the Thomas Gage Papers at the William L. Clements Library, University of Michigan, the Forbes Library, Northampton, the Beinecke Library, Yale, and the Connecticut Historical Society, Hartford, yielded several essential items. Lastly, the printed *Collections* and *Proceedings* of the Massachusetts Historical Society were a mine of information. Where I have used modern works I have acknowledged my dependence in the text.

# ✣ *INDEX*

## A

Abercromby, Gen. James, 102, 106

Adams, John, 123, 135–136, 154, 161; *Novanglus* pamphlet, 45; evaluations of James Otis, Sr., 72; and James Otis, Jr., 132, 177, 179; opposes Stamp Act, 157–158; Michael Corbet case, 175

Adams, Samuel, and Stamp Act riots, 157; newspaper role, 161; James Otis, Jr.'s fear of, 173, 177–178; "Massachusetts Convention," 174–175

Aix-la-Chapelle, 95

Alden, John, 42

Alien, Bozoun, 22, 24, 25, 26

Allen, Dr. Daniel, 46

Allen, James, 92, 94, 95, 101, 137

Allen, Jeremiah, 81

Allyne, Mary, 63

Amiel, John, 91

Andrews, Joseph, 15

Andrews, Thomas, 7

Antigua, 127

Articles of Confederation, 195

Attleborough, Mass., 71

Attorney generalship, 98

Auchmuty, Robert, 71, 87

Avery, Dr. Benjamin, 97

## B

Bacon, Edward, protégé of James Otis, Sr., 103–104, 107; representative, 104, 192, 195; against Independence and war, 188, 191; exclusion, 193

Bacon, Mary, 38

Bacon, Nathaniel, 38, 42, 49

Bailyn, Bernard, 50, 58, 132, 133, 134

Barnstable, Mass., 35–36, 38–41, 44–46, 56–60, 66, 68, 70, 90, 107, 116, 131, 166; land distribution, 48–50; economy, 51, 95, 100, 125, 128, 192–193; political structure, 61–63, 75, 78–79, 148–149, 164, 180, 185, 194–196; centennial celebration (1739), 65; land bank, 74; Indians, 98; French and Indian War, 102–104; nonimportation, 177; intolerable acts, 184–185; Revolutionary War, 187–190, 193–197; Independence, 188, 194, 206; loyalists, 191–193

Barnstable County, Mass., 50, 80, 204; early population, 47; excise politics, 78; representation, 85; mores, 110; James Otis, Sr.'s role, 185

Barnstable fleet, 51

Barnstaple, Eng., 5, 6

# AMERICAN HISTORY TITLES IN THE NORTON LIBRARY